SOCIOLOGISTS' TALES

Contemporary narratives on sociological thought and practice

Edited by
Katherine Twamley
Mark Doidge
Andrea Scott

D1610390

First published in Great Britain in 2015 by

Policy Press
University of Bristol
1-9 Old Park Hill
Bristol
BS2 8BB
UK
t: +44 (0)117 954 5940
pp-info@bristol.ac.uk
www.policypress.co.uk

North America office:
Policy Press
c/o The University of Chicago Press
1427 East 60th Street
Chicago, IL 60637, USA
t: +1 773 702 7700
f: +1 773 702 9756
sales@press.uchicago.edu
www.press.uchicago.edu

© British Sociological Association 2015

British Library Cataloguing in Publication Data
A catalogue record for this book is available from the British Library

Library of Congress Cataloging-in-Publication Data
A catalog record for this book has been requested

ISBN 978-1-4473-1866-8 hardcover
ISBN 978-1-4473-1867-5 paperback

The right of Katherine Twamley, Mark Doidge and Andrea Scott to be identified as editors of this work has been asserted by them in accordance with the Copyright, Designs and Patents Act 1988.

The British Sociological Association (www.britsoc.co.uk) is a professional membership association for sociologists in the UK. Founded in 1951, it is a registered charity and also a company limited by guarantee. Registered charity number: 1080235. Company number: 3890729. Registered in England and Wales.

All rights reserved: no part of this publication may be reproduced, stored in a retrieval system, or transmitted in any form or by any means, electronic, mechanical, photocopying, recording, or otherwise without the prior permission of Policy Press.

The statements and opinions contained within this publication are solely those of the contributors and editors and not of the University of Bristol, Policy Press or British Sociological Association. The University of Bristol, Policy Press and British Sociological Association disclaim responsibility for any injury to persons or property resulting from any material published in this publication.

Policy Press works to counter discrimination on grounds of gender, race, disability, age and sexuality.

Cover design by Andrew Corbett
Front cover image kindly supplied by Gareth Humpage
(www.garethhumpagephotography.co.uk)
Printed and bound in Great Britain by CMP, Poole
Policy Press uses environmentally responsible print partners

Contents

Part 3 How does one become a sociologist?

Contents

Acknowledgements

The editors wish to thank the British Sociological Association, in particular Alison Danforth, and the staff at Policy Press for their support in bringing this book together.

Foreword

Judith Mudd, Chief Executive, British Sociological Association

At the British Sociological Association, we often ask ourselves 'How do we explain the fascination of sociology?', 'How do sociologists learn their trade?' and 'How do we support and nurture our successors?' *Sociologists' Tales* provides answers to all of these questions. Full of compelling descriptions of sociology, inspirational examples of sociological research and candid insights into the lives of sociologists, it is an invaluable resource. In it, the contributors tell us how they came to sociology, revealing often riveting twists and turns in their journeys, highlighting what made a difference to their career trajectories and offering sound advice for newcomers including sign-posting to other helpful resources.

I have worked with many talented, enthusiastic, generous people across the sociological journey but I am struck by the willingness, openness and generosity of all of the authors who contributed to this book. The foresight and tenacity of the editors in suggesting and bringing this work to fruition is remarkable. In producing the book they have made a significant and positive contribution to the knowledge, development and understanding of sociology, and a chapter has been written in their own sociological tales.

This book is a fascinating read for sociologists old and new, and is 'mentoring in your pocket' for anyone setting out on their sociological apprenticeship.

Introduction

Mark Doidge, Katherine Twamley and Andrea Scott

'Making the familiar strange and the strange familiar.'
(C Wright Mills)

'But he isn't wearing anything at all!', shrieked the young child. Among the throngs of well-wishers and dignitaries, the Emperor strolled triumphantly through the streets for all to admire his resplendent attire. He had just been made the finest clothes by two tailors who had procured the most beautiful threads; so wonderful was this finery that it was invisible to the naked eye. The Emperor's ministers and admirers all noted the exceptional workmanship and sumptuous detail of the new clothes so that they would not highlight their stupidity in front of their superior. It was not until a child declared that actually the Emperor was naked that the myth surrounding the vain leader began to unravel.

Hans Christian Andersen's fable of the Emperor's New Clothes provides a useful metaphor for the discipline of sociology. As sociologists we untangle the invisible threads through our analyses, showing them for what they are – pure air spun by the structures of power and inequality – revealing to the world what they knew, but didn't know they knew. Such unravelling is not just about uncovering truths, but about challenging the very structures that uphold such truths. As Marx (1970) famously said, 'The philosophers have only interpreted the world, in various ways; the point is to change it.' How much change (or 'impact') our research really makes is debatable, but that sociologists' strive for this change cannot be refuted.

It is this sense of discovery, insight and transformation that flows through the narratives that are contained within *Sociologists' Tales*. In this book, 33 sociologists tell us their tales of a life in sociology.

They share with us their ideas and passions, their daily practices and challenges, and their tips for those aspiring a similar career. The result is a book both about sociology *and* sociological practice. Together the narratives provide an overview of the questions and concerns that are driving contemporary British sociologists, while also giving advice to the 'next generation' of sociologists. Through these accounts, the reader can discern a story of sociology as a discipline, and how biography and the political economic context shape scholars' research and careers. This book will be of interest to anyone with an attraction to sociology: for established sociologists there are insights from some renowned exponents of the discipline. For mid- and early-career sociologists there are overviews and opinions about charting a career in higher education. And last but not least, for students and those inquisitive about the discipline there are ideas about what it means to be a sociologist.

The origins of sociology: the story so far (abridged)

Sociology originated as the science of modern society. As Western Europe moved from traditional rural communities to modern urban societies, the discipline of sociology emerged to understand how human beings operated in this brave new world. The early proponents of sociology, like Comte, Spencer and Durkheim, as well as later members of the Chicago school, focused on establishing sociology as a legitimate discipline in the academy alongside the natural sciences, history, anthropology and philosophy. A second wave of sociology occurred in the 1960s thanks to an interest in the New Left, and fuelled by the student protests of 1968, marked by a surging interest in class politics. The importance of this date re-occurs in several of the biographies within *Sociologists' Tales*, drawing authors into a sociological career, funnelling their desire for change into their work and opening up new opportunities for a university education and career. For example, John Brewer was drawn to sociology at this time through his growing awareness of inequalities, racism and anti-Vietnam sentiments.

In the 1970s feminism drew attention to the gendered nature of the discipline and its theories. More importantly, feminism gave (female) sociologists the theoretical support to challenge the status quo and enabled women to argue for the relevance of 'women's lives and work' to sociology. The legacy and influence of feminism is difficult to underestimate. Around this time too, poststructuralist theorists challenged notions of knowledge, theory and method. Theorists such as Michel Foucault proffered new ways of critically analysing the world and this helped reinforce the work of those engaged with gender and sexuality research.

Subsequent scholars lamented a perceived shift away from a methodological or theoretical consensus, especially when compared to the natural sciences (Turner and Turner, 1990; Horowitz, 1993; Goldthorpe, 2000; Cole, 2001; Berger, 2002). Without a set of established methods they felt that it was harder to ascertain a core knowledge with which to communicate with students and the public. Much of this comes from an anxiety that has existed since Comte and Spencer that sociology should be a 'science'. This positivist approach permeated the discipline until the multiple challenges that arose in the 1970s from feminists and poststructuralists.

Sociology is now a broad church that covers a range of methods and theories. Ritzer (1975) argues that sociology is 'a multiple paradigm science', with scholars drawing on different epistemologies and ontologies in their research, resulting in a rich variety of methodologies and theories. Meanwhile, Urry (1981) goes so far as to say that sociology is 'parasitic', feeding off other disciplines. Despite this rather unappealing term, it highlights that the discipline is inherently interdisciplinary and open to new ideas, spawning 'hybridic sociologies' as Stanley (2005) calls them. Several of our authors exemplify the ideal of a hybridic sociologist, such as Sasha Roseneil who uses a psychosocial approach in her work, even going so far as to retrain in group psychotherapy to hone her skills. In other cases, sociology provided a 'home' to academics from other disciplines, allowing them to carve out a hybridic sociology of their own – such as Yvonne Robinson who calls herself a 'sociographer' having originally studied geography.

What is constant, at least in this book, is the attachment to C Wright Mills's vision of *The sociological imagination* (1959). The central principle of the sociological imagination is to be able to see micro interactions and macro society in unison – rather than the actions of individuals or groups as independent of other social processes. C Wright Mills argued, 'the sociological imagination enables us to grasp history and biography and the relations between the two within society' (1959,12). The contributors to this book hold true to this vision in their narratives, unpacking their own biographies and career trajectories within the wider structures of the academe and the socio–political context around them.

Another legacy of C Wright Mills can be seen in the authors' commitment to public engagement. This was a central theme of the book (picked up again in more detail below) and a key motivation for many to study and work in sociology. Some sociologists have criticised the political approach of the discipline. Parsons (1959) argued that for the discipline to be a true science, it must retain value-free objectivity. Similarly, Berger (2002) laments the political agenda that has entered the discipline and argues that sociologists should be impartial observers, rationally and scientifically analysing society without proscription. As many of the authors in this book discuss, however, politics (in its broadest sense of the word) is often a motivation for joining the discipline. Becker argues that it is impossible for social scientists to undertake research 'uncontaminated by personal and political sympathies' (1967, 240). Similarly, Burawoy (2005) argues against this 'pure science' position by suggesting that 'antipolitics' is still political. In effect, the purpose of sociology is to make society better.

Reflection is vital in order to alleviate accusations of personal bias. As this book is about reflective sociologists, the chapters illustrate how these practitioners situate themselves within this wider political economic context. Gouldner (1968) suggests that being reflexive of one's own political position is precisely how we as sociologists can remain 'objective'. By acknowledging our own position, and keeping this at the forefront of our mind, we can ensure that our research is not adversely affected by our own preconceptions. 'Objectivity', as Gouldner (1968, 114) argues, 'consists in the capacity to know and to use – to seek out, or at least accept it when it is otherwise provided – information inimical to our own desires and values, and to overcome our own fear of such information'. Because we are aware of our own position, we seek out contrary information so that we can present the whole picture in an objective fashion. Such reflexivity then is common in sociological studies, whereby the researcher attempts to unpack his/ her political, theoretical and biographical baggage that they carry with them. The contributions in this book are an example of reflexivity in action, as researchers attempt to unravel how their personal lives and convictions have shaped their careers and research trajectories.

The idea for the book

This book was originally conceived as an attempt to bring together scholars from a range of backgrounds to give advice and inspiration to early career sociologists, such as us. The three editors are convenors of the British Sociological Association (BSA) Early Career Forum. Through interactions with our members, we felt that a book from more established scholars could encourage, advise and enthuse our members. Each of us is committed to a sociological career and we seek to hear others' stories about how they have managed to carve one out. Already among the three editors there is evidence of diverse career trajectories and discipline interests. Mark started his career in a warehouse before moving into logistics management. Following redundancy he studied for a master's degree in ancient history before discovering sociology. Andrea's experiences as an athlete led her to study a sports science undergraduate degree. Her journey into sociology began after becoming frustrated by the 'black and white' nature of the 'natural' sciences and renewed by a discipline such as sociology that questioned the 'grey areas'. While Katherine has perhaps taken the most conventional route from sociology undergraduate to PhD to 'postdoc', with some travelling in between. We knew how our biographies had shaped these paths, and we thought it would be interesting to consider whether the same was true of other people. In particular, we were eager to get the 'tales' of those from different generations. We hoped that by inviting sociologists from across the decades, we could discern patterns across the years. In the end, there were both similarities and differences within and between 'generations', though there is no doubt that personal biography and the historical (both socio-political and theoretical) had a profound effect on our contributors' interests, theoretical inclinations and career pathways.

At the same time, we were aware that in the current economic climate young people are more and more concerned with 'employability'. We envisioned a book that celebrated the merits of sociology as a discipline, while also giving realistic career advice to encourage a new generation of would-be sociologists. What comes across in the pages contained within this book is the passion that our authors have for sociology, and the rewards of a sociological career. These were the aims of this book, and our contributors answered with gusto.

How we went about making this book

The solicitation for contributions to this book did not follow any specific logic or plan. We aimed to include authors from a range of backgrounds, ages and disciplinary interests. Our only criterion was that the contributor should be minimally 'established' in her/his career; no students or postdocs have been included. It is not that we feel such people have nothing to contribute; rather, we sought to include the advice of those who have already 'made it' into a 'permanent' post. As this project has been completed in association with the BSA, many contributors are members, or actively recruited by the association. It is for this reason that the focus has been on British sociology and sociologists. Beyond this, we were keen to ensure that contributors of 'minoritised' groups were included, including minority ethnic, female and LGBT sociologists. In retrospect, the narratives are not as diverse as we had hoped, particularly in regards to tales from minority ethnic sociologists. It is to be hoped that this is something that can be rectified in a future volume.

All of the contributors were asked to address the same questions in writing their chapters:

- What is sociology to you?
- Why study sociology? (Why did you?)
- Why 'be' a sociologist – what does that mean?
- Looking back on your career, what would you have done differently?
- What advice would you give to someone starting out in a career in sociology?

Additionally, authors were asked to be mindful to write chapters that would be accessible and useful for students and early career sociologists, who are potentially facing similar opportunities and challenges to those they faced themselves.

The enthusiasm of scholars to contribute to this book both surprised and delighted us, especially given the busy time upon which we called on them (around REF deadlines);[1] several commented on the therapeutic and rewarding experience of writing their piece. Nonetheless, there was also a certain level of anxiety from scholars more used to writing about others than themselves. Several wrote to us asking for further information on 'style' and queried how 'academic' or not their chapter should be. Three asked to see other's contributions before embarking on their own. While some may have been simply courteous and attempting to 'please' the editors, others were clearly nervous about writing something different from their usual research 'outputs'.

Due to the relatively open guidelines given to the authors, we have amassed a group of chapters that approach the topic in varying ways, both thematically and stylistically, but primarily the questions provoked biographical narratives, with authors situating their own views and experiences of sociology alongside key experiences in their lives. Many, for example, talked about their first 'exposure' to sociological ideas, or how early experiences or their social positionings sparked the questions that drove their sociological enquiry.

What emerges in the personal biographies that follow are, however, not individual accounts of individual lives. The influence of others, and their impact on the author, clearly come across. No auto/biography is independent of others. As Cotterill and Letherby (1993, 74) state,

> Life histories…'tell it like is' from the lived experience of the narrator. They are invaluable because they do not fracture life experiences, but provide a means of evaluating the present, re-evaluating the past, and anticipating the future.

C Wright Mills argued that, 'no social study that does not come back to the problems of biography, of history, and of their intersections within a society, has completed its intellectual journey' (Mills, 1959, 12). This book seeks, in some small way, to do that with sociologists themselves. We are presenting the personal reflections and biographies of various sociologists. In keeping with their sociological training, they reflect on the wider social and historical aspects within their stories.

The danger of our approach is that by eliciting stories without guaranteeing anonymity, we limit the possibility of 'negative' stories, and encourage stories of success and positivity. We acknowledge these are limitations, though we feel that anonymous tales would have resulted in rather sanitised accounts – as discussed above, research foci and personal biography were often intertwined so anonymisation would have necessitated quite significant deletions and omissions. At any rate, not all of the accounts are biographical, and some of the biographical accounts describe significant failures and setbacks, though within the context of ultimately holding a 'permanent position' in one way or another. The diversity of tales reflects the diverse group we managed to recruit, in the hope that their stories will help and/or encourage others.

Description of the book

The chapters that follow tell a story about sociology in the UK today. They tell us where sociologists are coming from, and where they are going. While nearly all the stories reflect on the autobiographical journey of the author, as any sociologist knows, society is not comprised of isolated individuals. This is neatly reflected in how the writers have interwoven their wider understanding of society into their personal biography. But the study of sociology or exposure to sociological ideas can also shape one's own life, and was used by many to understand their own life trajectories and social situations. Such overlaps show that, perhaps more than in any other discipline, sociologists' lives and works have a symbiotic relationship as we study everyday life and the world around us.

We have divided the chapters into three sections: What can sociology do?; What does it mean to be a sociologist?; and How does one become a sociologist? This division of chapters is not to suggest that each chapter in that section only addresses that particular theme, rather, they have primarily focused on that aspect in answering our questions outlined above.

Part 1: What can sociology do?

What emerges from the narratives in this section is the centrality of social activism to the sociologists' work; they have a desire to do more than 'just' analyse. Although the discipline provides a range of tools and skills with which to investigate the world around us, the outcome of this research for these contributors is intended to affect it. This is perfectly illustrated by Liza Schuster's powerful discussion of conducting research with vulnerable populations who have very difficult tales of injustice to tell her. Schuster tells us that she is 'committed to the search for understanding, to the resolution of social problems and to the formulation of public policies that will do more good than harm', but confronted with her participants she feels at times like a 'voyeur'. This conundrum pushes her to develop a way of being a sociologist that allows her to combine academic work with activism.

Schuster's chapter is followed by Mark Featherstone's exposition on the importance of sociology to explain social change. He argues that this makes sociology vital in today's world and he never loses sight of sociology as a utopian discipline that can make the world better.

The importance of public sociology is reiterated in a chapter from one of the most pre-eminent public sociologists in Britain: Zygmunt Bauman. Bauman refers to Burawoy's call for 'public sociology' (2004; 2005) and argues that 'sociological wisdom is needed more than at any other time of modern history'. Understanding the tumultuous world we live in will help us understand our own place within it and make us happier.

The following two chapters highlight the revelatory nature of sociology. Anthony Giddens describes how sociology looks at the mundane everyday interactions while simultaneously unpacking wider social structures and institutions. It is this sociological perspective that gives us wonder. For Bev Skeggs, sociology provides a range of perspectives, which allow us to understand the wider world. We need curiosity and imagination to push the boundaries of knowledge. More particularly, Skeggs argues that you have to 'stick to your instincts' and say things that may be unpopular in the wider public, or the academy; in her case it was to continue to talk about the concept of class.

Wider social movements can have a dramatic impact on sociology and sociological careers. John Holmwood discusses how feminism's emergence in the 1970s showed that class was not the only form of inequality in society. Understanding this inequality was important in order to challenge wider assumptions. He has put this into practice through the 'Campaign for the Public University' to challenge the current changes to higher education. Political activism has been also central to Sasha Roseneil's career. In her interview, Roseneil discusses how her feminism and anti-nuclear politics engaged her to research Greenham Common. She felt at home in the discipline, while also working on its 'edges'.

Communicating these social changes is a vital aspect of sociology. John Brewer's tale describes how 'communicating sociology's capacity to be both life-changing and life-empowering is what I see as the essential purpose of sociology teaching and research'. This is not just a rational response to provide impact for the managerial culture that impresses upon higher education. It is a moral imperative to improve the lives of those whose voices are muted. Similarly, Judith Burnett suggests that studying sociology allowed her to pass 'through the looking glass' into a new world. This personal journey and awareness should not just be used to influence our students, she argues, but policy makers as well.

The section ends with an interview with Les Back entitled 'Living sociology'. Like others in this book, Back did not start out in sociology, but in this interview he describes how he found a 'home' in sociology, helping him to make sense of his upbringing in a large public housing estate on the outskirts of London. His sociological interest continues to be driven by social questions, telling us that 'sociology is nothing if it is not concerned urgently with the key problems of what it means to live in the twenty-first century', and describing how he strives for new modes of sociological writing and representation to answer these questions.

Part 2: What does it mean to be a sociologist?

Authors in this section focused more on their identity as a sociologist, some relating a troubled claim to that identity, whether because of feeling 'outside' mainstream sociology, or because of other disciplinary backgrounds. Yvette Taylor's thought-provoking chapter poses the question of professional identity and how it is represented and misrepresented, bringing the reader to consider the 'absences and presence' in academia and to (re)consider failure and success. Ann Oakley continues this interrogation of 'success' and even a 'career', suggesting that it is a particularly gendered notion. She describes how she has struggled to work by feminist ideals in a 'masculine intellectual tradition'. In doing so, Oakley pushes the reader to turn her/his sociological eye on the academe, and on the very ambitions of sociologists and our readers.

Linsey McGoey's engaging tale refocuses on 'failure', but in a more humorous way, telling the reader that as an academic she strives to 'fail better'. We found this idea of failing better an engaging one to consider in the work of an academic given that so much of our work entails 'failure' and learning. Like Oakley, however, McGoey also describes how she strives to be a more 'purposeful' sociologist speaking 'truth to power'.

The next four chapters focus more on disciplinary boundaries. These writers ask us to consider what are the limits and particular strengths of sociology, and how one can identify a 'sociologist' or lay claim to being a 'proper' sociologist. Yvonne Robinson started out as a geographer, but charts her increasing identity as a sociologist. Like Taylor, she unpacks who is absent and present in the discipline, finding sociology more open to herself as a black woman, but ultimately describing herself as a 'sociographer'. Maxwell and Hodkinson meanwhile reflect on whether and how they can describe themselves as sociologists, having both come to their present position through different disciplines. They explore the 'fluid boundaries' of sociology (Maxwell), and how they have carved a space within those boundaries. Both Maxwell and Hodkinson also discuss 'the pressures and realities of research and writing in a national higher education context' (Hodkinson), each giving their own particular advice for early career academics. Scott's narrative perhaps provides the most 'sociological' tale in this section, the most assured in his sociological identity. He describes his career from the 1970s, always within sociology, but a sociology that has witnessed great change in that time, tracking how the political and cultural context has shaped his sociological practice.

Eileen Green also describes a career in sociology that began in the 1970s, but her story is quite different to Scott's: Green explicitly charts how her gender has had an impact on her career trajectory, and how feminism enabled her progression. Green's piece is also informative in the sense that she describes the myriad activities in which sociologists in the academe take part, and the juggling involved in managing these. Gayle Letherby also discusses the impact of being a relative outsider in academic sociology, but her chapter concentrates more on how her methodological experiments have potentially created this antagonism – without any regret for having made them! Letherby also charts how her personal life, in particular her experience of miscarriage, has shaped her sociological interests and enquiries.

The section ends with Ann Phoenix's discussion on the interdisciplinarity of her sociological approach. Ann Phoenix studied psychology before discovering sociology. She felt that the former overly focused on the individual while the latter looked at the structures of society. For Phoenix, it is important to understand society and the individual as inextricably linked. Interdisciplinarity helps foster that understanding.

Part 3: How does one become a sociologist?

This final section emphasises the career trajectories of active sociologists in the academy, with authors highlighting the various trials and tribulations that working in sociology can bring both professionally and personally. Each author provides powerful advice to young scholars seeking to 'make it' in sociology, and the peaks and troughs of this type of career. While most tales are encouraging, some are necessarily cautionary yet provide a significant lesson to those who seek the challenge.

In the first tale, Berry Mayall describes how her dual role as a mother and an academic has shaped her sociological career and tells us as much about her passion for a discipline as about her personal history. She calls for young academics to experience 'real world dilemmas faced by people' in order to grasp important sociological ideas. In a similar vein, Jocelyn Cornwell's interview explores a number of stops and starts in her own trajectory as a sociologist, retreating and returning to a discipline that seemingly never truly leaves you. Like Mayall, Cornwell argues that these 'real world' experiences are as much a part of a sociological learning process as work within the academy. She describes having no real strategy to her career but a 'thread' by which she moved from one interesting thing to the next.

Mel Bartley offers a cautionary tale of perseverance despite many setbacks to maintain her relationship with a subject for which she has great passion. Her tale is one of striving for permanence in the academy and the personal trials that have followed. Killick's experiences are as much informed by the negative as the positive and poses a story of emotional labour and upheaval when attempting to fit into new academic environments. She explores her position as 'foreigner' working in a new country and her negotiation of this unknown terrain.

Carol McNaughton Nicholls provides a celebration of her career in sociology by describing how much of a privilege it remains to lead the research that she does. She offers a considered advice section to young academics that focuses on communication, engagement with the world, being broad in your approach to research and caring deeply about what you do. Similarly, Kate Woothorpe's enthusiasm for sociology is the focus of her piece. She highlights how her appetite for sociology stems from its ability to allow you to understand why things happen, to challenge entrenched ideas and to 'find your own feet'. Her tale is one of some good fortune and timing but, centrally, hard work and persistence by getting to know different institutional methods and how to navigate within these. Anthony Heath's interview emphasises how an enthusiasm for solving life's problems makes for a good career in sociology. He describes how he has drawn on different kinds of sociology in tackling 'real world' problems, which were inspired by the social inequalities he observed among miners growing up in north-east England.

Drawing on personal experience, Richard Giulianotti and Rob Mears discuss how academic departments influence career trajectories. In the former tale, a key research culture in one department allowed for creativity and the ability to foster internal and external collaborations while the latter tale discusses the importance of theory to an academic's understanding of the social world.

Eric Harrison and Daniela Sime go on to describe how finding a career that you are passionate about can be as much about accident as design. Harrison notes that it 'never entered my head that I might become an academic' while Sime believes that she 'never decided to become a sociologist, sociology found me'. In a similar vein Jeffrey Weeks claims that he became a 'mistaken sociologist', finding a home in sociology after being ostracised from other disciplines. In these periods of exile, Weeks continued to write and suggests this as a central piece of advice to budding sociologists.

This section closes with Howard Wollman's reminiscent account of a varied career that has allowed him to work in many parts of the UK and experience multiple roles in research, teaching and management. He stresses the diverse opportunities that sociology can bring in a changing higher education market and the continuing need for a critical and challenging sociology that can help to change the world.

Embedded within these broad sections are a number of other themes. The current situation in UK higher education in particular is a spectre that haunts many of the accounts. The contemporary picture is reminiscent of the 1980s, with sharp funding cuts, a tough job market, and the dissolution or 'merging' of sociology departments. Increasingly sociologists have been asked to defend their discipline by demonstrating 'impact' and told they must 'publish or perish'. While authors demonstrated an enthusiasm to 'make the world a better place', and many enjoy the process of writing, these pressures can have the unfortunate tendency to push out early career academics who are overworked and often underpaid in insecure positions. The contributors to this book are in 'permanent' positions, but they are not immune to these pressures. A few discuss the difficulties, particularly for early career sociologists, in striking a balance between buying into these market driven ideas of higher education in order to 'make it', and being true to one's own ideals. Ultimately there is no one right answer, but it appears that the overarching advice is to at a minimum conduct the kind of research or teaching that interests and engages you.

On a more positive note, authors celebrate sociology and a sociological career, despite the setbacks and difficulties they encounter. For many there is a joy in intellectual puzzling which is grounded in the everyday questions of our time. Their decision to study sociology was often sparked by questions which emerged from the world around them, and in their narratives they celebrate the new (and continuously renewed) understanding which sociology brings to their lives. As Les Back tells us in his interview, sociology does not address just 'academic problems', but 'problems about how to live life.'

For their gems of advice and words of wisdom, we would like to thank all the contributors to this book. We hope that we have done justice to their work, and that our readers find as much enjoyment in reading the chapters as we have.

Note

[1] The REF is the Research Excellence Framework, the system for assessing the quality of research in UK higher education institutions. The research 'output' (for example, publications) for each institution is assessed, both internally and externally, to determine the amount of research funding to confer on institutions.

References

Becker, H, 1967, Whose side are we on?, *Social Problems* 14, 3, 239–47

Berger, P, 2002, Whatever happened to sociology, in *First Things* October

Burawoy, M, 2004, Public sociologies: Contradictions, dilemmas, and possibilities, *Social Forces* 82, 4, 1603–18

Burawoy, M, 2005, For public sociology, *American Sociological Review* 70, 1, 4–28

Cole, S, 2001, *What's wrong with sociology?*, Piscataway, NJ: Transaction Publishers

Cotterill, P, Letherby, G, 1993, Weaving stories: personal auto/biographies in feminist research, *Sociology*, 27, 1, 67–79

Goldthorpe, J, 2000, *On sociology: Numbers, narratives, and the integration of research and theory*, Oxford: Oxford University Press

Gouldner, A, 1968, The sociologist as partisan: Sociology and the welfare state, *The American Sociologist* 3, 2, 103–16

Horowitz, I, 1993, The *Decomposition of sociology*, Oxford: Oxford University Press

Marx, K, 1970, *The German ideology*, London: Lawrence & Wishart

Mills, CW, 1959, *The sociological imagination*, Oxford: Oxford University Press

Parsons, T, 1959, Some problems confronting sociology as a profession, *American Sociological Review* 24, 547–59

Ritzer, G, 1975, Sociology: A multiple paradigm science, *The American Sociologist* 10, 3, 156–67

Stanley, L, 2005, A child of its time: Hybridic perspectives on othering in sociology, *Sociological Research Online* 10(3)

Turner, S, Turner, J, 1990, *The impossible science*, London: SAGE

Urry, J, 1981, Sociology as a parasite: Some vices and virtues, in P Abrams, R Deem, J Finch, P Rock (eds) *Practice and progress: British sociology, 1950–1980*, London: George Allen and Unwin

Part 1
What can sociology do?

ONE

The sociologist as voyeur

Liza Schuster

Liza Schuster is a reader in the Department of Sociology at City University London. Her research interests include asylum and migration at local, national, European and global levels and exploring the interactions between them. She has conducted research in a number of European countries, in Morocco and Uganda, and more recently has carried out fieldwork in Afghanistan, examining the impact of deportation and the migration decision-making of families.

I was in Italy embarking on the first stage of a post-doctoral project that marked a shift to sociology, having completed my PhD in political science. After my first interview, I called John Solomos, who had been my PhD supervisor and was now managing this project, to say I couldn't do it – I couldn't be a sociologist. I felt ashamed, guilty, sleazy and above all, impotent. About 20 minutes into the interview with Rita, the tears had started flowing, first hers then mine, as she told me of her flight to Rome, the first night in 30 years that she had not shared a bed with her husband, the calls with her son demanding to know why she had left him when he needed her. I apologised for intruding and said we should stop, but she insisted on continuing, telling me that it was good to be able to put into words all that she had had to hide from her family during the weekly telephone calls. There was an unspoken agreement that when she and the other domestic workers met up on their Sunday afternoons in a park, they would not bring each other down by talking of their loneliness, how much they missed their husbands, their children and their lives back home. She told me she didn't need or want anything more from me, except that I listen to what she could not say to anyone she knew.

John offered reassurance, stressing the importance of listening to those about whom we write no matter how difficult the experience. Years later in the Moroccan desert, I was confronted by an angry man wanting to know why he should talk to me – what good would it bring him, stuck as he was in limbo, trying to return to a country that had deported him. I told him truthfully – 'None. If you speak to me, you will give me a gift I cannot repay.' He demanded I hand over my bag, and having examined the contents took a card and told me to leave. Some hours later, I received an email. He had made his way to the nearest town, and in an internet café had googled me. He had done his research and on the basis of my writings so far, decided that he would meet me after all, because he trusted me with his story. We met in a dusty café, surrounded by other men in a similar situation who took turns to tell me how they had left home, the journeys they had made and their plans, before turning the questions back on me – insisting that I explain why 'Europe' had deported them, didn't want them, refused to allow them to work, to look after their families, 'to live like Europeans'. And again, the question why did I want to talk to them, what was I going to do with the information?

For over 20 years, I have regularly been asked, and asked of myself, 'what is sociology for?' Teaching introductory sociology courses, I have lost count of the number of times I have read that sociology is the study of social facts, social relations, that it is about understanding social phenomena. I accept and am committed to the search for understanding, to the resolution of social problems and to the formulation of public policies that will do more good than harm, and also accept that these are necessary and sufficient reasons for becoming a sociologist.

And yet…in the field, they can feel very abstract. In the field, witnessing the personal challenges, difficulties and experiences of fellow human beings, it is easy to feel like a thief or a voyeur. This is especially so when using qualitative methods, encouraging people to share what are often the intimate details of their lives before thanking them and returning to a desk to write a paper or a book that improves the chances of promotion, but has little chance of making any difference to those without whom said paper would be impossible. And so the question – what is sociology for? – seems a very pertinent one. So too is the question of how to be a sociologist in a way that respects those with whom I work.

I don't dare to speak for sociology as a discipline – only for myself. I am an academic because I want to understand – and change – the way things are. Finding myself in Germany in 1992–93 I followed the asylum debate and the attacks on migrant hostels with bewilderment. Returning to Britain to find the same rhetoric but only a tenth of the asylum seekers, I found myself asking 'Why?' – why were wealthy, liberal states so hostile to people fleeing war and persecution? Given the focus on the state, and an undergraduate degree in politics and languages, I chose to pursue that question via a PhD in political science, but afterwards, thanks to John's influence, switched to sociology.

An approach that consistently asks 'Why?' must challenge the way things are, especially when calling into question norms, roles and practices that seem 'natural' or 'given' to those involved in them; an approach that uncovers relations of power that are invisible must call into question the operation of power whether at the micro- or macro-level. For me therefore, the practice of sociology is always and inevitably critical and political. I had been told on starting my PhD, that I would have to choose between academia and activism. John provided calm reassurance that this was not so. Why study social problems unless it is to contribute to their resolution? This does not necessarily mean going on demonstrations or campaigning against government policy, and some of my best friends draw strict boundaries between academic and political work, but it is possible to combine the two. I have had the good fortune to be mentored by Stan Cohen during my fellowship at the LSE, whose loss I continue to mourn.

Stan combined an intellectual rigour with serious moral commitment. Through his own work, especially *States of denial*, and long conversations in his office and the LSE common room, Stan showed me that the desire to alleviate or reduce human suffering was a legitimate motivation for becoming a sociologist.

Increasingly, I am working with vulnerable populations who have little education and who are sometimes illiterate, but who trust me even when they have no way of understanding what sociology is or what I will do with what they tell me. This creates a moral pressure to develop a way of *being a sociologist* that allows me to rebalance what often feels like (is?) an exploitative relationship. There are plenty of guidelines, right back to Weber, emphasising the importance of putting aside personal bias and stepping into the shoes of those being studied, to Bourdieu demanding that the sociologist objectivises him/herself and acknowledges the extent to which the world we describe is a production of our 'theoretical gaze' (Bourdieu and Wacquant, 1992, 69). But what does all of this mean practically? For me, it means a) using the knowledge and skills that I have to analyse and work with the data I am given, b) following where the data and the analyses lead, c) finding ways to open my analysis to my participants' critique and d) allowing those I am studying to make demands on me.

Allowing people to get close to me means allowing them to make demands on me and on my time. It means ceding control of the conversation and waiting until the person I am speaking to is ready to tell me what is important to them. I find much of my fieldwork now consists of conversations in which I respond to at least as many questions as I ask – about myself, my migration history, my family and my work, but also about visa regimes and migration destinations, about life in Europe and about whether I can help with letters of invitation, work, accommodation and contacts. And providing accurate information about issues that interest my interlocutors offers a way of recompensing people for the time and stories they share with me. It is not always a comfortable way of working, but the discomfort of this openness and proximity is infinitely preferable to the superficial comfort of adopting the pose and distance of the 'expert'.

The acquisition of data (and of funding) creates an obligation, however. The stories of migrants are vital to an understanding of migration but, contrary to what some seem to believe, do not speak for themselves. It is not enough to claim that one is allowing the voiceless to speak by presenting chunks of raw data harvested in the field. While people are the experts of their own lives, being a migrant does not mean that one understands migration as a social phenomenon. Understandably, most people are too mired in the quotidian challenges of working, caring for families, *living*, to be able to locate our experiences – migratory or otherwise – within a broader social context. As sociologists, we have the luxury of time to read, to study, to reflect on social phenomenon and probe common sense understandings. It is important not just to engage with people, but also with what they and other scholars tell us, to test our understanding against the understanding of others working in the field. As C Wright Mills (2000) suggests, we need to use our information to produce lucid summaries of what is going on in the world, to connect history and biography, to use our sociological imagination.

Finally, increasingly I try to test out my analyses and conclusions on those I am studying, asking if what I have said makes sense to them, whether I have represented their views or perspectives accurately, and where necessary I defend or amend my conclusions. Again, I don't suggest I am alone in working this way or offer this solution as a model, only an example of how one sociologist has, however tentatively, tried to resolve the challenges of doing sociology for herself.

Perhaps I have reinvented a fully functioning wheel, perhaps I would have found better solutions, perhaps I could have spared myself, and my interlocutors, my long journey towards this compromise, if I had actually studied sociology, but I learned my sociology through teaching it. For a long time I felt diffident describing myself as a sociologist. I don't regret having studied political science but a degree in sociology would have given me much more confidence in terms of methodology and ethics. And while it is important not to become hung up on methodology, I do wish I could at least understand more than basic quantitative methods. I have a continuing scepticism towards statisticians whose data seems to hide as much, if not more, than it reveals…and yet numbers wield incredibly seductive power. I wish I could rely more on solid knowledge than informed intuition when evaluating such 'hard' data and so if I was starting out, I would do an MSc in qualitative and quantitative methodology. Though often the least popular undergraduate courses, I do think every sociologist should grapple with them.

It is difficult to choose one book to recommend to a new sociologist – instead I would urge any sociologist to read widely and far beyond their area of special interest. Read the works of philosophers and historians, geographers and economists, political scientists and psychologists.

References

Bourdieu, P and Wacquant, L, 1992, *An invitation to reflexive sociology*, Chicago, IL: University of Chicago Press

Cohen, S, 2001, *States of denial: Knowing about atrocities and suffering*, Cambridge: Polity

Mills, C Wright, 1959/2000, *The sociological imagination*, Oxford: Oxford University Press

TWO

Why sociology?

Mark Featherstone

Mark Featherstone is senior lecturer in sociology at Keele University.
He has also worked in Canada and Japan. His areas of specialism are
social theory, cultural studies and psychoanalysis and he has written
widely on utopias, dystopias and globalisation.

Let me open my 'sociological tale' by explaining why I think we need sociology today, as this will shed light on my own background in the discipline and my views about what it means to be a sociologist. In our post-modern society where everything must have instrumental value, the question of the *usefulness* of sociology has come to haunt the discipline. How we answer this question will in many ways define the future of the sociological project in the UK and beyond. However, before we answer the question 'Why sociology?', perhaps a more fundamental question is 'Why *Why sociology*?' In other words, why is the question of the value of sociology, which has caused so many ruptures between those who regard sociology as a critical normative discipline, and those who believe it is an objective methodology for the accumulation of facts to be used by others in the creation of policy, such a serious one today? Although it is possible to trace this debate back to the founders of the discipline and explore differences between Marx, Weber and Durkheim in their view of the purpose of intellectual work, I think that it is also possible to relate the crisis of sociology, if we may call the troubling question of the usefulness of the discipline *a crisis*, back to much more recent social and political transformations which took place in the 1970s and which Zygmunt Bauman explains through the idea of *individualisation*.

These transformations, which Bauman connects to Thatcherism and the emergence of what we now call neoliberal capitalism, created a society premised on a view of the importance of the individual, self-realisation and the competitive spirit. In the wake of this shift from the social, which was, in Europe at least, largely understood through the concept of class and the idea of class struggle, to the individual, who has now become the focus of everything, it is not surprising that sociology has today become a kind of spectral discipline, a discipline haunted by questions of its own value and importance, but which also haunts contemporary society and the academy like a ghost from the past. What is the place of sociology in a society of individuals where the question of social relations is largely foreclosed? The answer to this question seems uncertain, undecidable. Ironically, I think that it is precisely because of this undecidability that sociology matters today. In a largely individualised society, where we normally think in terms of individuals outside of social relations, and we are continually thrown back upon our own resources, I think that it is even more essential to seek to understand the position of the individual in their social environment and think about the ways in which this is constructed by power relations.

In my view, it is the very spectrality of sociology, the fact that it is a discipline in crisis that seems *out of time*, unsure of its core purpose, that paradoxically confirms its importance and value as perhaps *the* critical discipline today. In this way I think that sociology is essential because it comes from some other place. It is an *outsider* discipline able to develop sociological analyses which cut against the grain, and are, by their very nature, critical in a kind of *asociety* that turns a blind eye to the existence of groups. Without sociology we are largely blind to the ways in which the individual is constructed and produced by others and its environment. I would also claim that this blindness is *the* problem of our age, a kind of areflexive, acritical, asocial lack of vision, which means that we cannot easily think about our place within the human-built environment and take charge of our collective fate. The current age of austerity is a classic example of this condition, where the market, a reified construct of human relations, becomes a *reason* for plunging entire nations, such as Greece, into dire poverty.

My view is that without some sociology the individual is lost in a manufactured human-built state of nature. In this way, I think that sociology, even if it is simply a kind of banal sociology, is necessary for individuals to find and situate themselves in the world. We need Marx, Weber, Durkheim, and their ideas, such as capital, rationality and anomie, because without them we have no purchase on our social world. In my own work, I have extended my theoretical toolbox to include others, including Freud, Heidegger, Lacan and Deleuze, because they have proved useful to me for understanding the social environment. There has never been a debate in my mind about whether or not these figures are sociologists, philosophers or psychoanalysts, and thus relevant to my work. The reason for this is that I have always taken the view that what matters is the usefulness of ideas for understanding basic sociological questions and enabling us to situate the individual in this thing called society which makes it possible to understand how they are made through their relation to, and contact with, others.

Beyond any expert, or technical, view of the value of sociology, I believe that sociology is about 'making sense of the world' and this is how I first encountered the discipline in the 1980s. Growing up in the period of transformation Bauman associates with the rise of neoliberalism and the individualised society in the 1970s and 1980s, I had a child's view of the decline of industry, the end of class war and the social decline of my home town of Hull in north-east England. It was, of course, impossible for a child to understand these changes in any technical sense, but I came to understand their effects first hand through the experience of family unemployment and depression and community decay and decline. Looking back I recognise that a heavy, depressed mood hung over the council estate where I was raised. I now understand the effect this had on my family and even on my own approach to social relations. At the time I was largely unaware of the weight of social change. It was simply part of life; I knew nothing else. Indeed, it formed a stark contrast to the normal, carefree attitude with which I, like every child, encountered the world as I learned about and entered into society through processes of socialisation. Later, as friends and their families moved away having bought houses under the Conservative push to expand the idea of a property owning democracy, I learned first-hand about community dislocation, and began to inherit a Marxist understanding of the world from my family who spoke in terms of workers and bosses and inequality and power.

As a follower of Freud, Klein and the basic idea of psychoanalysis, I have always believed in the formative influence of childhood experiences. My formative years and early experiences shaped my mature political orientation, approach to sociology, and also my methodological assumptions about the conduct of the discipline itself. In my view, sociology is a discipline rooted in embodiment and our relation to the human-built environment through our bodies which live, eat, go hungry, love and feel miserable and depressed. Against those who argue for sociology as a technical discipline, which can produce facts, I have always responded through reference to Heidegger and Merleau-Ponty – the 'I' is, and must be, situated. There is no view from nowhere, there is no objective position, because all knowledge is the product of the particular vantage point of some embodied mind or other.

Essentially, then, I have always thought, and tried to teach students that sociology is a *concrete* discipline rooted in experiences of the world, and for this reason nobody should feel overawed by sociological or conceptual language. There is no incorrect experience and the task of the sociologist is to learn how to express their experiences or understandings of the social world in such a way that they can connect to and be understood by others. Sociology is an essentially democratic discipline because it *must* be about the communication of experiences of the social world to others who may have different experiences. I do not think it can be anything else. However, in the same way that sociology is a concrete discipline, it is also fundamentally imaginative and metaphorical, aiming to understand the experience of others through empathic projections where I put myself in the other's shoes. Here, I become other in order to reach them.

This approach to sociology has been heavily influenced by Marcuse, who wrote about imagination, art and aesthetics, C Wright Mills, who discussed the sociological imagination and the ability to relate private issues to public problems, and Bauman, who explains the value of thinking sociologically, which relies on similar imaginative processes. I first encountered these thinkers in my undergraduate studies, but only really came to understand them much later on under the guidance of the Canadian sociologist, John O'Neill. He gave me the greatest gift that any teacher could ever give a student – the confidence to think freely and express his or her experiences. I feel privileged to have been taught by him. This imaginative, artistic element of sociology needs to be emphasised in the contemporary discipline where it has been played down especially since the empirical turn, which associates knowledge with some objective truth 'out there', rather than art and imagination as I have discussed it. This balance needs to be redressed, especially today in our end of history post-modern society, where it feels as though there are no new ideas, and society seems to lack the kind of imagination, direction and hope that characterised the modern period of history.

As my own career developed I focused on the idea of hope and the concept of utopia, and started to write about the ways in which these notions can be seen to relate to contemporary social experience. In terms of my broader understanding of my discipline, I have also come to regard sociology as a utopian discipline with a very clear mission, which is to first, diagnose social problems, second, critically analyse these problems, and third, seek to create interventions to resolve these problems in the invention of a better social future. Although this vision of sociology has been shaped by a range of thinkers, including some of those mentioned above, but also others including the psychoanalysts Melanie Klein and Donald Winnicott who wrote about the importance of objects, environment and hope in the world, I am also aware that, despite everything, very little has changed since my childhood encounters with my parents' basic version of Marx – a thinker who was, and is, able to validate everyday experience and provide a hopeful vision of a possible future free of the exploitation and daily humiliation that characterises today.

This approach to sociology has sustained me through my career and enabled me to maintain my belief in theoretical, culturally orientated work in the face of the empirical turn. My belief in and fidelity to this approach concerned with sociology as creativity means that there is very little about my career that I would change. On the basis of my experience, this would be my advice to new sociologists: have the courage to follow your beliefs. Apart from this, I think that it is important to understand the history of sociology and related disciplines such as philosophy, and not take this intellectual tradition for granted or imagine that it is no longer relevant. Tradition is necessary to innovation; we must be situated in a cultural history in order to move forward into the future. Along the same lines, I think that it is important to observe a kind of Socratic humility before tradition and remember that there is much that we do not know. Arrogance is a dangerous enemy. When I meet academics who seem very sure of the irrelevance of what has gone before, and assume that they already know everything, I take the view that they probably know nothing.

In order to avoid this situation I think that the good sociologist must continue to read, study and ask questions in order to keep their discipline alive. In this respect, I would warn against a fall into, what Alvin Gouldner called, *methodolatry* – where technique thinks so we no longer have to. I would also argue that sociology is a communicative discipline, concerned with critical engagement with society. However, I think that sociologists must remember that they are more than the handmaidens of the state and must be free to be creative, imaginative and independent in their thinking. Finally, I do not think that there is any way to disengage teaching from research. I do not believe that one can be a good teacher without research to teach or be a good researcher without the capacity to communicate to those learning about sociology. In my view sociologists have an ethical responsibility to teach in order to communicate their work to the next generation of intellectuals.

How to respond to my initial question then, 'Why sociology?' The answer is that sociology is necessary to keep society alive and prevent it from becoming unreflective and stupid. In this way, sociology is society's mirror. Through study, diagnosis, critique and intervention sociology can ensure responsible, active, social change. I think that this is sociology's utopian mission.

THREE

Sociology as a science/technology of freedom

Zygmunt Bauman

Zygmunt Bauman is professor emeritus of sociology, University of Leeds. His latest publications (all published by Polity) are: *What use is sociology?* (with Michael Hviid Jakobsen and Keith Tester), 2014; *Does the richness of the few benefit us all?*, 2013; *Liquid surveillance* (with David Lyon), 2013; *Moral blindness* (with Leonidas Donskis), 2013.

It was Michael Burawoy who almost two decades ago alerted us all that sociology was losing its link to the public arena…Following his hint, I suggested then that the extant academic sociology groomed and honed to serve managerial reason was singularly unfit to properly service the emergence of a radically different public composed of individuals burdened now with functions abandoned and 'subsidiarised' down the line in the course of the on-going 'managerial revolution mark two'; and that a thorough re-adjustment of sociology (of its agenda and problematics, strategic goals, language) is for it now, literally, a life-or-death matter. What was and still is called for is a fully and truly watershed change of its status and character from a science/technology of un-freedom to the science/technology of freedom: admittedly a highly demanding endeavour – yet one capable of opening up to sociology an unprecedentedly vast public and set an equally unprecedented public demand for its services.

At all times of its two-centuries long history sociology focused on the aspects of human condition deriving from the fact of being a '*social* animal' – living in society, in the company of others, interacting with others, and so on: 'sociality' of humans is and cannot but be for sociologists that 'difference that made its difference' of other humanities. Long before C Wright Mills, Albion Small, one of the pioneers of sociology in the US, pointed out that sociology was born of the *desire to improve society* – the tacit premise being Aristotle's proposition that 'good life' is conceivable solely inside a good polis and that only beasts or angels can live outside a polis. Want to do something about the quality of human life? Then start from doing something about the quality of society which shapes humans, while being shaped by them. There was, so to speak, a sort of 'elective affinity' between such an understanding of the services sociology was bent on rendering and promising to render, and the 'managerial reason' of the time, bent on determining desirable human actions by manipulating their probability of being chosen – through manipulating the setting in which the actions are to be designed, undertaken, conducted and seen through; a manipulation calculated to limit, narrow down and best of all eliminate altogether the actors' choice…

Managerial reason has changed since, alongside the strategy of domination – shifting from the emphasis on 'hard power' (extricating discipline through coercion or its threat) to 'soft power' (relying more on temptation and seduction). In a nutshell, the idea of 'good life' nowadays is cut out from the idea of 'good society' and turned into a DIY job, a matter of individual concern and individual performance: no longer it is the question of 'improving society' but of finding/

constructing a relatively comfortable niche in a badly discomforting social setting largely beyond repair. The resulting radical change in human condition confronts sociology with the need to re-think and recompose its vocation…In the present-day society, individualised by the decree of fate aided and abetted by the second managerial revolution (consisting, by and large, in the managers 'subsidiarising' their managerial tasks to the managed), sociology faces, however, the demand and a chance of turning, for a change, into a *science/technology of freedom*: of the ways and means through which individuals-*by-decree* and *de jure* of the liquid-modern times may be lifted to the rank of individuals-*by-choice* and *de facto*.

Under the new circumstances, the business of sociology is a continuous, un-ending and indeed two-sided conversation/exchange with 'common sense' construed by and invested into human experiences – and that means with the rank and file practitioners of life, not with the spokesmen for one or another profession, including our own; in our thoroughly deregulated, individualised age more than at any other stage in the history of sociology. In that conversation/exchange we appear in the dual role of teachers and pupils and we enter it with no up-front guarantee of being in the right. In order to be listened to and heard in that sort of exchange, one needs to learn the art of listening and hearing what is said. Practicing our vocation requires a balanced blend of self-confidence with demureness. It also takes some courage: interpreting human experiences it is not the kind of life I would recommend to weather-cocks.

In my view, the crucial objective of such an on-going conversation is in the long run the breaking of the widespread, perhaps even nearly universal habit of 'non-sociologists' (known otherwise as 'ordinary folks in their ordinary life') to evade the 'in order to' category of explanation and deploying instead a 'because of' type of argument when it comes to reporting their conduct (a habit noted and discussed at length by Alfred Schütz). Behind that habit there is a tacit, occasionally articulated though mostly un-reflected upon and hardly ever questioned presumption that 'things are as they are', 'nature is what it is – full stop', and a conviction that there is little if not nothing that actors – singly, severally or collectively – can change in nature's verdicts. What results is an inert worldview immune to argument while entailing a truly deadly mixture of two beliefs: in indomitability of the order of things, human nature or the state of human affairs – and in human weakness boarding on impotence. That duo of beliefs prompts an attitude which can be only described as 'surrender before the battle started'. Etienne la Boétie famously gave that attitude the name of 'voluntary servitude'. In his *Diary of a bad year* (Vintage Books 2007) JM Coetzee objected: 'La Boétie gets it wrong.' And he proceeded to spell out what was missing in that four-centuries old observation yet gains fast in consequentiality in our times: 'The alternatives are not placid servitude on the one hand and revolt against servitude on the other. There is a third way, chosen by thousands and millions of people every day. It is the way of quietism, of willed obscurity, of inner emigration' (p 12). People go through the moves, docile to their daily routine and resigned in advance to the impossibility of changing it, and above all convinced in the irrelevance and ineffectiveness of their own actions or their refusal to act.

And how to accomplish such passage? What is the strategy to follow? The strategy consists in engaging in an ongoing dialogue with '*doxa*' or 'actor's knowledge' (which sociology, attuned to the old-style managerial reason, denied cognitive value and set out to 'debunk', 'uproot' and 'correct'), while observing the principles recently suggested by Richard Sennett in his essay on the present meaning of 'humanism': precepts of informality, openness and cooperation. 'Informality' means the rules of dialogue are not pre-designed; they emerge in the course of the dialogue. 'Openness' means: no one enters the dialogue certain of his/her truth and tasked with convincing the others (holders, a priori, of wrong ideas). And 'cooperation' means: in that dialogue all participants are simultaneously teachers and learners, while there are neither winners nor losers…The price to be collectively paid for neglecting, collectively, that advice, can be the (collective) irrelevance of sociology.

Alongside the questioning of the worldview that underpins such 'quietism', the sociological variety of conversation aimed at the expansion of individual freedom and the collective potential of humanity pursues the task of revealing and unravelling the features of the world which, however deceptive and misleading they might be, supply nevertheless some grounds for a kind of worldview that sustains and continuously galvanises 'quietist' attitudes. 'Relativisation' aims at both sides of human experience – external ('what happens to me') and internal ('how do I live through it'): it is the dialectics of their interaction that could be named as the conversation's ultimate objective.

Sociology, as the rest of society whose dynamics it is called on to unravel and grasp, lives currently in what professor Keith Tester of Hull University, drawing on the Italian philosopher Antonio Gramsci, has described as a period of 'interregnum': of such time in which old ways of doing things manifest daily their inadequacy, whereas new and more effective ways hoped to replace them have not yet reached a planning stage… This is a time when everything or almost everything can happen – but little if anything can be undertaken with certainty, or even high probability of success. I suspect that predicting the destination toward which we move under such conditions (and even less the destination to which we are bound to arrive in their result) is irresponsible and misleading, as the impossibility of a purposeful action reaching the roots of liquid-modern problems, and the absence of agencies able to undertake it and see it through, is precisely what defines those conditions.

This does not mean however that we should stop trying; but it does mean that while never stopping to try we need to treat every successive attempt as another interim settlement: one more experiment, in need of thorough testing before it is proclaimed a 'final destination', or a 'fulfilment' of our vocation.

Can the labours of sociology help people in their pursuits of meaningful, gratifying and altogether happy lives? They can – if seeing-through the social world that we shape and that shapes us, our condition and our intentions and dreams, makes one happier than s/he otherwise would've been…On the other hand, there is little chance of happiness in closing one's eyes on the intricate mechanism of such reciprocal conditioning, or in turning them the other way. And a fleeting chance it would necessarily be, just as in inebriation or drugging – with a heavy price in the currency of frustration to pay once the moment of sobering up (inevitably) arrives.

In our times of massive deregulation resulting in the condition on uncertainty and perhaps misleading, but all the same widespread and deeply harrowing feeling of individual impotence in the face of unpredictable turns of events, sociological wisdom is needed more than at any other time of modern history.

FOUR

Why sociology matters

Anthony Giddens

Anthony Giddens is a fellow of King's College, Cambridge, former professor of sociology at Cambridge and former director of the London School of Economics and Political Science. Among other works, he is the author of an introductory textbook, *Sociology*, now in its seventh edition (2013, Polity).

The most important maxim in sociology – indeed in the social sciences as a whole – is that human society is infinitely greater than the sum of the individuals whose activities compose it. It was Durkheim's main contribution to the subject, but it is often misunderstood. In my eyes at least it does not mean that society is some sort of grand entity, or that the subject-matter of sociology is only about the large-scale institutions, such as the political system or the economy. On the contrary, society is there in the smallest of individual gestures and the most personal of thoughts – and the reverse also applies. You open up your mobile phone and check whether you have any text messages or emails. It is an everyday action and in some respects a private and personal one. Just sit back and think for a moment what such an everyday action involves – it is quite stupendous. It presumes years of technological advance in electronics and computer science, themselves quintessentially collective activities. It presumes a whole history of social time management. Time was not standardised until well into the nineteenth century, even on a national level. Until about the 1840s different parts of the country had their own local times. There was no national railway timetable, for example, until quite late on. There were no internationally-accepted time zones until much later in the century. They were established by a congress that met in 1884 in Washington. International travel and communications were fragmented affairs until then. Many activities we take for granted now were simply impossible. Today you can email or call anyone anywhere in the world on your phone, or get on a plane and know the time it will arrive at its destination. It is so familiar that more or less everyone takes it for granted. Yet the complexity and level of global co-ordination that lies behind those simple actions is simply stunning.

Sociology is revelatory in a way that most other subjects simply can't match. The main point of sociology, as I would see it, is to prise open the mundane, the everyday, and disclose the richness of what lies behind them. It is to look at the interaction between personal life and the great sweeps of history and institutional change that it presumes but also in some sense contributes to. This is the reason why, if it is well taught, sociology exerts such a grip on anyone coming to the subject for the first time. You fall in love with someone and begin a relationship. It would seem one of the most elemental of human experiences. Yet did you know that the term 'relationship' – meaning an emotional tie with another person – did not even exist in the modern sense only 50 years ago? The idea of romantic love has a long history, as does the institution of marriage; but the two were only rarely tied together. For most of the past, and in most cultures, marriage was contracted on the basis of property, influence or prestige. Most often, marriages were arranged by parents or other kin, not freely contracted by the couples involved. Arranged marriages, of course, still exist in many parts of the world, but for many people today marriage is the outcome of a 'relationship' – based on personal and sexual appeal.

Sociology presumes studying social life and institutions in an objective and impartial way. This perspective often means that what is taken to be 'common-sense' in a particular social context is in fact either invalid or too ambiguous to really offer a satisfactory explanation of a particular activity. Robert K Merton pointed out that common sense explains little or anything most of the time. The reason is that common-sense sayings are usually deployed after the event, depending upon what seems to have taken place. Suppose someone makes an investment on the stock-market and it goes disastrously wrong. His or her friend might say 'Look before you leap!' However, if the move had been successful, the investor might admonish those who urged caution, declaring: 'He who hesitates is lost!' The explanations are of no value, because all the options are covered.

The sociologist, in other words, takes a scientific approach to social life. There are long-standing arguments within the field, however, about how the word 'scientific' should be interpreted. Some argue that sociology should aspire to be as close to the natural sciences as possible. For them, the best sociological research is highly quantitative. Others, including myself, take a more relaxed view. Quantitative research is indeed highly important and there are some areas, such as the study of social mobility for example, where it is indispensable. Yet there are at least as many contexts where the intensive study of a few individuals can yield insights that no amount of number-crunching could reveal. Very often the two approaches in fact need to be combined. For example, to properly understand social mobility we need to study the phenomenon statistically but also enquire into the personal experience and attitudes of the individuals involved.

I would like to be able to say that I was drawn to sociology because of its revelatory nature as described above – as a result of a naturally enquiring mind. Yet it wouldn't be true at all. I had never heard of sociology when I was at school. There was no A-level sociology in those days. I wasn't in any way academically-minded. My results were mediocre to say the least. I managed to get to stay on in the sixth form but because I was far from being an ideal pupil it was against the opposition of the school more than with its support. Out of a large sixth form, only three of us were not made prefects, which meant we had to roam the school during breaks between lessons looking for an empty classroom in which to sit. The prefects had their own room to go to. I determined to try to go to university, but to this day I can't remember really why. I think I saw it vaguely as a sort of rebellion. No-one in my family had been to college before. The school gave me very little help. I had to go to the local library and check out universities. Latin was needed in many universities at that time for arts subjects, and as a student of Latin I was an abject failure. I managed to find three universities where Latin was not required and applied to them. Two of them turned me down flat. I was given an interview and accepted by the third, the University of Hull.

I applied to study philosophy, a subject in which I'd got interested precisely because it wasn't taught at school. I had no real idea what philosophy was. I acquired some books in Indian philosophy that I had stumbled across in a second-hand bookstore. It seemed to impress those who interviewed me. Unfortunately there was only one main lecturer in philosophy at Hull in those days, and he was away in Sweden for the academic year. I tried to switch to English but the department wouldn't accept me. There were places available to do a joint degree in psychology and sociology and so that was what I opted to do, without knowing what these endeavours were about. I was extremely lucky. The two departments at Hull were outstanding. Each boasted an inspirational teacher – Peter Worsley in the case of sociology and in psychology, George Westby. I owe a great deal to both. While at Hull I wrote my first published academic paper. It was a study of the hall of residence in which I lived, a few miles away from the university itself. Peter Worsley encouraged me to submit it to the *Sociological Review* which, amazingly, accepted it.

The experience didn't make a scholar of me. Peter suggested that I apply as a graduate student to the London School of Economics. I did so, and was accepted. Many years later I was to become director of the School; but my experience there as a student was not a particularly happy one. I cannot in any way blame the LSE for that. I had no intention of pursuing an academic career and did not choose a 'significant' subject to study. I opted to pursue the sociology of sport, which in those days was non-existent as a respectable academic subject. I wrote a lengthy dissertation for a master's degree, but was not accepted to proceed to a full PhD. Insofar as I had any career in mind at all, I was thinking of trying to become a civil servant. My academic career started by accident. A friend saw an ad for a post at the University of Leicester and suggested I apply for it, which after some humming and hawing I did. Luck and contingency play a very large part in most peoples' lives, no matter how much they might find a pattern or a driving force looking back. There was probably no other sociology department in the country that would have offered a job to a 22-year old with a master's degree in the sociology of sport. However, in the Sociology Department at Leicester there were again two outstanding individuals – Ilya Neustadt and Norbert Elias. They attracted a range of exceptional individuals to the Department.

What was more important from my point of view, they had an interest in areas that weren't seen elsewhere as significant: including the sociology of sport and play. So I squeezed in and my academic career started from there. At Leicester I imbibed much of the passion that Neustadt and Elias brought to their engagement with the social world.

What advice would I offer to someone embarking on the study of sociology today? (1) Don't drift into the subject in the way in which I did! Think through your aspirations at a much earlier stage than I was able to do, at least if you possibly can. Most will find, however, as I have done, that there is a lot of contingency in life. (2) Don't take sociology thinking that it is an easy option. It isn't. You will have to master statistical method as well as deal with esoteric forms of social theory, and master a lot of comparative data from different countries and parts of the world. (3) Sociology is most rewarding, however, if it is not treated as just another academic endeavour: it is also a path of self-exploration, at least if explored with enthusiasm. You will find that the world doesn't look quite the same as before, or your own place in it. (4) Don't lose hold of the sociological perspective when your studies are over. Continue to look at the everyday and the mundane with a sense of wonder.

FIVE

Passion, curiosity and integrity

Beverley Skeggs

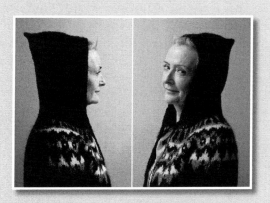

Beverley Skeggs is an ESRC professorial fellow in sociology at
Goldsmiths, University of London. She has worked in the areas
of women's studies and cultural studies. Her main publications
include *The media* (1992, Macmillan), *Feminist cultural theory* (1995,
Manchester University Press), *Formations of class and gender* (1997,
Sage), *Transformations: Thinking through feminism* (2000, Routledge);
Class, self, culture (2004, Routledge), *Sexuality and the politics of violence
and safety* (2004, Routledge) (with Les Moran, Paul Tyrer and Karen
Corteen), *Feminism after Bourdieu* (2004, Blackwell, with Lisa Adkins),
Reality TV and class (2011, BFI/Palgrave) and *Reacting to reality
television: Audience, performance, value* (2012, Routledge) (both with
Helen Wood). She is the co-editor of *The Sociological Review*.

To me sociology is a way of approaching the world; it's not only a perspective but also a passion. It's a way of understanding who we are, how we are and how to understand other elements such as people, organisation and technology. It's a way of understanding that moves through different scales, from the individual (as it is constructed in its singularity through the idea of the self) to the multiple global scales of capitalism operating throughout the world. I love the way sociology enables us to move through scales with specific forms of understanding. For instance, sociology shows us how the self is produced as an *idea* over time, repeated until it appears as common sense – so that we do not notice that it is a very specific idea, based on promoting and consolidating the interests of a particular group against its constitutive opposite – the mass. We grow up hearing, seeing and learning to believe in such ideas and use them to make sense of our lives and then suddenly we encounter sociology which enables us to see how the self is a fabrication, a way of insulating ourselves from others, a way of owning property in ourselves, of becoming a 'proper person' and a way of blocking off other ways of seeing. When C Wright Mills talks of the sociological imagination he is talking about perspectives – what we can and cannot see and how.

I love the way that sociology never ceases to surprise me, of how it enables me to switch into new ways of seeing. I excitedly anticipate being exposed to the assumptions I take for granted that will be blown apart in the future. This is why I love finding new books, new articles and hearing people talk about new areas. I remember when I first came across Marx as an O-level student (aged 16 years old in a College of Further Education) and it literally changed my life. It made me understand the world differently. As did Pierre Bourdieu's understanding of 'cultural capital'. The same happened when I came across different forms of feminism – they enable me to see the world differently. I was offered new forms of interpretation, understanding and new ways of doing and being.

Sociological knowledge can enable switches in perspective by offering a range of ways of understanding. This range is incredibly useful when doing research, operating as a theoretical tool kit, enabling one to work out which explanations are the most useful, which ones have 'explanatory power' and which theories cannot make sense of what is happening and what matters.

The metaphor of seeing translates into experience. By seeing things differently one experiences the world differently. Going to a very posh university with very posh people made me feel like matter out of place. Marx, feminism and Bourdieu, however, enabled me to connect my shame and discomfort to how the world operated and provided me with life-long research questions, such as how some people can and want to invest in their own superiority at the expense of others.

Many of my sociological inquiries have led me to the question of why we consent to power. That is a great (Gramscian) sociological question which pushed me into different sociological explanations – is it because of a lack of alternatives? (What would alternatives look like?) Is it because of psychic fear and insecurity? (What would security look like?) Is it because of different relationships to the past and to the future? Do we actually know what we are doing? Are we just caught up in performing ourselves without knowing? Being pushed into concepts in order to answer questions is a positive experience. They put us to work, extending us and taking us into different domains.

This is also why I love doing empirical research. People are complex creatures. We live multiple contradictions over time and space. This is why I'm less keen on the hit and run one-off interview approach that can only capture a moment of a speech act produced through a contrived encounter. To understand whom we and others can be we need to concentrate our attention over time. I did a longitudinal ethnographic study of subjective formation (*Formations of class and gender*), to understand how class and gender shaped who, what and how we could be and do. I loved exploring the gaps between words and deeds, always evident when you spend time with people. I was often perplexed but most of all I loved being surprised. When the research participants said things or behaved in ways I could not understand, I'd be forced to *make* sense, ditching preconceived assumptions and theories.

There is a great sociological delight in making things make sense when they don't appear to do so. In a study of the LA Watts riots in the 1960s Guy Debord (2008) notes how people were looting fridges even after the area had been burnt down and there was no electricity. What a great act to understand the desire for impractical objects to those who have no access to them. The London rioters of 2011 were much more practical.

I also really appreciate how latent and lurking thoughts are made manifest. When we were doing the research project on reality TV (*Reacting to reality TV: Audience, performance, value,* with Helen Wood) I had been reading lots on affect which linked me back to a memory of something I'd read years ago (Larry Grossberg, on affect as the missing link in ideology – on popular music). I tracked it down, it was from 1988, and it helped me make sense of reality TV as a sensation-generating form that manipulated emotional responses from our participants. But what a lot of theories did not explain was how affect was converted: what happened to it after it was expressed. This gave us a great way to explore what affect *does* and unexpectedly led to a whole challenge to theories of ideology.

This analysis also took me back to thinking about value and judgement, which made me realise that all my work has been about e/valuation and value formations and it made me further question Bourdieu's analysis (which began in depth when I tried to make Bourdieu connect to feminism; an experiment that failed as Bourdieu does not understand how gender proceeds through ambiguity (see Skeggs, 2004). I'm now trying to develop this further and have just embarked on an ESRC fellowship on 'a sociology of value and values', which will be the culmination of all my research pushed in new directions (how digital social relationships and prosperity theology connect value to values: see https://values.doc.gold.ac.uk/).

It is the interrogation, not just of common sense but of sociological sense, that I think makes us push the barriers to our knowledge. To be a good sociologist I truly believe that you have to be open and curious and to do so you need a range of sociological tools (Latimer and Skeggs, 2011). These range from detailed conceptual understanding (always define your terms, always know why you are using a particular idea/concept, know its etymology and applications), to historical knowledge of how things appear to be the way they appear to be, why people do the things they do (alternatives, investment and incitements) to a methodological tool kit for understanding why people speak in a particular way (discursive framing), and are likely to tell and perform in the research encounter.

Sociology is a relational way of understanding the world – whether it's the relations between capital and labour, or mothers and daughters. It is the social relations that shape our conditions of possibility. And 'conditions of possibility' is such a useful frame for understanding. Possibility will always be complex because we are located in many social relations, but it is by interrogating the complexity of those relations that we forge new ways of understanding.

For somebody starting out in sociology I'd say 'stick to your instincts'. When I've come across new ideas via new books, papers and so on, sometimes they speak directly to me (for me Marx, feminism, Bourdieu), but sometimes I feel they are instinctively wrong. For instance, those who just theorise their own experience and somehow seem trapped in their own privilege. They talk about there being no such thing as class (as they try and promote their own brand of banal theory instead). Even when they become fashionable, usually as a result of banality – see (McLennan, 2004) and everybody cites them

I'll stubbornly refuse. Concepts must have explanatory power not just trending status. Sometimes I'll be forced to mount a critique but frankly I'd much rather work with good ideas to build on or modify than waste my time taking apart rubbish.

So it's a matter of working with what makes sense but also recognising that some ideas take time to work. I was sceptical about performativity when I first came across Judith Butler in the early 1990s but instinctively felt there was something in it. Applying it to my ethnographic research showed how it lacked an understanding of class: conscious performance can blow apart performativity (unconscious iteration) as class disrupts gender and sexuality. The 'forced' performances spectacularly revealed by reality TV intensify this breakdown, challenging how we come to understand different forms of classed gender. Some things are worth spending time on.

It's also great going back to things you found interesting and re-reading – they often offer up new perspectives. It's sad that as academics we have been under so much pressure since the 1990s to publish not fully worked out ideas in order to be REF-able (the method that measures our productivity from writing, research grants and impact, and like McDonald's burger chain rewards us with stars that are then collectivised to our departments, universities and lead to the distribution of government funds). We don't need to keep finding new ways of saying the same thing as is often the case. Sometimes it's good to dwell with ideas. I now see all my writing as work in progress rather than a fully formed product. It is an engagement and an intervention in a debate rather than a steadfast result, product or truth.

A connected point to trusting instincts is to 'keep integrity'. When people continuously said to me 'class doesn't matter' – from the 1980s fashion of post-modernism into 1990s Foucault and Latour, I stuck to my guns. I was able to argue why it did. And now I've learnt that every time a new theory comes along it's not very hard to work out its class production. I've fought hard to keep class on the agenda in both feminism and sociology and now as we enter horrific austerity (where people are having to use food banks to survive in the seventh richest country in the world), we have plenty of understanding of how and why the term is useful.

Class is not just a category but a complex idea about value that enables us to speak and understand inequality. I'm completely aware of how class is a rhetorical device but I'm also aware of how economic injustices make people feel if they have no form for political critique that can explain their circumstances. Hence, why every government for the last 30 years (sadly supported by some sociologists) has tried to deny that class exists. I'm still angry, frustrated and upset by these issues.

Also, if things are not happening in your sociological world make them happen – organise things to surround yourself with the people and debates you want to hear. There is something very nurturing about heralding people to discuss the things that matter. The struggle to establish feminism within sociology was not easy and continues (Skeggs, 2008).

I'd also say, however, learn how the world of sociology works. Read all the great work on audit and metrics (for example, Burrows, 2012) the REF, the way universities as institutions work and why and how the government intervenes. I never cease to be amazed by the people who work in sociology departments who do not understand the conditions in which they work – being a head of department has been very revealing of how those who study power do not often understand their own location in it.

Most importantly remember what matters. Stick with your project. Think about what you really want to do and how to make it happen. It takes time. I began with three part-time jobs in three different institutions. I knew where I wanted to be – Lancaster Women's Studies. I know I like to be surrounded by people who are really smart so that I can learn from them. There's a huge pleasure in enjoying just the corridor conversation with colleagues. I also love teaching, without teaching I am not tested to fully explain my ideas: there is nothing like a group of smart students telling you that you don't make sense to force a radical re-think.

Is there anything I'd do differently? Plenty. I'd not be so precocious and mean in book reviews. I'd not be terrified by the proper posh male Marxists that made me feel that I had nothing to offer their incredibly limited critiques. I'd learn more quickly that just because people can speak well does not mean they have anything clever to say; I'd spot snobbery as a disguise for lack of sharpness rather than revealing of it. I'd be more generous to those with whom I disagreed. And I'd learn to say 'No'. Insecurity and curiosity are a lethal combination. I'm very proud of being a sociologist and doing sociology. It changed my life and hopefully it will change others.

References

Burrows, R, 2012, Living with the h-index? Metric assemblages in the contemporary academy, *The Sociological Review* 60, 2, 355–72

Debord, G, 2008, The decline and fall of the 'spectacular' commodity-economy, *A Sick Planet*, Oxford: Seagull Books

Grossberg, L, 1988, *It's a sin: Essays on postmodernism, politics and culture*, New York, NY: Power Publications

Latimer, J, Skeggs, B, 2011, Introduction. The politics of imagination: Keeping open, curious and critical, *The Sociological Review*, 59, 3, 393–410

McClintock, A, 1995, *Imperial leather: Race, gender and sexuality in the colonial context*, London: Routledge

McLennan, G, 2004, Travelling with vehicular ideas: The case of the Third Way, *Economy and Society* 33, 4, 484–99

Skeggs, B, 2004, Introducing Pierre Bourdieu's analysis of class, gender and sexuality, *The Sociological Review Monograph*, 52, 2, 9–13

Skeggs, B, 2008, The dirty history of feminism and sociology: Or the war of conceptual attrition, *Sociological Review* 56, 4, 670–89

SIX

Sociology as democratic knowledge

John Holmwood

John Holmwood is professor of sociology at the University of
Nottingham. He did his undergraduate and postgraduate studies at
the University of Cambridge, with an interlude as teaching assistant at
the University of California, Los Angeles. He has held appointments
at the universities of Tasmania, Edinburgh, Sussex and Birmingham.
He has been chair of the Council of UK Heads and Professors of
Sociology (2007–12) and president of the BSA (2012–14). He is co-
founder of the Campaign for the Public University and co-founder
and joint managing editor of the free online magazine of social
research, commentary and policy analysis, *Discover Society.*

What sociology is to me is best understood in terms of my biography and career in sociology. I have come to see sociology as an expression of democratic citizenship and as centrally concerned with facilitating public debate over pressing social issues. Unsurprisingly, perhaps, given my involvement in forming the Campaign for the Public University, and my advocacy of public higher education, my commitment to sociology cannot be separated from my commitment to public education more broadly. This, too, has a biographical aspect – like others of my generation, I was a beneficiary of the 1944 Education Act and the 1963 Robbins Report and the expansion of public higher education supported by grants.

I went up to University in 1969 from a state grammar school (comprehensive schools were introduced for the cohort directly behind me) to 'read' the Economic Tripos at Cambridge University. Sociology was not available, but a Part 2 Social and Political Sciences Tripos with a strong emphasis on sociology had just been introduced and it was possible to change into it after the first year.

My family background was in tailoring (father and grandfather), very left-wing – communist leaning, in fact – but also socially conservative (my mother was the daughter of a prison warden and brought up in Wandsworth prison) and formed by the 'spirit of '45'. However, I must have been the only student at the time – the height of the student movement, sit-ins and demonstrations – to announce that I was changing from economics to sociology only for my father to say, 'but sociology is just bourgeois ideology'. 'Exactly,' I replied, 'that's why I want to do it!'

Steeped as I was in Marxism – virtually the only literature in our house was Left Book Club books and Marxist pamphlets – and having a daily diet of arguments about capitalism, I was attracted by the sociological alternative. The possibility of reforming capitalism, the promotion of progressive social reform and a different conception of freedom seemed to me to be central to sociology. Broadly, I was attracted to Durkheim, Mead and TH Marshall and found in my teachers precisely that sensibility. Reading the Marxist critiques of sociology that came to prominence as part of post-1968 reactions to sociological orthodoxies merely affirmed for me the significance and distinctiveness of the sociological imagination.

Oddly, my favourite author as an A-level student was EM Forster and what most resonated was his vision of resolving unsatisfactory dualisms and making connections as articulated through the character of Helen Wilcox in his novel, *Howards End* – 'Only connect! That was the whole of her sermon. Only connect the prose and the passion, and both will be exalted, and human love will be seen at its height. Live in fragments no longer.' That seemed to me to be at the heart of sociology, too, with its emphasis on the social self and complex interdependence.

On graduation, I went to study sociology at UCLA, at the height of the ethnomethodological movement. I took classes from Garfinkel and Schegloff, but the real influence was Melvin Pollner. One seminar stood out. He was recounting setting up fieldwork in a local mental hospital. He arrived in the lobby, where there was someone at reception. 'I am Dr Pollner,' he announced to the 'receptionist', 'here to see the Director.' 'That's interesting,' came the reply, 'because, I am also Dr Pollner and here to see the Director.' 'You don't understand,' said Melvin, 'I am Dr Melvin Pollner, from UCLA, and I have an appointment,' only to be met with the response, 'But I do understand because I am also from UCLA and I have an appointment.' There were several more iterations and Melvin described getting more and more exasperated and gesticulating with greater force, only to catch out of the corner of his eye, someone behind a plate glass door mimicking all his gestures. At this point, Melvin stopped. There was a pause. We asked for the conclusion of the story. 'The conclusion,' he said, 'is that *social reality is awesome.'*

The capacity for social life to be surprising, and for sociology to be surprising in turn, have, for me, been lasting pleasures of the discipline. This has been so, even when the surprises have come with a hard thwack. The eruption of feminism in the 1970s and 1980s was a shock. As a graduate student and after, I had been a member of the Cambridge social stratification seminar and the discovery that inequality was not only about class, but also was gendered, was both a shock to my intellectual system and an accusation against my sociological practice.

If, however, EM Forster had provided a lesson in the need to overcome class condescension and that, at the same time, it was a painful process, this provided a useful lesson in overcoming other condescensions of one's own privilege. Making connections and understanding that the sociological journey was one of self-discovery was one of the great lessons of feminism, usefully applied to other encounters that followed feminism's challenge to the academy and wider social relations. It reinforced my interest in Mead's (1899) account of reform and that social transformation also involved the disintegration and re-integration of the self.

It also, however, brought me an understanding that this process might all too easily become a routinised and ordinary part of our sociological life – that we can be unreflectingly reflexive – and that social change is frequently a source of anxiety, precisely because of its challenge to the sense of self and identity. I recall telling my mother that the 'left' stood for feminism and gay rights, as much as for hostility to capitalism. 'Don't be ridiculous,' she said, 'you are making it up!'

Of course, one of the purposes of family is to remind you, that, even as a professor, you might just be 'making it up'. The sociological imagination is about making imaginative connections and imagining different possibilities, but we also have to be attuned to the possibility that our imaginings are the consequence of our particular locations and experiences in the relatively privileged space of the university and may not resonate much beyond those locations.

Social change can produce different experiences and possibilities and displace even those who think themselves privy to the future. It would be hard to represent a career in sociology that traversed the 1970s to the present without addressing the external environment of wider social changes and ideological reconfiguration. For much of my career, and past the time when I should have known better, it seemed straightforward to me that social reform, amelioration and the public purposes of the university were all aligned with the development of the discipline. After all, the Robbins reforms of the 1960s brought about an expansion of universities and the great growth of sociology as a discipline – new departments, new appointments – but this brave new world began to fracture from the 1980s onwards.

By 1978, it was difficult to get an academic job – bizarrely, to anyone reflecting on current circumstances, I had been offered a lectureship directly after my undergraduate degree – and I moved to the University of Tasmania as part of the setting up of a new Department of Sociology. I returned to a post at the University of Edinburgh in 1980. This was one of the last permanent posts for over a decade. The 1980s were hard for sociology. The Thatcherite attack upon the welfare state also included sociology as a discipline that seemed peculiarly aligned with it, notwithstanding that many sociologists were also critical, albeit from a different political position.

Like many, I regarded Thatcherism as temporary and reversible in the normal cycle of party politics. Even the adoption of neoliberalism by New Labour did not initially dissuade me from a view of the cyclical nature of the political process. Now I am much less sanguine. Finally, I understand the anger of my parents – their anger at inequality and poverty, their anger at the corruption of political elites. Along with a sociological conviviality, I now express a sociological anger. Social reality is not only awesome, it is also distressing for many and sociology ought not avert its gaze and lose its sense of purpose in the improvement of the circumstances of publics and the deepening of democracy.

With a government committed to the reduction of public functions to the market, I fear we live in a profoundly anti-democratic age in which the anti-social sciences are promoted at the cost of the sciences of social structure. Evidence-based policy has become reduced to policy-based evidence, where what is wanted is a social science that accepts inequality as given and describes possible interventions to change individual behaviour. Sociology, for its part, necessarily imagines a different society.

As might be guessed from this short biography, I am an unapologetic advocate of sociology and defender of the discipline. I don't have much time for equivocal self-description in terms of some separate field of study or interdisciplinary identity. Like a stick of rock, sociology is written in me all the way through!

What is now under threat is the critical engagement and ways of understanding that the discipline represents and these need to be defended. I have been a member of the BSA since graduating and I have been actively involved in it. Part of this is simply the enjoyment of the company of fellow sociologists – as Durkheim said, 'to have the pleasure of communing, to make one out of the many, which is to say, finally, to lead the same moral life together' (1964, p 15). But as universities become unremittingly managerial and collegiality is undermined, its last bastion is the professional association. It is not necessary to join the BSA, but for any who complain about managerialism, it is incumbent on them to join some body that represents the meaning of academic life beyond a particular university's corporate branding.

I do think these are difficult times to start out in sociology. Perhaps surprisingly, I do not think the pressure will be that of getting a job, but rather the difficulties are all about the purposes that are enjoined upon academics under a neoliberal knowledge regime. But all situations, however negative, create niches and opportunities that give respite from the dominant trends. As ever for sociology, career cannot be all – and it is best to let one happen rather than to pursue one, to the neglect of the personal meaning derived from being an academic and sociologist. First and foremost, identify your own purposes and find the niche in which they can flourish.

What would I have done differently? Not very much. I would probably not believe everything I read in books. I read in Habermas that it was not possible to understand the nature of the problems confronting sociological theory without proper consideration of Parsons's work. I made the mistake of writing about Parsons, and subsequently found it difficult to persuade others that my interest was in the pathologies of sociological theory, not as an advocate of his approach.

More seriously, I wish I had fought the neoliberal onslaught on universities earlier, but this would probably have been to no greater effect. It is doubtful if academics are ever ready to look up from their studies and notice the impact of what is near at hand and most threatening to their ability to engage in those studies. I could be reconciled to that as our loss, but just for once the defence of sociology and of the public university has a greater cause than our own discipline and jobs and a greater consequence, namely the possibility of contributing to the imagination of a different society and the defence of fellow citizens against a partisan politics of austerity.

References

Durkheim, E, 1964, Preface to the second edition: Some notes on occupational groups in *The division of labour in society*, New York, Free Press

Mead, GH, 1899, The working hypothesis in social reform, *American Journal of Sociology* 5, 367–71

SEVEN

Pushing at the boundaries of the discipline: politics, personal life and the psychosocial

Sasha Roseneil in conversation with Katherine Twamley

Sasha Roseneil is professor of sociology and social theory, head of the Department of Psychosocial Studies and director of the Birkbeck Institute for Social Research, at Birkbeck, University of London. She is also a group analyst and psychoanalytic psychotherapist. She has written extensively on social movements (particularly feminist, peace and lesbian and gay movements), intimacy, sexuality and personal life, and the politics and practice of care, community and citizenship. Her recent books are *Remaking citizenship: Women's movements, gender and diversity* (edited with Beatrice Halsaa and Sevil Sumer, 2012, Palgrave) and *Beyond citizenship? Feminism and the transformation of belonging* (edited, 2013, Palgrave).

Katherine: Okay, so the first question, as well as the obvious question is: how did you come to be a sociologist? How did you come to be in the situation you are in now?

Sasha: I think one can always tell a lot of different stories in answer to a question like that, but one of the defining moments was when I was doing history A-level and we were studying mercantilism in early modern Europe, and I remember asking a question in class about why capitalism had developed as it did, in the West, in Europe. And my history teacher said, "That's not really the sort of question that we deal with. It's not a relevant question." And somehow, and I don't know quite how, I came to realise that it was exactly the sort of question that sociology asked. When it came to applying for university, I had been very, very keen on history at school, but I was also politically active and socially concerned in a way that it was hard not to be during Thatcherism, and I came to the realisation that I wanted to do something that was sociological and political.

I applied to Cambridge, under quite a lot of pressure from school, and that meant having to study something else first because, at that point, you couldn't do social and political sciences straightaway at Cambridge. So I applied to do History Part 1, and Social and Political Sciences Part II, and I got a place. But then, after taking the Cambridge entrance exams, and one term into the second year of the 6th form, I left school and went to live at Greenham Common. I had been involved in various anarchist, peace and animal rights groups in Northampton, and the world felt as if it were on the eve of destruction, and going to Cambridge really didn't seem very relevant. So, I left school – well, I was 'asked to leave', because I had been spending more and more time not at school, but on anti-nuclear demos and at Greenham. And so I went to live at Greenham. And after I had spent over a year living at Greenham, being part of this incredible social movement, living outside normality in so many ways, the idea of going to Cambridge just didn't compute. I couldn't go from all that to Cambridge. And also, I really didn't want to do history. I was quite clear by that point that I wanted to do sociology. So I applied to LSE, because I could carry on doing all the politics I was doing, which by that time was in London, and I could do sociology straight away.

Sociology has always felt like the right place for me, but it has also always never quite seemed like enough. So those parts of me that are interested in history and that are interested in politics have always been there; I've always been interested in the intersections with other disciplines. And I somehow made the right decision in going to LSE where they had the BSc (Econ) degree, which was a broad-based degree that required to you to study across the social sciences. My 'special subject' was sociology but I got to do quite a lot of history, and I did courses in government, law, the history of European ideas and German. I went on straight away to do a PhD after my undergraduate degree. I stayed at LSE, because I wanted to continue living in London, and I had realised that no one had really written anything about Greenham, and I really felt it needed to be written about and I thought, in the Greenham spirit of taking personal responsibility for what needed to be done, well, I should do it then. So I applied for an ESRC studentship, and as a back-up plan I applied for a law conversion course, and thought that if I didn't get a studentship I would become a barrister – which was also clearly related to my experiences with the legal system at Greenham. But I did get funding, and so I wrote my PhD about Greenham, in order to try and make sense of this incredibly important, world-changing, life-changing instance of feminist political action. And during my PhD I read a lot of international relations, and politics and history. It was the end of the 1980s and there wasn't much gender studies, or women's studies, around – it was a question of finding the bits that you could in different disciplines. I was very interested in questions of identity and subjectivity and there was a literature starting to emerge, a critical post-structuralist literature in psychology, and so I was piecing things together for my PhD from different places, and drawing especially on feminist theory, particularly American feminist theory, and the beginnings of queer theory, which emerged just as I was finishing my PhD.

And that mixture of all these different components is my academic world, my formation. It's not mainstream sociology, but it's the sociology I do. And over the past ten or fifteen years I became more and more interested in that space that is now psychosocial studies – the intersection between sociology and psychology, that really challenges the nineteenth century disciplinary structures that work against understanding all sorts of complex social phenomena and human experiences.

In some ways I was seduced, very early on, by the Comtean idea of sociology as queen of the social sciences, and in fact I still think that sociologists should be able to think about psychic life, we should be able to think about history, we should be able to think about politics, and law, and policy, and about space. And not all the tools for this are in sociology already, but social relations and the social formation are made through all these things, and human experience is made of all these things, so it should be within our remit to seek to understand these aspects of social life and social reality. It might be a bit of an imperialist notion of sociology but I do hold on to the idea that what I do is sociology even though it's at all these edges of other disciplines.

Katherine: You talked briefly about being an activist and then Greenham, although I actually don't know much about Greenham.

Sasha: That's an age thing!

Katherine: But actually, your narrative has mostly been about theory and ideas. Have they come together for you, or is it theory and ideas, and the 'why?' questions that you were talking about earlier on, that have mostly mattered?

Sasha: For me, I suppose, the politics and the theory have always been completely enmeshed. The kind of theoretical questions that I was asking – that I've always asked – are, for me, also political questions. I mean, it is the old Marxist point that in order to change the world we have to understand it, but that it's not enough just to understand the world – the point is to change it. But I also don't think there's any simple relationship between understanding things and managing to change them.

Very early on when I started my PhD, I was very anxious that I would be expelled by my Greenham feminist community, where there was quite a lot of anti-intellectualism, quite a lot of hostility to academia, and to the students who had come to Greenham saying, "We are doing a dissertation. Will you answer my questions? I've got a questionnaire." And the response was always, "No, we won't fill out your questionnaire. If you want to understand what Greenham is about, come and live here and see what it's like. Be part of it. You can't understand it from the outside." And I was really concerned about what it would be like when I told people that I was doing research on Greenham. There was the fear that I would be accused of appropriating their experience and using it for my own advancement and ends, and that I would fail to adequately represent the diversity and complexity of Greenham. Actually, I ended up not really coming up against any hostility, which was probably to do with my insider status, although it may also be that it was there but not expressed to me.

Having been so involved in politics, however, I always thought that it was a bit simplistic to think that feminist work in the academy would really change the world, as often seemed to be claimed in the early days of women's studies. I think it's politics and social movements that change the world, and the everyday actions of ordinary people. Academic work can make small in-roads into the project of trying to see things differently, but I think the grand claims made for feminist intellectual work are really overblown. There is a real difference between what we do when we write papers and books and go to conferences, and politics on the ground – which isn't to say that the academic work isn't political. It *is*. But we make a mistake if we think that somehow we really do political work in the academy.

So I think the relationship between theory and practice, between academia and the world of politics and social movements, is really complex. Dialogues across those divides can be difficult as well. I remember reading Alain Touraine's work when I was first starting my PhD and he had this, I thought, very grandiose idea of the sociologist taking sociology to the social movement, and with it bringing true understanding and reflexivity to the project of political change. I found that kind of sociological arrogance very uncomfortable. It went against my feminist politics, and the anti-hierarchical, anarchist politics in which I had been involved, and my distaste for this work, which was very important in the sociology of social movements in Europe at the time, actually fuelled my research on Greenham. I didn't think that I was going to offer great insight back to Greenham, or to feminist activism, about itself. What I thought I might offer was some understanding to the academy of how social movements, especially feminist movements, work, and of the difference that they make in the world, so that we might understand better how social and political change are brought about.

So, I think that what we might have to offer as sociologists to the world of practice is not straightforward. I think that we take from, and learn from, people's everyday lived lives, their politics and their struggles, and how much we have to give back is not clear, however much there is, at the moment, a discourse about 'impact' and 'knowledge transfer'.

Katherine: As you're talking, you are referring to ideas you had when you started your PhD and to ideas you're having now, so has your idea of sociology or your work as a social researcher remained constant over the years?

Sasha: Oh gosh no. I'm sure it's changed enormously in all sorts of ways. I mean, I started my PhD in 1988 and at that point, there wasn't much feminist scholarship. There was *some*. There were some on the syllabus at LSE. I also did a wonderful course, which I didn't fully really understand the importance of at the time, in my third year. It was called 'Women and the Law', which sounds really boring and old-fashioned now, but actually, it was a rather powerful post-structuralist course that was quite cutting-edge. I think it was over the heads of most of us at the time, but it was one of those courses that, kind of, settled, that grew on me and made more sense over the years. Right at the end of my undergraduate studies I had this feminist introduction to post-structuralism, to Foucault, and Donzelot, and so on. Now, I've never been a card-carrying Foucaultian or post-structuralist – I've been too much of an anarchist to carry a card – but I was very much shaped by those ideas, and they have been very important to me.

The first journal article I published, however, which was an article in the *British Journal of Sociology* that came out in 1995 – it was all much slower then, there was much less pressure to publish early in your career – was a set of critical reflections on the impact of post-structuralism on feminist sociology. I was trying to grapple with the cultural turn, and I was basically saying that we need to focus on both culture *and* materiality, we need to analyse discourse *and* practice. It does, perhaps, seem like a perfectly obvious argument now, but it was a moment when post-structuralism was in the ascendant, particularly within feminism, and I felt that it was important that sociology held on to material lived practice, everyday life and experience. And so my work has always tried to attend to both everyday lived practices and material conditions of existence *and* to subjective experience, identity and meaning-making.

What is more recent is my interest in psychoanalysis, which was not at all part of my training in sociology, or in any discipline, at LSE, and which was strongly repudiated in the feminism in which I was schooled in the 1980s and 1990s. Psychoanalysis was really outside the boundaries of what was considered acceptable sociology, especially by feminist sociologists. And there is still a lot of hostility among feminist sociologists to psychoanalysis. Psychoanalysis is seen through a rather narrow reading of Freud as the ultimate patriarch, that I think doesn't hold up, and doesn't do justice to the complexities in Freud's thinking, and certainly doesn't take into account the radical, feminist, critical and relational developments in psychoanalysis that have taken place since the 1940s.

I was really lucky to be part of an ESRC Research Group when I was at Leeds, CAVA – Care, Values and the Future of Welfare. We got funding from the ESRC for a five-year feminist project that was asking a set of questions about the future of welfare in relation to changing practices of parenting and partnering, changing practices of intimate life. The central question was: what sort of forms of welfare do we need, given the radical changes that have gone on in family relations and personal relationships since the founding of the welfare state? What the ESRC funding for CAVA gave us, which was incredibly precious for me, I think, at that point in my career, was some time to talk and think, and to engage in a collective research process. I'd been on this early career treadmill. When I started my lectureship, there was no let up, no allowance made for new lecturers. You had more work than anyone else, rather than less and it was really gruelling. Then we got this research money, and built into it, there was time for seminars. We had these regular monthly seminars where we sat around on Fridays and we spent the whole day talking.

One of my two projects in CAVA was about practices of care and intimacy outside conventional families and I was particularly interested in friendship, which came very much from my own experience. I was quite a bit younger than most of the people in the project and living, I felt, a bit of a different life that wasn't being recognised in this project. It was very much framed around changes in families – motherhood and employment, the breakup of heterosexual couples, and how they dealt with care afterwards, grand-parenting and extended kin, and so on. My project was about people who don't live with a partner, people who are single and people in LAT relationships (living apart together relationships), including lesbians and gay men, and I had this hunch that friendship was really important for this group of people living outside conventional couples.

And so I'd been doing these pilot interviews, piloting a fairly traditional, semi-structured interview, and what I was getting were these answers that sounded really like people were parroting the theme tune of 'Friends', which was really big at the time: "My friends are always there for me, through good times and bad times, they'll look after me. I can turn to them when things are tough." And it was all very uplifting. It was nice, because this is what I thought I might find, but it also felt like there was something really missing from that discourse, something about the less positive aspects of living outside conventional couples, about pain and disappointment, about friends *not* always being there for you. It was interesting, because it said something about the relationship between culturally available discourses and people's ways of speaking about their lives – perhaps how 'Friends' offered a language that made sense to a certain group of people. And I talked about all this in the CAVA Friday seminar, and about my sense of dissatisfaction with the data that the interviews were producing, and Wendy Hollway, who was a member of the research group, and who is a critical psychologist, said,

"Oh, I've just sent this book to the publisher. You can have a look at the proofs. It's about the problem of discourse and about how the way we ask questions in interviews produces certain discursive formations and doesn't get at the more ambivalent, conflicted, complex aspects of human experience and subjectivity."

Anyway, I read this manuscript [*Doing qualitative research differently*] and it changed the way that I then went ahead and did that project. I used a version of what she and Tony [Jefferson] called 'the free association narrative interview'. I must have been open to this form of psychosocial thinking that she was developing, and I found it really exciting, really challenging and it did radically change how I then went ahead with that project.

And it marked a real shift in my work because that was the point at which I thought, "Actually, I do need to get to grips somehow with psychoanalysis." And the more I realised how much there was to read and learn, the more I realised that I was effectively taking on another training. And I did eventually undertake a formal training – I trained as a group analyst. I thought, "How do I develop a really deep understanding of this, of psychoanalysis, of human subjectivity and experience, and its complexity?" And I decided that I wanted to develop a clinical practice-based understanding as well. So I looked around for quite a while to see what sort of training I wanted to do. Did I want to do a classical psychoanalytic training or a psychoanalytic psychotherapy training? And I stumbled across group analysis, partly because of the work of Ian Craib, who was a sociologist at Essex, who has since, sadly, died. He had written a wonderful book called, *The importance of disappointment*, which I read about this time, at about the time Wendy gave me her book.

So I picked up this book by Ian Craib – somehow the title must have spoken to me. He was a well-known social theorist; he had written a lot on classical social theory but he had also trained as a group analyst and he wrote this book about disappointment, and about psychoanalysis and about why some sociology needed to take both seriously. He was also making some very interesting interventions around the nascent sociology of emotions that was happening around that time. He was arguing against what he saw as the tyranny of a very strong social constructionism, and the way it obliterated psychic life, and the complexity of psychic life: if everything's socially constructed, then what about internal conflict? What about the experience that people have of their inner worlds not matching the social world in which they exist?

All this made a lot of sense because a lot of my work, particularly my PhD, had been about identity and subjectivity, and the struggles that women experienced when they were changing, and the complexity of desire, but I hadn't had any access to a psychoanalytical way of thinking at that point, and I didn't really need it for what I was doing then. But for this work that I was going on to do, which was about personal life and intimate relationships, then ways of understanding ambivalence, and conflict, and thinking about being torn between love and hate, especially when caring for someone who is dependent, and who conjures our own vulnerabilities, for that I began to see that I needed psychoanalysis.

Anyway, Ian Craib's work was important to me at this time. I noticed on the back of his book or somewhere that he was a group analyst so I had a look into what this was. And the way that group analysis thinks of itself is that it's the meeting point of psychoanalysis and sociology, and that really appealed to me, and the idea that it was an analytic way of working in groups was also really attractive, as I've always been interested in groups. My whole engagement in feminist and anarchist politics, and a lot of what I was interested in about social movements and particularly Greenham, was about how small groups work. How does the small group, the political group, relate to the larger group, the wider society? How can it produce change in the larger group? How do we deal with power conflicts within small groups? How do we negotiate and mediate difference within groups? These were all the sorts of things that group analysis deals with. And it was also, I found, a very powerful medium for personal change – for encountering the self and others, and for producing better understandings and new ways of being. So I embarked on my training in group analysis, which was very long. I started it in 2006 and finally qualified as a group analyst in 2013.

Katherine: Gosh!

Sasha: The training involved seeing individual patients as a psychoanalytic psychotherapist, as well as running a long-term clinical group and a more applied shorter-term group. The training has been very demanding of my time and energy, but incredibly enriching. I did my clinical work in an inner London NHS psychotherapy department, so I've had this new experience of working in the NHS, with an incredibly diverse patient population, which has been very interesting.

I've been carrying on with my sociological research on one hand and I've been doing this training and seeing individual patients and running groups on the other hand. Having got to the end of the training, I've started to think, "Well, how do I bring these two together?" because I've still got quite a lot of career ahead of me and they somehow have to come together because they came out of the same set of interests and concerns. Undoubtedly, that training has fed into the work I've been doing using biographical narrative interview methods and developing psychosocial methodologies and ways of understanding the world. But I also feel like there's 20 years work ahead, trying to see what to do with those two things now.

I think one thing I would say to academics at a certain point in their career is that it's really good to be a student again, you know, to reconnect with what it's like to be a student again after you've not been a student for quite a while. And it's not very nice, quite a lot of it. You get off your pedestal, off the podium, and you're put in the position of a learner, explicitly, structurally: being assessed. And on a clinical training you are being constantly surveilled. One of the best things about finishing the training is that I've stopped being almost constantly in supervision. I was in supervision on my training course. I was in clinical supervision in the NHS. I was in supervision for my work with individual patients with an individual supervisor. So there was this constant Foucaultian sense of being surveilled, and being assessed, with no one ever quite telling you whether you're doing it well, or okay, or even if you were doing terrible damage to people. I mean, I hope I wasn't, but actually being put back in touch with that kind of anxiety, which is the real experience of PhD students sometimes, quite a lot of the time probably – there was something good about doing that. I think it is good to be a student again and to remember what it's like to not really know whether you're doing things right and whether your work is good enough. It's probably made me a bit more of a sensitive supervisor. I hope.

Katherine: That, sort of, brings me on to my next question, which is, would you advise somebody now to study sociology if you met yourself when you were 18 or if you met somebody else who was 18 or a person just starting at university or something?

Sasha: Well, I suppose, I have now done enough psychoanalytic training not to *advise* anyone much about anything, but rather I would try to hear from them about who they are, explore what they want and, kind of, let them unpick and think about their desires, their hopes, their dreams, and from there, talk with them about all of this. If I met someone who is a bit like I was at 18 – I had very powerful ideas about changing the world and about injustices of all sorts, and I perhaps tended to see the world in rather straightforward binary terms, good and bad, black and white – then I probably would think that sociology was a good thing, a good trajectory, for them.

Because hopefully, at its best, what sociology will do is allow you to follow those interests and politically-inspired concerns about social justice and making the world better, but also it's about developing the capacity to see the complexities of those positions and the difficulties that there are in actually realising those goals of a more just society, and all the things that get in the way. I wouldn't want anyone who I've talked to in that way to come out of our discussions thinking sociology would give them the answers to the problems they see in the world, but rather that it might help them to see how complex it all is. That's what I think a sociology degree should do. It should help people to see how complex the world is and in the process not make them so depressed that they think it's impossible to change, because actually, sociology is, or should be, full of examples of the world changing and of people bringing about change for the better. At the same time, it is also full of examples of things sliding back, and things not turning out as we'd hoped. 'Unintended consequences' was one of the first concepts that was introduced on my undergraduate sociology degree, and I still think it is a key concept.

If the young person I was talking to was primarily concerned about having a career, you know, fitting easily into the world as it's structured at the moment, then I'd probably not think sociology was the right thing for them. They'd be better off going straight away to study accountancy or law. It's not the right thing for everyone, by any means, and I think it really does require a capacity to tolerate uncertainty and ambiguity and not everyone is up for that. Actually, not all academic sociologists are up for it either, but I think the best sociology is able to really live with the ambiguities of things.

The 18-year-old who spoke politically and passionately might not be very keen on ambiguity, but they may develop that. It's not a bad place for a sociology student to start – with a set of passions about changing the world.

Katherine: What about when sociology students get a bit older and now they're doing their PhD or finishing their PhD or doing their first postdoc or first teaching position. What advice would you give to them if they've already decided they want to have a career in sociology?

Sasha: Okay, if they really want to do it, they're going to have to be able and willing to work very hard. The demands, I think, have got greater and greater. You know, it felt really hard when I started my first job in 1991 at Leeds and there were no structural concessions to the early career lecturer but at the same time, there were not the same pressures to publish. No one ever told me I needed to publish. I mean, I somehow realised it, but I didn't do it very quickly and I didn't do it very much, whereas young academics now know right from the outset that they've got to publish and they've got to get at least four papers in their first full REF cycle.

There's a lot more pressure around research and publishing, around earning grants and if anyone is embarking on a career as an academic sociologist, they need to see the academic world realistically. It is no ivory tower. At the same time, I was advised...I remember going and talking to my third year personal tutor at LSE about this idea I had for doing a PhD, and Ian Roxborough said, "You're crazy! You don't want to do a PhD." He left LSE soon afterwards for a job in the States. This was in 1987. There hadn't been any jobs in academia for years and in sociology there weren't really any jobs during the 1980s. There was, for a while, a lot of talk about this lost generation of sociologists who didn't get jobs during that period. When I got my job in Leeds, there had been one new appointment in the previous five years and one in the five years previous to that. There had been hardly anyone appointed between the mid-1970s and me getting appointed in the early 1990s but I was pig-headed enough to just want to go ahead and try, to apply for this ESRC studentship to write my PhD about Greenham. And I went ahead with it and I've never regretted that. The job is stressful. I mean, I feel the responsibilities of the job very strongly, but I'm not in court every day, as I would have been if I'd become a barrister. At the end of the day, no one's life, no one's incarceration, hangs on whether I have written those emails or finished that paper, so in spite of all the pressures on academics now, it's still a very privileged life in lots of ways, compared to other things, and that's why so many people want to do it.

It's still very appealing, the life of the mind, the chance during the summer to organise your days in the way you want. Yes, there's a lot of pressure to get stuff written, but this summer I could go out for a run first thing in the morning, or have a swim, and then have a leisurely coffee and then work late in the evening. There is a lot of freedom. But the cost of that is, there's this expectation on us to be producing that has increased and is ever increasing. It is an expectation that the young academic needs to develop the resources to deal with.

I think that those resources have to be individual, personal, but they also have to be collective and relational. It's really important to have networks of colleagues who are friends. I think that is important to make connections with other academics. But I also think it's really, really important to have some friends who aren't academics as well, and see what other people's lives are like and keep connected to other worlds. I think it's important to take care of your mind and body, and that can go quite easily by the board at particular points. I mean, there are times when it really needs to, like the last few months of writing a PhD – that's fine, but they have to be short periods. The problem is, an academic career could, if you let it, become like always trying to finish a PhD. That pressure can be felt so intensely. And developing the ability to say 'No' and to set your own boundaries, that's the constant struggle, I think, because no one else is going to do it for you. Pretty much no academic has a manager who is going to look after them and protect them from over-work. You are just going to be pushed further and further, and not just external pressures from the university but your internal pressures about what you think you should be doing. I don't have any magical solution for that but I think that developing good habits early on, and having time off is so important. Work–life balance has been constructed as if it was an issue just for women with children of a certain age, but it's an issue for everyone, especially for academics.

Apart from all those sort of issues – the psychic life of contemporary academia – I would say it's really important to do the research that you want to do. Of course, we don't all get to do that all of the time, especially if you're a research fellow on someone else's project. I have had quite a lot of researchers work with me on projects, *for me* really, and it has been really important to appoint people to those jobs who were really interested in the work, and it felt important to try and give them a bit of space to shape the research, but at the same time, I had to hold on to what the project was about and what the funding was for. I think, once people have hopefully passed the position of working on other people's projects and are able to shape their own work, I would encourage them to try to work on the things they really want to work on, and not to just follow intellectual fashion or just to follow the funding. Of course, we can't escape fashion and we can't escape the exigencies of funding, but to find the issues that really motivate you and to pursue those, even if they're not fashionable. To have confidence that people will be interested in *your* issues, to believe that you can make them interesting. I think that's really important, because what will sustain an academic life is doing the work that matters to you.

One of the things I always try to ascertain with prospective PhD students is their motivation for their research. "Why do you want to do this? Where's it coming from? Is this really the project that you want to do?" Quite often in interviews I find out that this isn't really the project the student wants to do, the one for which they've written their proposal, it's the one they think is appropriate. And then quite quickly, in the discussion, they're coming up with something that's quite different. But I think it's hard to know what it is you want to work on – education in our society isn't really about encouraging people to develop their own interests and ask their own questions, and sometimes people only discover what they are really interested in after quite a long time. I think that there is a process of becoming, as an academic, which is about finding out what it is you really want to work on.

So, yes, looking after yourself and your mental health, having good networks inside and outside academia, and finding the things to work on that really matter to you. Then there's a huge amount of luck. There's that sad truth that not everyone gets the job and not everyone will get the job they want.

Being prepared to move, I suppose, is another thing. I was in London for my undergraduate degree and my PhD, and then I got a job at Leeds, I moved to Leeds. I'd never been to Leeds, apart from for an interview at the university when I was 17, but as it turned out, it was a great place to get a first job. Leeds is a wonderful city. I was really happy there for 16 years, not happy every moment of it, but it was a great place to work for 16 years. I ended up having all sorts of opportunities to do things there and it was a really great city, and I completely fell in love with Yorkshire. So I was lucky. What would have happened if the only job I could have got was somewhere that really was unappealing to me? I don't know if I'd have stuck at academia. You know, I might then have gone and done that law conversion because I was quite picky about where I would live. And so there's an element of questioning how much does one want to be an academic? If you want it enough, you'll go and live anywhere, and in America, where it is a hugely competitive academic job market, people I know have moved to places that they've ended up hating, small college towns, where they don't fit in, as single or queer people, in a hugely family-orientated culture. They've been trained in the big cities in San Francisco, in Chicago, or New York but then they have to get jobs in states they never dreamt of living in, and often with their partner living a very long way away. And I know people who've then thought again about this after ten years and given it all up. I think being able to change direction and change gear are some of the best life skills.

Katherine: Okay and looking back on your career, is there something that you would have done differently now, looking back?

Sasha: Not really. I mean, I think I have been lucky. I was very lucky to get that job at Leeds. I hadn't finished my PhD. I didn't finish my PhD for quite a while after I got the job at Leeds because the job was so overwhelming, but I got a job at Leeds at a point where the department was going through a lot of change. Zygmunt Bauman had just retired, and Carol Smart had just been appointed. I was able to be part of this shifting, newly emerging department, in which sociology and social policy had been merged, right at the beginning of my career. That was a huge opportunity for me and actually, the university was quite open and I was able to kick-start and get together a gender studies centre, the Centre for Interdisciplinary Gender Studies. It was a great university at which to have my first job, and it was so good that I was able to stay there. I went on a one-year contract and I stayed for 16 years.

It was also good to leave. I do remember in my first year or two seeing people who were probably only the age I am now, or younger, who I thought were completely entrenched, impossible to change, who just moaned all the time about everything and I thought, "God, I never want to stay here long enough that I become like that." I think I just moved in time, maybe not quite in time! It was really good to be able to come and be somewhere very different, and Birkbeck is very different from Leeds. It's in the centre of London. It's got a very different constituency. We do our teaching in the evening. We teach very different sorts of students, mature students, whereas Leeds was largely 18–21 year olds. Birkbeck's really different. It's a much smaller place. It's very critical and politically-engaged and it's exciting to be working in London and, again, I think what I've been able to do at Birkbeck is be part of building a new institute for social research, the BISR [Birkbeck Institute for Social Research], and being part of a new department of psychosocial studies. And it's been really good to be able to situate my research in a context where there are lots of people interested in new, critical forms of psychoanalysis.

EIGHT

Growing up as a sociologist in rural Shropshire

John D Brewer

John Brewer is professor of post conflict studies at Queen's University Belfast and works on the sociology of peace processes. He was president of the British Sociological Association and is now honorary life vice president. He is a member of the United Nations Roster of Global Experts and is a member of national academies in three countries.

Sir Edward Elgar, born in the neighbouring county of Worcestershire and still Britain's best-known and accomplished composer, described himself on one occasion as an amateur. He immediately qualified the remark by saying it was because he truly loved his work. In an age of professionalism, when the appellation 'professional' seems so important to status and credibility (for good sociological reasons that lie in the authority it confers), describing oneself as an amateur might appear foolish and using it to depict others is likely to be taken as highly offensive. Yet I love sociology to the point where I would be happy to appropriate Elgar's meaning; and I still do so even though I am now well into my fifth decade as a practitioner, having left school in 1968 to transfer to a further education college on a 22-mile round trip every day deliberately to study it at A-level when it was not then available in the school curriculum.

I was head boy at my village school in Shropshire but I was fond only of PE, history and English, and on my last day when visiting teachers to say goodbye, which we did in a pack of eager and excited leavers, I recall being asked by my English master what I was doing next. On telling him that I would be attending FE college to study sociology (I remember well that I did not mention economics or politics as my other A-level subjects), he retorted dismissively that I did not even know what the word meant. 'It's the study of society, Sir', I replied proudly, shutting him up for the first time in five years and feeling smug as I did so. Strangely enough, 45 years later, I still think that is the best quick definition of the subject. What has changed, I believe, is simply how we conceptualise and understand society. Society is a more intricate entity than I once envisaged or then imagined, but sociologists are still the experts in unravelling its complexity.

I now know, of course, that the 1960s was a period of rapid expansion in sociology in Britain and it had by then entered public consciousness for its strident critique of contemporary society. I would like to be able to say that as a 16-year-old in 1968, I was drawn to the subject because it fitted my growing teenage awareness of injustice, inequality, anti-Vietnam war sentiment and anti-racism, issues very topical at the time – I do recall writing a poem as part of an English language exercise in school about the contradiction in the treatment of African Americans in US society and the number killed fighting in Vietnam for the very country that rejected them; as well as another poem that transposed the Christmas story in Bethlehem to the experience of homeless people in Britain in the 1960s (and feeling terribly disappointed when the aforementioned English master was not impressed by it). But such a claim would be aggrandisement. Sociology was attractive for biographical and thus highly personal reasons. As a boy, I was fascinated by society – by its past, its people, social relations, and social practices and behaviour. I enjoyed sitting at the feet of elderly relatives and listening to stories of the past. Sociology also was very different from what I could do at school – and I rather liked being the unusual one who left to attend a further education college to study this rebelliously new thing. Paradoxically, I studied the very subject that shows us to be social animals because I was a bit of an individualist.

There is another very strong recollection that lives with me still about my interest in and commitment to sociology. To this day I recall vividly, when attending first year lectures in sociology at Nottingham University in September 1970, watching Danny Lawrence walking down the steps in the large lecture theatre to talk to us about power in what were our first set of lectures, and thinking to myself that I would not mind that job too. Becoming a university lecturer in sociology is what I set my heart on after just a few introductory encounters with the role. I never wavered from that early career choice.

It was not an untroubled or easy career progression though. It never is. Labour market conditions always combine with serendipity to determine the plot a career path takes. I came on the labour market in the first of the wave of university cuts and I went through the routine round of interview rejections, temporary appointments, publication disappointments and rejections and interpersonal stresses and strains, but I never lost sight of what it was that I wanted to be. Commitment to a career choice is truly as important as suitability to the role in determining success, which is a piece of advice I give to my own graduate students who encounter the same mix of labour market constraints and chance.

I have never regretted my career choice. Sociology has been good *to* me – I eventually became a professor, a head of school, president of the British Sociological Association, a member of the United Nations Roster of Global Experts, a member of four learned societies, including the national academies in three countries, and a member of Council for both the Academy of Social Sciences and the Irish Research Council, among other things. Much more important though, sociology has been good *for* me.

Sociology has enabled me to make sense of my life. It helped me understand the kind of upbringing I had in a rural community on the Welsh–English border where there remained the remnant of a coal mining industry as an outcrop of the Shropshire coalfield; an industry in which my father was sadly killed when I was two years old, when there was not much of a welfare state but a strong occupational camaraderie. I have reflected on these biographical encounters, which I call 'spaces of selfhood', on an earlier occasion and noted their impact on my interest in sociology and the work I do on the sociology of peace processes (Brewer, 2009), and here I would like to draw out their general implications for my approach to sociology.

Communicating sociology's capacity to be both life-changing and life-empowering is what I see as the essential purpose of sociology teaching and research. It changes lives and enriches them at the same time. We do this in our teaching so that we enhance the lives of our students by our enthusiasm for the subject and its potential. We also do this in our research as we strive to achieve two things through our work: to enable the ordinary men and women whom we study to make sense of their own lives; and through better understanding of the structural constraints that operate on their lives, improve them at the same time. The life-enhancing connections I see between individual biographical experiences, social structure, history and power in my own life is an insight available to all through the application of the sociological imagination.

Charles Wright Mills in the late 1950s called this the promise of the sociological imagination; Michael Burawoy at the turn of the new millennium termed it public sociology. I have referred to it as the new public social science (Brewer, 2013). But whatever the phrase, sociology has a normative purpose at its very core. This is a controversial suggestion but only because it is misinterpreted to mean that sociologists are antithetical to science and let their values shape the evidence they collect. It is important that sociology remains scientific. However, there is no incompatibility between science and value, for moral purposes can be interrogated scientifically. Even more importantly, it is essential that sociology continually refines its scientific practice and methods in order to better meet its normative obligations and to ensure that its research is robust enough so that sociology is as revelatory and life enhancing as current scientific methods permit. Sociology's normative purposes are not advanced if sociology becomes ideological and unscientific but neither does this commitment to science preclude our data contributing to moral debates and serving moral ends.

The interface between value and science is one of the most important challenges the discipline faces in the future given that so many of the complex problems the twentieth century has bequeathed the twenty-first have such strong moral dimensions. Climate change, the elimination of world hunger, human rights and the like, touch upon moral principles like equality, compassion, empathy and justice, and sorely test the ethical frameworks people in the Global North operate when responding to the suffering of 'distant others' in the Global South. So profound are these challenges that the French sociologist Luc Boltanski (1999) has suggested the need to reconfigure sociology's 'moral framework'. However, there is another profound challenge for sociology that follows when we begin to deal with the complex problems facing the future of humankind.

Despite all its life-changing and life-empowering capacities for the individuals who study sociology and are affected by its research, if it is to make a difference to the global challenges ahead, sociology has to work more closely with the other disciplines whose subject matter also contributes to their solution. The future is thus one of growing collaboration between the disciplines not the practice of disciplinary closure that cuts each one off from the other behind ever higher intellectual fences. Sociology has a significant part to play in analysing, diagnosing and ameliorating the social condition in advanced modernity despite these structural conditions no longer privileging sociology in the way that they did in nineteenth-century industrial society. This is because these conditions will throw into particularly high relief the moral dimensions to twenty-first century global insecurity, inequality and injustice, but in helping to deal with them, sociology must work alongside human rights lawyers, climate change scientists, medics, environmentalists, food nutritionists and the like.

I believe the emancipatory nature of the sociological imagination, evident in my own life and to which I have alluded throughout these short reflections, makes sociologists particularly sensitive to the changed conditions of late modernity in which new forms of analysis, diagnosis and amelioration are necessary. Sociologists will thus be at the vanguard of the new public social science, as they have always been, but the nature of the complex problems the twenty-first century will be dealing with means that sociology will no longer be *sui generis*, unique unto itself and capable alone of changing the world. Of course, sociology never was capable of doing this but the rhetoric of some sociologists appeared to suggest otherwise. The role for sociological teaching and research in the twenty-first century is still to change people's lives and to empower them, but now also to encourage them to recognise that social change requires that the insights of sociology be placed alongside those of others – including those whom sociology considered strangers in the past – who can all meaningfully contribute to analysis, diagnosis and amelioration of the human condition.

Would I do it all again? Of course I would. Sociology illuminates the world around me in a way no other subject does. Would I change anything? Well, universities are not the places they once were. The march of the market has fundamentally changed the nature of the lecturer role and the working culture of modern universities, although in some respects they have also changed for the good. But universities are not the only place where sociologists are needed. People educated in sociology and knowledgeable about its research are needed in politics, in law, in humanitarian agencies and human rights organisations, in climate change science and throughout the civil sphere. The job for sociology remains immense; I envy the new generation and what they will be able to achieve with the sociological imagination. I wish I were starting out again; I envy your introduction to sociology.

References

Boltanski, Luc, 1999, *Distant suffering*, Cambridge: Cambridge University Press

Brewer, John D, 2009, Space of selfhood, *Times Higher Education* 10 December, 40–2

Brewer, John D, 2013, *The public value of the social sciences*, London: Bloomsbury

NINE

On the right-of-way

Judith Burnett

Judith Burnett left school at the earliest school leaving age, studied on day release, and went to university aged 21. She was the first in her family to go to university and graduated in sociology from the University of Nottingham in 1986, followed by a Master's in politics. After a spell working in London, Burnett returned to academe and started lecturing at the University of East London, completing her PhD, 'All about thirtysomething: An exploration of the value of the concept of generations in sociology'. She later took up the position of dean at the University of Wolverhampton where she became professor of sociology and social change. She is currently pro vice chancellor (architecture, computing and the humanities) at the University of Greenwich.

It is a Sunday morning and I am writing this at home. The last day of a hot summer is gorgeously golden in the garden. It is peaceful, and I am in the mood for sociology. Sociology never leaves you; it is your choice if you leave it. Leaving it is sometimes helpful and even necessary. The return, with new eyes, can be a joyful thing. It can also be unsettling and challenging: from those moments of new engagements have come my own 'personal bests'. The first thing to say is that I have laboured under the belief that I was leaving sociology several times in my life and have insecure identity questions about being a sociologist at all. Like all identities it sits within and between social locations and is the site of games and negotiations. What is a real, proper, sociologist? What is sociology?

Coming across sociology in the first place seemed to me for many years to be accidental. Accident has become part of the pattern and is a custom of the (my) country. I would like to be able to say that I have always been socially generous and got involved hoping sociology to be a force for democratic good and essential to our social understanding. I own that I have also been self-interested and got into it in part because it was an industry which was recruiting. In any event, I view sociology as a road map to a different place. Sociologists might say that this individual experience is most likely a social pattern, and that the challenges are wrestled down by agency and structure. Since the individual biography is a kind of window on the world, here is my version.

I went to a girls' school in the first year after its conversion to grammar school status. In the late 1970s it held no truck with such a new-fangled craze as the social sciences at A-level, not that this was particularly relevant given that my class of 34 and my year group of 100 largely fled to work, motherhood or nothing in particular at the earliest possible school leaving age. My own transition was to a job in a bank, my cohort of leavers left in our wake a small group of hardy souls a few of whom would make it later to polytechnics and universities.

I took up day release and an evening class at the college of further education because I wanted to keep up my education. This was no proud or brave attempt to undo a wrong or sidestep a thwarted ambition. Rather, it was playing out a long tradition of country folk who read widely and deeply and knew all manner of things about a world in which they had not been formally educated beyond a minimum requirement.

The day arrived when I had to buy a book, the subject under investigation was the industrial revolution. I came across Haralambos' book *Sociology: Themes and perspectives*, the 1980 edition. At home parked on the settee with a cheese and pickle sandwich and a '*Price*

Right!' coffee, which I can still smell and taste, I had an exasperating hour or so – Haralambos was not like anything I had seen before and I thought I had wasted my money. It lacked anything useful like the date the Spinning Jenny was invented and carried no maps showing the location of 'the fast flowing rivers of the north of England' or 'the great cities of the industrial revolution'. I thought the chapter on work was interesting but I skipped the theory chapter completely on the basis that it was written in a foreign language for which I had no dictionary. The family chapter was, I felt, common sense which just left the chapter about social class. Here I found the founding fathers, the triumvirate of modern sociology (as constructed in those days), and I liked it. I think I appreciated the obsessional riff, all that mapping of the infinitesimal ways in which status is established and power wielded through the division of labour. I went into work on Monday and saw 'society' for the first time and had a name to call it by. So I passed through the looking glass and was hooked.

This world took me to public libraries where I somewhat randomly obtained books on social history, society and health, and the Second World War. Fortuitously, I fell to working my way through several volumes by Arthur Marwick. I found *Love on the dole* by Walter Greenwood (1933) and got to the welfare policy shelf and the postwar world via Nye Bevan *In place of fear* (1952).

In my free-wheeling style of education I had moved on to English A-level at evening classes, where I was dutifully trying to keep up appearances. I had obtained *Room at the top* (the 1959 film directed by Jack Clayton the advertisement for which read 'A savage story of lust and ambition') from the video shop to save having to read the book (Braine, 1957). The essay was returned with a note carefully typed on very thin, 'typing paper' appended, suggesting that I might not be suited to 'a career in the arts and literature' and that I should consider transferring to sociology, since they had some places. I remember the tutor saying that they were argumentative and interested in Marx, so I would like it.

I didn't do an A-level in sociology but I eventually went to university for a degree in sociology. Sociology was taught in blocks, 'Women and Work' 'Industrial Society' 'Society and Development' and so on. A discovery was that numbers were something marvellous and useful. When I was introduced to *Social Trends* I noted with more than a passing interest that my household class of origin meant a good few years difference in life expectancy from my middle-class peers and that there were patterns to which hideous illness or condition would lead to my demise. Quietly in the library after hours, I began my long march through books and journals and changed my habits of solitary and self-directed study. I got over lots of things, and a few folk from the middle classes turned into some of my oldest friends.

I graduated, worked, and took a Master's in politics in the evenings. I enjoyed it immensely but found sociology hard to shake off. I left again before arriving at the gates of academe for a third time. As a mature PhD student I took the sociology of generations as my subject and was kindly supervised by folk who knew sociology inside out and back to front. I became a full time lecturer and settled into teaching in the multicultural London institution of UEL. It was a tough and rewarding time, and I learned about all sorts of things, including the social sciences. I delighted in the engagement with the region and the concept that sociology and the social sciences in all its forms was a force for social and economic good. I was lucky enough to work with urban geographers, social policy makers and thinkers of every kind and perspective, sometimes working at the edges of disciplines and in the gaps left behind by the more traditional and staid departments of other institutions. I came of academic age in a cultural environment which was challenging and robust, unafraid of experimentation, and able to stand its ground having looked at the evidence before opening its mouth. I was finally able to lay claim to the idea that universities are also for the likes of me, and grew strong in an environment where this was supported. I widened my reading and learned some major insights from Maya Angelou (1969) and Meera Syal (1999) as well as from the many colleagues writing and working at that time. It was during this time that I first encountered the British Sociological Association (BSA) and we hosted one of the large BSA Annual Conferences. I became more involved with the Association, and have welcomed the proximity to new research and a lively community. These things I took forwards with me when I left to go on to the University of Wolverhampton, where I worked with a good crowd trying to do something in one of the more disadvantaged areas in Britain, and by and large succeeding with boisterous good humour and a cheery lack of deference.

I have worked with and been most interested in the institutions with hefty numbers of first generation students with a greater representation (in comparison to other institutions) of working-class, BME and mature learners. I was delighted in the sometimes non-traditional lines of enquiry and detraditionalising ways of being at university, learned about high aspiration and determined ambition, and was concerned when I saw lack of confidence and limited awareness of what was necessary for success. A hidden problem for higher education is that so few would cross the great divide into postgraduate work, and even fewer would make it to a research career.

Tips? Entering academic management roles I watched the male sex ask for permanent jobs, higher salaries and upgraded work more often and more persistently than the female (still). I became aware that mature students and 'late' entrant members of staff sometimes suffer from the feeling that they need to catch up, positioned as they can be as never having enough of anything (publications; experience; gravitas; funds; time). Young PhD graduates and new members of staff might despair too deeply too quickly labouring under the misapprehension that their sometimes rocky experiences of first teaching are somehow unique to them, a dirty little secret that they dare not share (you should). More positively, remember that sociologists and our many fellow friends found both in and outside academe could provide a greater and more significant social service than is allowed by current conditions and our social scripts: speak truth to power and focus on what you can do rather than what you can't.

Nowadays I work in academic management and my challenges remain those around enabling success and access including teaching and what is nowadays called student experience. I spend some of my time dealing with the changing world of policy decisions, including the recent crop of major changes around student funding, and the tightness of the research funding regime. The extent to which a good dose of the sociology of education and well executed social research would significantly assist policy makers and leaders at every level, and their reluctance to countenance such a prescription, still surprises me.

Other challenges include the labour involved and the resources needed to deal with the amount of regulation and audit in its various guises, including from bodies such as the QAA, HEFCE and HESA and, given that some of the regulation is less useful than others, the tension between dealing with this at an institutional level while meeting the needs of students, the academic workforce and thus what for me remains the primacy of our focus on teaching and research which is what this very special sector is really all about. I have enjoyed all the jobs I have had in academe, each has presented different kinds of rewards and challenges, and offers unique insights into the system. Having said that, universities are also curious places to work. The creative and academic environment is usually interesting, and the student body engaging and rewarding to be around. However the fragmentation, rigidity and disorganisation can be quite challenging and the power struggles daunting. It is important to not be thrown off stride by the shenanigans which can go on. Postgraduates entering the system may find it helpful to take the view that it makes for good data, rather than, for example, taking things to heart.

For me, I am glad I walked through the looking glass. My ego and its corporeal reality says 'This is my story and it is surely all my own work.' But sociology shows that statistically a certain number of us break through, and social explanations can be put together which show that the opportunities and barriers, and both plans and accidents are more patterned than it may first seem from our vantage point on the ground.

The golden day is fading, and breezes have sent the first leaves to the back door. My take out is that there is nothing remarkable in this account of my journeying along this particular right-of-way. The account is affirmation of the thought act which is sociology. It is this which allows us to name the social and show with evidence that it still counts.

References

Angelou, M, 1969, *I know why the caged bird sings*, London: Hachette

Bevan, A, 1952, *In place of fear*, London: William Heinemann

Braine, J, 1957, *Room at the top*, London: Eyre & Spottiswoode

Greenwood, W, 1933, *Love on the dole: A tale of two cities*, London: Jonathan Cape

Haralambos, M, Heald, RM, 1980, *Sociology: Themes and perspectives*, London: University Tutorial Press

Syal, M, 1999, *Life isn't all ha ha hee hee*, London: Doubleday

TEN

Living sociology

Les Back in conversation with Katherine Twamley

Les Back is a professor of sociology at Goldsmiths, University of London. His sociological tale begins in the 1980s when he started a PhD in social anthropology. Since then he has conducted a wide range of empirical work, largely based in Britain, and published books on social theory and research methodology. He has taught undergraduate cultural studies and sociology and between 2009–13 he was dean of Goldsmiths Graduate School.

His main areas of interest are the sociology of racism, popular and digital culture and city life.

Les Back's work aspires to create a sensuous or live sociology committed to searching for new modes of sociological writing and representation. This approach is outlined in his books *Live methods* (Back and Puwar, 2012) and *The art of listening* (Back, 2007). He also writes journalism and has made documentary films. Between 2006 and 2008 along with Celia Lury he coordinated the ESRC-funded *Live Sociology* programme which offered training in the use of multi-media in qualitative research as part of Researcher Development Initiative and in 2011–12 they set up Real Time Research network for methodological innovation.

The conversation started with a discussion of the threats and opportunities faced by the sociological imagination today.

Les: I think academic sociology faces both profound challenges and real openings. So there is an unevenness in the Republic of Sociological Letters, a combination of opening up new opportunities to imagine sociology differently and a kind of conservatism which also closes things down. There are real threats to the life of the mind, while at the same time there are unprecedented opportunities to do sociology differently. The corporatising impulse is transforming the university and it is hard not to become possessed by the metrics of auditing and measuring intellectual value and worth. There are many people who are trying to defend a space and defend each other in order to avoid committing either institutional or intellectual suicide. That seems to be really what is happening.

Katherine: I want to hear a bit more about your trajectory. How did you come to be a professor of sociology and dean of a graduate school?

Les: Well those kind of elevated titles associated with my name mean that miracles are possible. My trajectory is a very eccentric one. It is one that is certainly not something that I would recommend to anyone. I started out at Goldsmiths College in the early 1980s studying geography, actually. I hated geography, mainly because it was a dreadful department full of right-wing teachers. This is very unusual for Goldsmiths in terms of what it has become.

A wonderful woman called Nici Nelson who taught Social Anthropology 101 came to speak one day introducing the first year options, however. I remember it so clearly; she said: "If rocks and strata make your heart beat faster then anthropology isn't for you!" I immediately thought, "Where do I sign? How do I join?" I'd discovered social anthropology. I remember reading Marcel Mauss's *The gift* and it was a complete revelation and had a huge impact on me (Mauss, 1954).

I had always been interested in social issues partly because of my own biography. I grew up on the fringes of South London; my family is kind of a classic Young and Willmott story of the suburbanisation of working-class culture (Young and Willmott, 1957).

We were moved out in the 1960s to the edge of London to a large public housing estate called New Addington, which has become notorious in recent times. It is where the Tia Sharp murder happened and the Emma West case when she was recorded spouting a racist rant on the tram. The estate was also featured on Secret Millionaire, the reality show. Anyway, as a young person, I was desperate to understand how I had ended up there, how my family had ended up in the nowhere place without a sense of history, really. *The art of listening* includes an attempt to make sociological sense of that experience (Back, 2007, especially Chapter 3).

I was growing up in a kind of culture quake in the 1970s, when popular racism was very intense, the National Front were leafleting outside of my school, but I had very close black friends. So, it was a very confusing thing to come of age in a place like that. I was the first in my family to go to university and I went to Goldsmiths College and geography was the closest thing I did at school that connected to the world I lived in – I enjoyed that, I was interested in the cultural and social sides of geography. Anyway, I ended up at Goldsmiths doing the wrong degree and Nici Nelson walked into the classroom and changed the course of my life.

She offered me a route into anthropology. I didn't know what that was, but it really caught my imagination. So then I went from geography to anthropology, and eventually I did a PhD in social anthropology with Pat Caplan who was a wonderful supervisor and I discovered cultural studies and particularly the work of Stuart Hall and Paul Gilroy. After I finished my PhD I worked in the Cultural Studies department at the University of Birmingham – which had been where Richard Hoggart and Stuart Hall set up the Centre for Contemporary Cultural Studies (CCCS).

I then ended up coming back to Goldsmiths to the sociology department, 20 years ago now. I feel very loyal to sociology because although I never studied it formally the discipline provided me with a hospitable intellectual home for the problems and things that I really cared about. How is a city like London both a place of living multiculture and at the same time where phobic, melancholic racisms are also socially alive? These seemingly contradictory impulses can exist on the same streets and even within a single person. I mean, that was my great obsession, I suppose, to try and make sense of this world in the ten miles between the edges of south London and the river Thames which was the great jugular vein of the empire. It was a world I felt very connected and proximate to and at the same time, estranged from. I both knew it like the back of my hand and I was completely lost within it at the same time.

I suppose sociology has always provided a space in which you can try and work those things out. My biggest sociological influence is C Wright Mills. I discovered him through one of my colleagues at Goldsmiths called Caroline Ramazanoglu – a wonderful woman, a feminist sociologist. She gave me Mills's book *The sociological imagination* (Mills, 1959) and said – "Read this: it will help you!" She was right. It did help and the first chapter, called 'The promise' still seems relevant today. I have tried to write a twenty-first century version of 'The promise' with my friend and colleague Nick Gane (Gane and Back, 2012). When I was a student there in the early 1980s, Goldsmiths was a very anarchic place and students could attend any lectures that they wanted to, so I used to go and sit in the back of sociology classes.

Katherine: Is it not like that anymore?

Les: It is less like that. I don't think it is quite as easy but it remains very hard to govern. I think education has become so much more instrumental. I used to sit and watch Vic Seidler lecture when he was writing all of his work about critical masculinity studies and teaching courses on Marx and Freud and nobody noticed. You just sat at the back and it was an extraordinary thing. In a way, I came into sociology through the back door. I feel incredibly grateful to sociology for that precious thing that it gave me, a space to work out – as C Wright Mills would say – the private troubles of a kid who grew up on a council estate in Croydon and the public issues that were contained within that experience. It resulted in my writing books about that world and others but also a kind of open conversation that then develops between that experience and teaching and doing work in public.

I always embrace any opportunity to go out and speak to people, whether it be in prisons or in schools – sometimes the two things seem very similar! Just that sense of asking the teenagers in the room: "Well, how do we make sense of this stuff?" I think that yearning to understand sociologically is very much alive in this generation. If it is presented in the right way and if you listen with care and respect, I am certain that the young people are striving for the same kinds of answers and struggling with the same problems of making sense of what is happening in the world. We are living at a time where human societies are producing more information, faster and with greater frequency than any other period in history. I think young people are desperate to figure out "What does it mean to enter that world?"

Katherine: On that, how do you see being a sociologist and the role of sociology in developing that kind of public kind of understanding or analysis?

Les: Sociology is nothing if it is not concerned urgently with the key problems of the twenty-first century. What kinds of human beings are we becoming? What is the relationship between the hyper-connected world and our personal relations? What does it mean that we are broadcasting ourselves, literally, to quote the great mantra of YouTube, at an unprecedented level and rate? How does surveillance and control operate in our time? These questions to me are the big ones. What does it mean to live in a world where there are greater chasms opening up between the very rich and the very poor? What does it mean to live in a world where the here of us sitting in this room is profoundly connected to so many others elsewhere around the globe? You know, these are not just academic problems; these are problems about how to live life.

What better place to try and figure those things out or to be able to say something useful to young people particularly, who I think have been betrayed by our generation. I think it means a much more urgent engagement with places where those kinds of dialogues can take place. I just mentioned a few off the top of my head, but they are almost infinite including, the relations between sexuality and gender, reproduction, parenting. All of these fundamental aspects of the human experience are all being transformed in our time.

Katherine: But does anybody listen to us?

Les: Yes, they do. There are some people, whose deafness is actually a trained sensibility. The social deafness of the powerful is cultivated. Can we expect them to want to listen? Perhaps not, but I go into schools all the time. There is a relationship we have with a sixth form college, called Christ the King in Lewisham. It has an incredibly charismatic sociology teacher and there are 300 students in the sixth form college doing AS- and A-level sociology, 300!

Every year, an academic conference is run for those 300 students in the school. I have done it several times and I love going and doing it. It is the most incredible thing. Academic researchers or writers come and give presentations to this packed room and then students write questions, they come up onto the stage and ask their questions in front of everybody: the academics or writers or whatever are then invited to respond. The school buys copies of the books of sociologists who give their time and give the books away to the students who ask the best questions. The thing that always blows my mind every year is how many of the students stay the whole day and then refuse to go home and the conversation goes on and on and on.

The last time I presented I talked about the significance of the prison and the criminalisation in this generation, which seems to me, one of the main social distinctions emerging in this generation for young people growing up in British cities. I remember this young man came up to talk afterwards and he said, "You know, it really made me think. I have got friends, who say 'No biggie, I have just done another six months. It's okay, you can watch TV, it is all right'" and that is the habitual routine quality for those young people and they are 17, 18, 19 and 20 years old. They are going in and out of prison, so much so that it becomes just a banal reality of life. The criminal justice system marks those young people and determines their future.

I think people are listening. They might not be the ones that we think are important, but I have come to the point now where I am less certain about the value of only channelling our desire to communicate towards those powerful interests in society many of whom cultivate a social deafness. Boris Johnson called it in the aftermath of the 2011 riots mere 'sociological justification', which elided explanation and understanding with making moral judgements. One key value in sociology is the questioning of moral judgements and their basis and veracity.

Katherine: Are you implying that we should be less concerned with 'academic terms of reference' and be more publicly engaged?

Les: I don't know about that, you know. I think sometimes those academic credentials are more symbolically valuable in public than we often realise. I always used to think the strictures of academic life were profoundly inhibiting. I started to realise that being 'an academic' also enables a certain kind of speaking position in the public debate.

Katherine: What do you mean exactly?

Les: For example, there was a piece of research that I did some years ago with my dear friend and mentor, John Solomos, who works at the

University of Warwick now. I was his researcher for many years and he was just a great, a wonderful person to work for and with. I did a kind of apprenticeship with John in the craft of social research. He was a fantastic colleague in the sense that it was always a partnership; it was always collaboration rather than just acting as a 'data miner'. We were doing a project about racism and politics in Birmingham in the 1990s and we stumbled across evidence that a white trade union candidate had rigged the Smallhealth parliamentary selection by using the union's 'block vote'. This constituency had a very large and important Pakistani/Kashmiri population that was active in labour party politics and some local candidates from within that community who were effectively frozen out as a result.

So what did we do? We wrote a paper about it, which was published, had huge press coverage locally and nationally (see Back and Solomos, 1994). There were very powerful interests within the Labour party in the House of Lords as well as in the House of Parliament, starting to put pressure on the then President of Birkbeck College, to get us to withdraw the article.

I walked into some very naive ambushes in the media, where we were being threatened with libel and all kinds of legal action and, of course, I barely had anything to my name. It was very scary and it was a lesson in how the stakes change when you are studying the powerful: they have the power to sue you if you step on the toes of their privilege!

What did we do? Well, we started to present ourselves as academics. We were not politically interested in this, we are just academics who are trying to make sense of the world. We, kind of, put on our white lab coats and pretended that we were in a scientific laboratory, just trying to do an experiment. I realised then that an academic speaking position in the public debate is not always a limitation. In this case, that sort of academic identity was a protection (Back and Solomos, 1993).

The end point of the story was happy though because what had happened in that whole sequence of events was that one of the local political activists had just basically delivered on my doorstep a paper bag stuffed with photocopies of all of the documentation that proved that the claims we were making were true, including the signatures and cheques that the union activist, who was the Parliamentary candidate, had signed and letters saying 'Here is a cheque for X amount of pounds for the subscriptions for those members who are going to be entered as part of the union block vote.'

Katherine: From what you are saying, it seems that your idea of sociology and what sociology is to you, would you say hasn't really changed?

Les: No. I think, in a way, I had a sociological sensibility before I realised that I was ever going to have a job as a sociologist. That was cultivated over a long period of time and in a way, what sociology, as a discipline, has provided for me is a way of making that sensibility a tool for paying attention to the world. I have been playing with Max Weber's famous essay about 'science as a vocation' and developing the idea of sociological attentiveness as a vocation and also a way to live.

How do you train an attentiveness that is furnished by theoretical ideas that help us see, hear and notice things differently in the social world? This is sociology as a craft sensibility that is cultivated through the ways in which we open out to the world and investigate it. It is not just about methodological tools and creating data but also a way of living. I am interested in the new opportunities there are for us to reimagine our craft.

I have just finished a book with my friend, Nirmal Puwar at Goldsmiths, called *Live methods* (2012), which is trying to say that actually, as difficult and as bleak as things are institutionally within the academy, there are unprecedented opportunities for us to reimagine our craft and what sociological research can be beyond the statistical survey or the qualitative interview. I think the digital era is an incredibly exciting time to be practicing our craft of sociological research.

A friend of mine, Yasmin Gunaratnam at Goldsmiths, does this extraordinary work on end of life care and she has worked very closely with a children's hospice in East London called Richard House. The children's hospice is such a poignant place because it is a place of refuge, it is both in a locality, but often local people feel an anxiety about that place because it is a place that they think of as tragedy and terrible sadness of lives prematurely cut short. The truth of the situation is that the young people living in those places are carrying on with their lives.

They are very seriously ill but life goes on for them and it is precious. Yasmin said "Well, how can we do one of these live sociology experiments using the idea of being able to broadcast findings almost instantaneously through using smart phones, taking digital images for recording digital sound?" So we came up with this slightly mad idea of recruiting a group of researchers, briefing them on how to use these tools, creating an online platform where researchers could go out into the local area, talk to people, make representations, make field notes and then post them, more or less, in real time. We took the curiosities of the patients for a walk and sent ethnographic dispatches back to them on a shared on-line space.

What we could do, in a sense, was take their interests out into the world, the places that they remembered or thought were interesting then bring that world into the space of the hospice where patients and carers could interact with what was being produced in *their own time*. That wouldn't be possible in an analogue era, not in quite the same way and so that is what excites me about the project; so it means, in a way, that it poses interesting questions about the relationship between research and time. It raises all kinds of interesting questions and opportunities about form and formats and it also raises all kinds of other interesting questions (see Gunaratnam and Back, forthcoming).

Katherine: Of interpretation?

Les: Yes, there are issues of interpretation but also it socialises that process of interpretation and analysis. It is a more sociable version of sociology, I think, that is one of my latest slogans – 'Wouldn't it be great if sociology was more sociable?' (Sinha and Back, 2013). Now that might be a threat to us because you think, right, okay, if there is a sociable version of sociology and lots more people are involved in it, then where does that leave us? Are we inventing a kind of sociology that means ultimately we will be unemployed?

No, I don't think that will happen and I don't think those anxieties are necessarily founded. I think there are really interesting opportunities. It does challenge the ways in which we understand the production of knowledge and who can be an author. I know that is easy for me to say given that I am in my 50s now and I got in through the back door during very austere times and have managed to stay employed. I have been lucky that I have had a future in that regard, although nobody expected to have a future in 1984 or 1985. There were no jobs. It was the high point of Thatcherism, you know, so I know that the damaging effects of the audit culture and the commercialisation of the university can't be somehow just glossed or brushed to one side. I have tried to be as outspoken against the commercialisation of the university as I can and to not be possessed by the tool in the way that some people are at the moment.

Katherine: What would you advise somebody who is trying to carve a career and has this anxiety or sensibility about the rules that we were talking about earlier but at the same time wants to be a professor some day or a working sociologist?

Les: I talk about it all the time to younger scholars and PhD students and I try and muster the best advice that I can. In 2011 I published a free on-line book called *The academic diary*, which is concerned with how to hold onto and defend the things that are precious in university life (Back, 2011). I still think that there is a way to navigate a course that is something like this – be mindful of those formats, spaces and kinds of research writing that are valued within the hierarchies of the audit culture. It is unspoken but it is an open secret. There is a hierarchy of value and the hierarchy changes around a bit but we know that somewhere at the top of that hierarchy of value is publishing in the key disciplinary journals of whatever field you are in, then writing monographic books, we know that is high up in the hierarchy of value too and then things that are in the lower gradations are book chapters, on-line journalism and probably last of all, blog posts.

Does that mean that you only do those things that are valued within the hierarchy I have just described? I think that is a heart-breaking recipe for intellectual death. I think on the one hand it is important to do things that are going to help young researchers make that transition into their first academic jobs. At the same time they have to keep their intellectual passions alive and curiosities awake. I have tried to keep both impulses alive.

I don't think that the structures of auditing value in the academy can only focus on the paper formats for much longer. I just don't think that it can sustain itself given the dynamism that we are in, the quality of the world that we are living in and in a sense, operating within. Something will have to give, I think, because there is so much sociological life in digital spaces of what we refer to as alternative media.

What is happening in that space of alternative media is very, very interesting in terms of how we attend to the world and how we decide to engage with it. Just to give you one example, terrible events that happened in Woolwich and the kind of pornography of violence that unfolded in the media the following day with headlines that the young man who had killed the soldier had his hands reddened with blood, probably enhanced digitally through the magic of Photoshop. So the next day, I am riding on the train from Catford to New Cross. Everybody on the platform is anxious, everybody is looking on the platform in ways that they have not looked at each other the day before and the choreography of multicultural life is thrown.

I just remember listening to two young black Londoners who were talking about this and what is going to come next. So on my phone, I am sending a whole bunch of tweets, mainly as a way of exorcising my thoughts. One gets retweeted 40 times within the space of an hour. It said that pornography of violence in the newspaper headlines was complicit with the violence rather than countering it. It struck some chord and got retweeted. Although none of the other tweets resonated, that one did.

I get into work and somebody from the press office said "I have just been approached by an online magazine, could you just write something? Anything you are thinking about?" I thought "No, I can't because I have got to do this and that and I have got to be here for a meeting with a very important person there that I can't put off" and so on.

I then suddenly thought, "No, now is the time." I didn't have time to do it but I cleared the space and I just wrote the article by taking a cue from the tweet that had resonated on Twitter. In the space of maybe 90 minutes I sent it and it was published (Back, 2013). The thing about digital media and what is interesting is that you can then really get a clear sense of who is reading it and where. It was read by thousands of people. There was a sociological conversation that was unfolding that I thought was quite precious, something else going on that couldn't have happened ten years ago.

Katherine: Yes, it is interesting what you are saying and it has made me think that there are, as you are calling them, alternative media or digital advances helping sociologists be more public sociologists.

Les: Well, if you want to be. If all you care about is your next article in *Theory, Culture and Society (TCS)* – and incidentally I do care about those things too – but if that is *all* that you care about then you have foreclosed that possibility. I think younger scholars are much more in touch with those possibilities and watching them do incredible things makes me incredibly hopeful. Even the most prestigious journals like *TCS* know that they have opportunities to be more inventive now and you can see that on their website. There is a wonderful project that Mark Carrigan does called *The sociological imagination*, http:// sociologicalimagination.org, which is a website, it is a Twitter feed, and you get news from sociological imagination every day. He is a postgraduate student who will have graduated by the time this book is published. He is just somebody who is passionate and curious about sociology. He is interested in interesting things and he has got thousands of people following him and following what he is doing and old lags like me saying, "You know, I would like to join in too."

I find it incredibly hopeful that in these threatening and austere times there is just so much intellectual vitality and you don't have to look hard to find it. I think the danger is that as the university becomes more corporatised and audited the risk is that we become much more timid and more conservative in our practice. There is no future for a timid and conservative sociology.

The energy that is in these spaces of academic discourse, public engagement, and people following their passions and communicating things that they are interested in is not timid and it is not conservative. There is something about that, which I find incredibly nourishing and important.

Katherine: Actually, there was another question I was thinking of. When you were talking about when you were younger and using geography and then anthropology and so on, you talked about having this sociological sensibility already. I was wondering if you think that is something that one has innately?

Les: I don't think that. The great success of sociology is that it proliferates and that popular culture becomes saturated with its ideas. C Wright Mills himself said that the sociological imagination would be more alive outside the academic discipline of sociology than within it. I am not sure we are as good as we might be in fostering those conversations. We might start using them as part of the process of doing research itself. I think there is a lot of opportunity for us to think about that now. I have been thinking about that a lot lately because I am writing a book with Shamser Sinha on the experience of 30 young adult migrants in London. It the story of London really through these 30 lives. The participants have become observers in their own lives, so they have made their own representations including making images and writing that Shamser and I are in dialogue with as well as working through what the participants say about what they make. So, it is an experiment doing sociology *with* people rather than doing sociology *on* them.

We are constantly surprised and fascinated by what emerges. How are they making sense of those things we have listened to and then tried to understand? One of the pieces of writing that we had just finished, which is going to be published in *Qualitative Research* focused on the reflections of one of the participants called Charlynne Ryan.

We arranged to meet Charlynne in a café to get some of her reactions to a draft article that we have written about her. So we sit there in a café in Leytonstone and have a very excited conversation for about 20 minutes. Shamser needs to use the bathroom, so we put the dialogue on 'pause'. We are just chatting and Charlynne leans over and says "I have to ask you – how do you know this stuff about me and my life?"

I said, "Well, we know it because you told us." I have asked her about it subsequently – through reading the representation of her own life offered in our paper she started to see herself differently. It was almost like a moment of sociological reckoning with her past, her present and what she hopes for in the future. I think her surprise was partly because she felt a sense of enchantment or re-enchantment.

I mean, it sounds like a very heady aspiration but I think that is what was alive in that moment in that café in Leytonstone as we were talking about the paper that we had written, which was referring to the things she had told us and the things that she had made and created.

Katherine: In terms of doing a project like that, I mean, something that I struggle with and I think I might have talked about it is the lies people tell themselves and the scepticism that you need to have about what they tell you and then how do you feed that back?

Les: That is a difficult question and a difficult problem because I think we all deceive ourselves, don't we?

Katherine: Totally yes, and not everyone wants to hear about it.

Les: No, not everybody wants to hear a deep reckoning within their own mystifications. That is a very difficult question and I am not sure I have got an easy answer. I do think that commitment to dialogue means that you have to try and continue with that, even in difficult circumstances where you are saying difficult critical things. It comes back to the challenge of how to balance dialogue and critique because sociology is nothing if it is not concerned with critique and thinking about those things that people do gloss and the mystifications that we all are prone to.

It becomes more complicated in that broadcasting yourself and having your name connected with the sentiments that you are broadcasting can implicate others so that sense of a sociable version of sociology might be good for some but it might mean even greater vulnerability for others. There are new ethical challenges that we are faced with in our new informational environment where self-disclosure is everywhere. The fact that these are self-authored doesn't mean that the ethical questions and the ethical problems that have been with the discipline since its inception somehow evaporate. They don't, they take on new forms. That is also why our work as researchers is valuable because facing ethical questions is compulsory and an inherent part of a sociological vocation.

So, I am arguing for a kind of living sociology that is vital and lively; both inventive in terms of its methods and techniques but also restless in its search for new opportunities and formats. I am also arguing that sociology is an orientation to life and a way to living in the world. Here sociological attentiveness becomes a vocation in itself as we notice and question what is before us. It is an invitation to live with doubt in the service of understanding. A sociological way of life necessitates taking our ideas, insights and findings out into the world to wherever the larger conversation is taking place about the kinds of human beings we are becoming and problems that need to be faced together.

References

Back, L, 2007, *The art of listening*, Oxford and New York: Berg Publishers

Back, L, 2011, *The academic diary*, London: Free Thought, www.academic-diary.co.uk

Back, L, 2013, Woolwich murder: The view from south-east London, *The Conversation*, 23 May 2013, 6.43pm BST, https://theconversation.com/woolwich-murder-the-view-from-south-east-london-14620

Back, L, Puwar, N (eds), 2012, *Live methods*, Oxford: Wiley-Blackwell/The Sociological Review

Back, L, Solomos, J, 1993, Doing research, writing politics: The dilemmas of political intervention in research on racism, *Economy and Society* 22, 2, 178–99

Back, L, Solomos, J, 1994, Labour and racism: Trade unions and the selection of parliamentary candidates, *Sociological Review* 42, 2, 165–201

Gane, N, Back, L, 2012, C Wright Mills 50 years on: The promise and craft of sociology revisited, *Theory, Culture and Society* 29, 7/8, 399–421

Gunaratnam, Y, Back, L, forthcoming, Every minute of every day: Mobilities, multiculture and time, in G Robson (ed) *Digital difference: Social media and intercultural experience*, Cambridge: Cambridge Scholars Publishing

Mauss, M, 1954, *The gift: Forms and functions of exchange in archaic societies*, New York: WW Norton Company

Mills, CW, 1959, *The sociological imagination*, New York: Oxford University Press

Sinha, S, Back, L, 2013, Making methods sociable: Dialogue, ethics and authorship in qualitative research, *Qualitative Research*, pre-published online, 24 June 2013, http://qrj.sagepub.com/content/early/2013/10/21/1468794113490717

Young, M, Willmott, P, 1957, *Family and kinship in East London*, Glencoe: The Free Press

Part 2
What does it mean to be a sociologist?

ELEVEN

Sociology for some, someone's sociology...

Yvette Taylor

Yvette Taylor is head of the Weeks Centre for Social and Policy Research, London South Bank University. She has three sole-authored books, including *Fitting into place? Class and gender geographies and temporalities* (Ashgate, 2012), *Lesbian and gay parents* (Palgrave, 2009) and *Working-class lesbian life* (Palgrave, 2007), and 11 edited collections.

Presences, positions, publics

We all, I think, know the danger in offering suggestive titles, as hoped-for audiences, listeners and engagements are pulled in (or pushed out) as the 'someone' to whom we should be responsive – and through whom we recognise ourselves. Titles (and job descriptions) have to live up to the name and, since deciding on the chapter title, I've had some time to pause on these words and to re-visit my intentions in conveying different journeys into and experience of and through 'sociology'. If sociology is to be 'someone's', to emerge from somewhere and be carried, sustained and challenged by 'sociologists', questions emerge of what it means to embody, labour or 'be' the discipline. Who is entitled to lay claims to this professional identity and who then does or disrupts 'sociology'? For feminist sociologists, including myself, these are enduring questions of professional mis-recognition, career arrival and academic–activist relevance; of legitimately being on the academic page as well as feeling that the page itself may already be restrictive (Santos, 2014).

In the *Art of listening*, following longstanding feminist questioning of personal–political implicatedness and forms of academic (dis) engagement, Les Back (2007) calls for a pause and a slow deliberate thoughtfulness – even in the midst of REF outputs, income tallies and other quick and urgent measures of success and 'failure'. So I'm at least going to pause on the words that are in my title, *Sociology for some, someone's sociology*. And to try *not* to reflect the 'sum' of sociology as already known in advance, as equated to income or output, as opposed to something much more contested and complex, personally and professionally provisional; as an invite to *do and disrupt* sociology. While I say this, I'm mindful of my own 'arrival' into sociology, seemingly professionally credentialised even as 'my' particular subject area (feminism, sexuality, gender, class) often means inhabiting a precarious presence, and a potential absence (Taylor, 2012a).

For example, in a recent academic forum, I was happily engaged in collegial conversations. In these settings, conversational exchanges can become conversions, allowing us to display, convey and circulate career capitals – or not. Such conversions, moving from conversations to careers, are perhaps more subtle than bringing out the CV. So, what's new? Why does it still surprise, and still stick, when academic conversations complicitly reproduce social inequalities, expectations and entitlements? Everyday judgements and distinctions are always being made manifest in social interactions, and academic settings are no exception. Many have written passionately and provocatively about the awkward encounters in academia where some seem to be versed and conversant, while others occupy marginal positions – and others aren't even in the room. We know this is a matter of structural inequality rather than simply not being able to appear and perform; in other words this is not just 'my problem' I'm trying to convey here, in pushing into the room. My problem is this: a lingering unease about a 'polite' even complimentary conversation, where I've maybe missed the 'joke', as the unhappy (Ms) feminist. Contrary to my own sense of academic 'fitting' and 'becoming', my colleague asserted, somewhat teasingly (I think) that I was 'Little Miss Perfect'.

Let's consider 'Little Miss Perfect' in academia. We know that she regularly still bangs her head on the academic ceiling; she earns less and often finds herself juggling multiple shifts, picking up domestic work, tasked endlessly with balancing and caring; her 'imperfections' are subject to much social commentary whether she's doing too much ('feminism gone too far') or not enough ('welfare mums'). As with gendered material inequality, many feminists have highlighted gendered cultural climates within academia: 'There is a cultural climate that favours men...Women are not recognised for their talents or abilities and are often forced to do low-level, high-volume administrative work, while many more men assume external-facing roles that have immediate...career gains...' (Morley, 2013). In the same *Times Higher* article, Morley asks 'Why are so many women missing from leading institutions, particularly at senior management levels?' Female professorial presence is both reduced and inflated as brightly coloured and exaggerated ('Little Miss Perfect'). So I am mindful of others who do not get to arrive in sociology, whose on-going labours, counted as individualised CV bullet points, still signal an ever-extended 'early career' status, as impermanence and precariousness become the normalised academic state (Taylor, 2012b).

So what are the forces that 'fit' the good, mobile academic to place and what shape can this take if the 'fit' is to reach beyond the individual (if queer) academic, to instead encompass questions of care, attentiveness and varied presence (Taylor and Addison, 2013)? I was excited to be invited to speak at 'The Rebirth of Feminism' conference, with the title posing potential... and, perhaps, problems or even pain. A 'rebirth' is loaded with prospects and (re)production, as enduring feminist labour. This is messy and, while something (and someone) 'arrives', the potential, problems and pain arguably carry on. I considered these concerns as I searched for an 'object' to bring to the conference, as instructed by the organisers. The chosen object was intended to foster discussion, deliberately deviating from a stand-and-speak format of knowing-feminist speaker versus feminist-in-training audience. Conscious of these knowledge exchanges, often bound up with generational positions, I chose to speak about my own retrieved school report cards, marking my own educational trajectory. Which I wouldn't easily describe – or feel – as an 'arrival'.

Report cards are something we've all likely experienced (arguably continued and self-audited as our own academic CVs). We've all been evaluated, and as educators, we all continuously evaluate, celebrating potential and lamenting failure. When the question of our own academic biographies intersects with questions of women's entry into the world of employment and education more generally, questions of potential can quickly become problematic – even recast as feminist failure. As McRobbie (2008) highlights in *The aftermath of feminism*, women's entry into the workforce, as beneficiaries of and achievers in education, has become a sign of 'arrival', that she has found her place in a (post)feminist world. But she can also go 'too far' and (some) women's achievement has also been seen as a cause and symptom of a male-underachievement and 'crisis of masculinity' (even with his pay differential).

In presenting, I hoped to remind everyone of this story beyond me, even as I placed my report cards on the floor, in the group circle; as we report on feminist potential (and failure) we must, of course, move beyond our own stories. But here is mine: I rediscovered my school report cards, held as valued and treasured objects, even though what they conveyed on the pages was frequently a 'failure' rather than a 'success'. In reading these educational (mis)representations of me, my initial curiosity moved to an anger and even dismay as I realised the emotional (and material) pull these stories still had for me as an adult. I am deeply sceptical of the story of meritocratic promise, of working really hard (and, romantically, 'against all the odds') and so I certainly didn't want to convey a problematic beginning, transformed by an educational 'becoming'. Instead, I wanted to query these official stories, which seem profoundly marked by classed and gendered terms and anticipated trajectories. My own reports are littered with 'lapses into idle chatter', of being 'easily distracted' and rather 'slap dash' in approach: the phrase 'continual underachievement' is, for one subject, underlined and in my physical education report a rather harsh judgement is made that I have, in fact, 'not mastered the basic skills' (of badminton).

Our presence comes from somewhere; we carry collective histories (and futures) as we take up space as the 'personal troubles' of biography can, and should be, transformed into public issues of society, or a public sociology. As Back notes, these histories and futures carry as we 'live in and across the histories and futures that they both carry and make on a daily basis' (2007, 148). But it is *with* colleagues that I am able to probe at intersectional dilemmas (and sociological questions of presence, absence and 'fit'), as an on-going collective effort rather than as an instance of self-reflexivity or researcher mobility (Robinson, 2013). When the 'girl with potential' becomes celebrated, anticipated *and* lamented, as a sign of educational and employment future/failure, we need to be attentive to the re-birthing and recirculation of enduring inequalities, so as to report feminist potential for everyone

This sense of going forward (and returning back) recently caused another pause for me when I was asked to do a Desert Island Discourse interview for the British Sociological Association's *Network* magazine. The purpose of the feature is to say what key works you would have with you in the unlikely event that you're stranded on a desert island. As a PhD student I'd done some of these interviews with my favourite academics. As someone being asked to provide this, I suddenly felt a weight about what to convey, what to display, when it was not just myself, my intelligence, my own good taste, that I was carrying. As we appear on the page (in the magazine, in the journal, in the book) we create certain presences and so we have to be careful to ask what else is carried with us? What – or who – can appear, and what is disappeared?

The interviewer asked me about my second choice, Beverley Skeggs' (1997) *Formations of class and gender* and I explained my choices, still hoping to be recognised on the sociological page:

> 'I'm going to continue with very much "alive" and present sociologists (at the risk of embarrassment)'.[1] So, this is the book I really remember grabbing off a shelf as an undergraduate at Edinburgh. I sat down on the library floor and read it there and then, something that rarely happens! While at Edinburgh I was doing care work, even though I'd "made it in time" in getting a maintenance grant; it seemed plausible to me that I would continue with a similar kind of work on leaving university as it was something I knew and could do well, where university had felt very unfamiliar and unexpected. This book made me question – as well as appreciate – these "cares" are also about class and gender. It gave me a validity in raising (albeit quietly at that point) questions about class in the classroom and the inside–outside academic spaces I occupied. And still occupy. Questions about class inequalities and feminist subjects

(and gaps) are ones followed through, I hope, in *Working-class lesbian life: Classed outsiders* (Taylor, 2007). *Formations of class and gender* was also key to my more recent book on *Lesbian and gay parenting: Securing social and educational capital* (Taylor, 2009), which showed that the middle-class "cares" of some are positioned as responsible and opposed to the "carelessness" of working-class parents – sexuality complicates the "success" and "failure" of these parental stories, and class positions.'

I should mention that one of my choices (even serious sociologists are allowed a frivolous, luxury item) was *Ramona the brave* by Beverly Cleary, which is part of a series of books about growing up, femininity, families, sibling rivalry, schooling, friendship and bullies. In the series there is a whole section about divorce, smoking and unemployment, as 'bad habits', which any good sociologist would surely need to rip out…But it's about negotiating place and belonging more generally – if the everyday world is problematic, fraught with gender and class inequalities, Ramona offers imagination, comfort – and strategies! I used to read this in a public library in Glasgow (which has sadly now shut down). I recently found a copy by chance and re-read meanings into Ramona's friendship with Daisy Kidd, her 'boisterous yet appealing' character, loud activities and, ultimately, her brave triumphs! There is something to be said for arriving in place, and being present…

'Visiting queer': awkward academics, trials and triumphs

But 'queer suicide' can perhaps be thought of an ultimate *absence*, yet one which provides a very present and persisting way of claiming LGBT rights as urgencies for some, where other lives – and those of black and minority ethnic groups – are already lost (Taylor, 2011).[2] In writing an article on 'queer suicide' in *Feminist Theory*, I described myself as a 'visiting queer academic', to locate myself, my implicatedness and standpoint within the field that I'd occupied and moved through. I'd realised later (of course, when the article is in print and thoughts are made public and a 'coming-out' has occurred) that describing myself as a 'visiting queer academic' was in fact a funny descriptor (in this un-funny event). Was I just passing through 'queer' as I visited this institution, was it (is it) the queerness of me/you which produces the queer place, or was 'queer' passing through me (and others) unsettling the happy mainstreamed campus: what can pass through, what facilitates this journey and what blockages – or sticking points – do we encounter? As academics, are we not all a little bit queer? Let me give you an example:

At a recent conference, I was making polite conversation. I was asked about my research and I talked about 'queer suicides' (Taylor, 2011), feeling recently compelled to think through the ways that, in celebrating new queer presences, 'others' are rendered absent, already lost to public/activist/institutional concern. I was so pleased that I hadn't scared away my new acquaintance. Yet as we talked I realised there was a profound mis-understanding between us. My new colleague thought that I was studying 'career suicide' and I was forced to repeat, then shout 'queer', to come out in the polite space. Polite exits were made. Queer, like class, can be an 'embarrassing and unsettling subject' (Sayer, 2005). Sexuality – and class – weigh heavily in the classroom and in the spaces, which the engaged university/researcher must increasingly take up, travel through and have an 'impact on' if they are to prove their diverse and distinctive capacity (Taylor, 2013). But class and sexuality constitute blockages where some more than others bear the weight of this labour, in coming up against normative institutional structures and in endlessly 'coming out' as queer. There is work to be done in the queering of these processes, beyond the individual uptake of space, self-telling or self-recognition (which 'coming out' implies even as it is often blocked). Efforts to challenge heteronormativity within higher educational settings can themselves reveal how identity and space are mutually constituted, reconfigured and re-embedded: *I come out and they, perhaps you, don't have to.*

What presences and absences are we complicit in reproducing in 'our' space and how are we – you and me – best placed to think through the intersectional–interactional dimensions of these, to make a sustained entrance, rather than a quick exit?

Consider these two stories:

Story 1: Triumphs

She'd just won a prestigious prize (at a prestigious conference): praise was rightfully delivered and she basked in the glory, in the surprise that seemed to say she'd arrived in academia (early career no more). But she was worried. Did this really signal a safety in arriving, a recognition of value, labour, contributions? Or did it signal more labour, maybe this time without recognition or value? When the stakes are set so high do we have no choice but to keep apace, to endlessly indicate, effect and fear our own (in)capacities? When we compete with colleagues in a competitive university-marketplace – and when competition is so close it is generated by-ourselves-for-ourselves (as 'keeping up', 'what next?')

– what cares, connections, capacities are rendered near and far? I tell her to add her award to her email signature, a neat summary quickly conveying who she is as a hyperlinked bio. But I pause. There's a borderline between the achieving academic, the celebrity star and the pretentious, (self)promotional subject. I pause over these laboured cares.

Trying: Story 2

'How long to keep trying, to just stay in the same place – to move around geographically, while staying on the same bottom rung?' After a sole-authored book and an edited collection, or two, she decided 'trying' had been long enough. She'd put in the long hours but was still stuck in the expanded category of 'early career'. She was leaving academia. She feared telling me, and other academics, feared that she would be letting the feminist side down. The sides in academia are often sharp and painful and despite our tries, these persist. 'Sides' stick out as barriers to entrance, as promotional hurdles, in recognised 'achievers' – or 'drop outs'. My colleague, contributor and competent academic feared she was on the wrong side: non-academic. Friends console, offer support, sympathise with the tough soul-searching and decision-making when academia is something more than just a job. We write our sympathies and supports in between emails as other urgencies come through our inbox (from students, colleagues, funders, unions). How much to keep trying and caring, with the inbox, the entrance and endurance in higher education as painful sides press against us.

The sides of these stories are not straightforwardly oppositional, as success versus failure, as enduring effort or ended potential; we are ever-encouraged to re-work our 'failures' as insights, to expand academic horizons as these are curtailed, and to be 'enterprising' as cure for structural dis-investment. These are intersecting 'stories to tell', which we all might recognise from our academic biographies and personal–professional investments, cares and capacities (Taylor, 2010). As an effort in 'trying' in, let's thinks about alternative stories that fracture the 'us' and 'them' of the successful/failing academic and institution. What other stories of academic cares and capacities can be shared beyond a story-of-self, of the hyperlinked academic with the good CV to be ever added to? How to hold doors open in arriving and fitting into place?

I started this chapter by thinking through my own presence and absence and the varied journeys, different labours and divided recognitions within and beyond academia, as rather 'careless' practices. The mobile academic may not be completely undone in these encounters but the critical differentials in processes of being and becoming often mean that some are unable to move into teaching-research landscapes, to move through and activate that terrain as their own, as properly academic. Others experience disjunctures in academic occupations, felt through research and teaching contexts. Being and 'becoming' on the academic map can involve emotional conflicts across time and place, felt in occupying academia, especially when this demands a mobility of practice and an entrepreneurial orientation to local–global markets (as 'outreach', 'widening participation', 'diverse publics'). I want to always be able to turn to sociology as an effort in public–professional–personal care, even as academic efforts necessarily sit on my own CV (and I'd want these there too).

Notes

[1] Typically the tradition is to discuss someone – mostly men – who are dead.

[2] The debates on same-sex marriage in the US frequently position a liberal white middle class as now about to 'come forward' into the sphere of public visibility and legitimacy as able to secure citizenship, rights and entitlements, but blocked by the 'backwardness' of black and minority ethnic and working-class communities. These debates, over the lives and deaths of queer community generally and queer youth in particular, continued during my research in the US – they were a big part of my own presence on campus, as the media took over Rutgers University as the site where Tyler Clementi experienced homophobia and committed suicide.

References

Back, L, 2007, *The art of listening*, Oxford: Berg Publishers

Cleary, B, 1975, *Ramona the brave*, New York, NY: William Morrow

McRobbie, A, 2008, *The aftermath of feminism: Gender, culture and social change*, London: SAGE

Morley, L, 2013, Global Gender Index, *Times Higher* www.timeshighereducation.co.uk/story.aspx?storyCode=2003517

Robinson, Y, 2013, Choreographing afropean bodies: The economy of West African dance and drumming in Italy, http://weekscentreforsocialandpolicyresearch.wordpress.com/2013/02/19/choreographing-afropean-bodies-the-economy-of-west-african-dance-and-drumming-in-italy/

Santos, AC, 2013, *Social movements and sexual citizenship in southern Europe*, London: Palgrave Macmillan

Santos, CA, 2014, 'Academia without walls? Multiple belongings and the implications of feminist and queer political engagement' in Y Taylor (ed) *The entrepreneurial university: Engaging publics, intersecting impacts*, Basingstoke: Palgrave, 20-40

Sayer, A, 2005, Class, moral worth and recognition, *sociology*, 39, 5, 947–63

Skeggs, B, 1997, *Formations of Class and Gender*, London: Sage

Taylor, Y, 2007, *Working-class lesbian life: Classed outsiders*, Basingstoke: Palgrave Macmillan

Taylor, Y, 2009, *Lesbian and gay parenting: Securing social and educational capital*, Basingstoke: Palgrave Macmillan

Taylor, Y, 2010, Stories to tell? (De)legitimised selves, *Qualitative Inquiry*, 16, 8, 633–41

Taylor, Y, 2011, Queer presences and absences: Citizenship, community, diversity – or death, *Feminist Theory* 12, 3, 335–41

Taylor, Y, 2012a, Class encounters: Again…, Editorial, *Social and Cultural Geography* 13, 6, 545–9

Taylor, Y, 2012b, *Fitting into place? Class and gender geographies and temporalities*, Farnham: Ashgate

Taylor, Y, 2012c, Enterprising, enduring, enabling? Early career efforts and 'winning' workshops, www.genderandeducation.com/tag/yvette-taylor/

Taylor, Y, 2013, Queer encounters of sexuality and class: Navigating emotional landscapes of academia, *Emotion, Space and Society*, http://dx.doi.org/10.1016/j.emospa.2012.08.001

Taylor, Y, Addison, M (eds), 2013, *Queer presences and absences*, Basingstoke: Palgrave Macmillan

TWELVE

Imagining social science

Ann Oakley

Ann Oakley's first degree was PPE at Somerville College, Oxford, in 1965, and her second a PhD in sociology at Bedford College, University of London in 1974. She has worked in university research for almost 50 years, and has published widely on gender, health, methodology and public policy. She is professor of sociology and social policy at the Institute of Education in London, and works in the Social Science Research Unit there, which she founded in 1990.

The stories we tell ourselves and each other about our lives are a mixture of edited memory and constructed narrative. The effort after truth is an effort after meaning, so the relationship between the stories and 'what actually happened' can sometimes be quite complex.

Today I think of myself not as a sociologist but as a social scientist. Over the last 30 years I have become convinced that the study of the social has so much in common with the material sciences that we ought not to see it as a special case. The task of all science is better to understand the place in which we find ourselves, with understanding being a pathway to prediction, control and improvement. Although I have spent most of my professional life in academia, I have never been interested in the life of the academy as such: the reason for being in this business of social science has always for me been a matter of public welfare, of trying to be part of that struggle whose broad underlying aim is a society based on what is essentially a moral vision of equality, peace and justice. As the social scientist and public servant, Barbara Wootton, pointed out, whatever one's commitment to science, judgements about the work that matters will derive ultimately from personally held principles and beliefs (Wootton, 1950).

'Becoming a sociologist'

Wootton also said, reflecting on her own professional life, that serendipity had played a much larger part in its direction than had informed choice (Wootton, 1967, 278). There was no moment when I decided to become a sociologist/social scientist. On the contrary, from very early childhood my ambition was always to be a writer (perhaps this is still the case). As an only child in an academic family, I spent a lot of time on my own, and the rest of it observing other people. There is a great deal of overlap between the qualities needed for effective writing, and those which are called into play doing social science (Oakley, 2009). In both cases, one must have the capacity to distance oneself from personal social context and circumstances, the ability to shift perspective and take on other points of view, and, above all, a passionate (but non-prurient) interest in the fabric of other people's lives. Writers and social scientists are both vehicles for producing accounts and stories composed of (of course differently balanced) fact and fiction.

As a teenage would-be writer, I was advised not to do an English literature degree, so I went to Oxford to study philosophy, politics and economics. Sociology was first taught to undergraduates at Oxford in 1964 as an option on the politics syllabus, and I chose to do it. After two years of symbolic logic, aridly taught political history, the peculiarly incestuous forms of philosophy and the nonsenses of neo-classical economics as practised at Oxford, it was a huge relief to be encouraged to study the real world. My tutors were AH (Chelly) Halsey and Bryan Wilson, and they could hardly have been more different. Bryan Wilson, whom I remember as a severe-suited acerbic theorist, was given to changing my tutorial dates when called to wine-tasting sessions at his College, All Souls. Chelly, a magnificent lion of a man, wore bright coloured jerseys, looked one straight in the eye, and enjoyed the industrial connotations of Nuffield College, having himself come to sociology as the child of a railway worker. The first text he set me to read was Ralf Dahrendorf's *Class and class conflict in industrial society* (1959), a book whose omission of gender stratification did not upset me then nearly as much as it did later.

Chelly Halsey also introduced me to an inspirational book which I have reread many times since, *The sociological imagination* by C Wright Mills. Its very title suggested to me an amalgamation of the (for me) newly discovered sociology with a writer's imagination. C Wright Mills calls 'the sociological imagination' a tool for grasping the social relations between history and biography, one capable of ranging from the most impersonal transformations to the most intimate features of people's lives. He is clear that this imagination is *not* confined to academic sociology, and is particularly wonderful on the deficits of what he calls 'grand theory'. In an unforgettable passage, he condemns the impenetrable verbosity of an American sociologist much read in the 1950s and 1960s, Talcott Parsons, reducing a one-page extract from Parsons' *The social system* (1952) to two short sentences. This has been a model for me ever since. So also has been C Wright Mills's advice about the dangers of 'abstracted empiricism' and about biases in sociological work: 'My biases are of course no more or no less biases than those I am going to examine,' he writes. 'Let those who do not care for mine use their rejections of them to make their own as explicit and as acknowledged as I am going to try to make mine' (Mills, 1959, 21). This proved a particularly apposite rule for a social scientist prone to pointing out the masculine bias of much sociology. *The sociological imagination's* Appendix, 'On intellectual craftsmanship' applies also to craftswomen, and is still the best statement I know of how to handle the relationships between personal experience and intellectual work and between thinking and writing in the doing of sociology. My advice to young sociologists today is to read, enjoy and take this to heart.

After an interlude devoted to writing and reproduction, I did a PhD on women's attitudes to housework at Bedford College in

London at a time when the only people who studied housework were fiction-writers. I attended few classes in how to do sociology and social research, learning chiefly by trial and error. I belong to that generation of sociologists/social scientists who *did* make most of it up: the institutional framework of sociology at that time was quite new (the British Sociological Association was founded in 1951, the Social Science Research Council in 1965), and formal training in methods was thin on the ground. As a result, we *were* probably rather undisciplined, but the joy of discovery and invention was intense; it might even have helped our work to have an impact (in the days before anyone tried to quantify this).

What kind of 'career'?

Just as I never decided to become a sociologist/social scientist, so I do not consider that the past 50 years have constituted 'a career'. I say this for two reasons. First, most of my work has been as a researcher, and researchers were in the 1960s and are still today unfortunately regarded as somewhat marginal to academic life. The second reason for being sceptical about having had a 'career' is what that concept means: a road or pathway from somewhere to somewhere, a progression from a lower point to some kind of 'advanced' status.

Most of my academic life has been spent doing research as a 'contract researcher'. Contract researchers are usually employed on fixed short-term contracts funded by external research grants. Until 1974 in the UK, they were not defined as academic staff at all; it took until 2002 for regulations to be enacted requiring that they be treated equally to other staff. Contract research is a 'culture of impermanence': its staff are still far more likely than other academics to have temporary posts.[1] Progression to permanent contracts and/or to readerships and professorships is difficult for contract researchers, most of whom are women, because the procedural rules are written for the teaching-and-research formula, where the main business of an academic is supposed to be teaching plus a little research on the side in order to generate a visible trail of peer-reviewed journal articles. On the negative side, I have spent years of my life fighting these rules and their implications, from the pejorative designation 'academic-related' deployed to describe researchers, to the stipulation that they deserve less room space, less annual leave, less access to libraries, more insecure contracts and other similar absurdities. On the positive side, I have immensely enjoyed the freedom of contract research – to choose topics for research, to solicit the support of sympathetic funders, to write up the results of research in imaginative ways.

Traditional notions of a 'career' speak to and about a gender-segregated world of work, one in which financial value and personal satisfaction are assigned to the world outside the home. In 1938, on the eve of the Second World War, Virginia Woolf published an outspoken essay called *Three guineas* in which she linked together the cultural attitudes allowing the rise of fascism with those that prevent the equal participation of women in public life, including in education. Woolf asked a question almost unknown at the time as to whether it is really such a good idea for women to become full members of a society which carries the imprint of masculine world views. She identified the values driving higher education as those of status-seeking, competition and acquisitiveness, suggesting that these values breed qualities of self-satisfaction and aggression towards others. 'Above all,' she inquired,

> where is it leading us, the procession of educated men?...Let us never cease from thinking – what is this "civilisation" in which we find ourselves? What are these ceremonies and why should we take part in them? What are these professions and why should we make money out of them? Where in short is it leading us, the procession of the sons of educated men? (Woolf, 1938, 240–1)

Aliens in the academy

The American writer Adrienne Rich wrote about the alternative of a 'woman-centered university' back in 1974. Rich sees universities as hierarchies with clusters of highly paid men at the top and a large base of ill-paid or unpaid women – administrators, cleaners, female partners, research and teaching assistants on whose labours those at the top depend. Most of the women employed in or by my own institution are cleaners, administrators, contract researchers, and/or other part-time staff. As Rich points out, the women who do reach the top appear to do so without the support of the same kind of retinue (either at work or at home).

What we are dealing with here is a masculine intellectual tradition which relies on ideologies of combat (a thesis is 'defended', a seminar resembles the 'primal horde' (Holmes, 1967), and so on and so forth). Unfortunately gender stereotyping works in such a way that the main alternative for academic women who want to do it differently is the motherhood/nurturing role. This is equally unsatisfactory. My own attempts in the 1990s to manage a research unit on non-hierarchical lines encountered problems from staff who misinterpreted my aversion to masculinist hierarchy as yet another attempt at mothering. Over the last few years, the growth of academic bureaucracy and the transformation of universities into capitalist businesses emphasising accountability, efficiency and the achievement of narrowly defined targets and outputs has generated what Mary Evans (1995) has termed 'managerial masculinity', a new form of masculinity superimposed on the old. These employment structures reinforce the cultural dynamics of gender, making a move towards a more progressive culture of gender parity even more difficult.

In his *Notes on a lifetime* Norbert Elias reflects on how the experience of, in some sense, being 'outside' the culture one lives in encourages the sociological imagination (Elias, 1984). This is the case, I think, for those of us (mainly marginal women) who have tried to promote a more egalitarian social science. My early work on housework and gender now has some kind of iconic status in the effort to change conversations about sociological interpretations of labour, biology and social life. This transition from barely-recognised-and-derided subject to established intellectual domain has also taught me that social scientists must always follow their noses in doing what they think is important work (even if nobody else thinks so at the time). This is how science works, and we are the same.

If I did it all again...

My life as a sociologist/researcher/social scientist has been one of both privilege and oppression. If I were to relive it I would choose not to work within those patriarchal structures to which women in the academy are forced to return again and again. Although I am seen as a successful academic woman, there have been many occasions when I have been discriminated against: in only one of these was I brave enough to launch any kind legal challenge. Like other attempts on the part of women to speak out, for example, women who have been raped, this is a matter of well-honed institutional strategies designed to drown out protest with background noise.

I would also wish – and this is really science fiction stuff – to live and work in a culture that is not so obsessed with ideologies of and about gender. The introduction of a feminist political vision into academic sociology/social science in the 1970s created a kind of mythology about 'qualitative' work as some sort of automatic corrective to masculine bias. My own sociology and social research has been forced into this mould, although it has always participated in both 'qualitative' and 'quantitative' paradigms (Oakley, 2000a). My advocacy of randomised controlled experiments and of systematic research reviews was (is?) earmarked as some kind of unforgivable desertion from the qualitative camp (Oakley, 2000b). All this paradigm squabbling is, in my view, a tiresome diversion from the task in hand, which is not to support the image of sociology/social science as 'just academic', but to think hard and well and methodologically and imaginatively to research the important questions of our time. Defining what is important comes first, and this must be a democratic exercise, involving both those who create knowledge as a product and those whose lives form the original production. Then we must know what kind of question we are asking, and choose approaches and methods which fit the question. Otherwise doing sociology is a waste of time, and we might just as well all write fiction instead.

Note

[1] 'Culture of impermanence' was a phrase used by Basil Bernstein, a professor of sociology at the Institute of Education, University of London.

References

Dahrendorf, D, 1959, *Class and class conflict in industrial society*, Stanford: Stanford University Press

Elias, N, 1984, Notes on a lifetime, in *Reflections on a life*, Cambridge: Polity, 1994

Evans, M, 1995, Ivory towers: Life in the mind, in L Morley, V Walsh (eds) *Feminist academics: Creative agents for change*, pp 7–21, London: Taylor and Francis

Holmes, R, 1967, The university seminar and the primal horde, *British Journal of Sociology* 18, 135–50

Mills, CW, 1959, *The sociological imagination*, New York: Oxford University Press

Oakley, A, 2000a, Paradigm wars: Some thoughts on a personal and public trajectory, *International Journal of Social Research Methodology* 2, 3, 247–54

Oakley, A, 2000b, *Experiments in knowing: Gender and method in the social sciences*, Chapter 1: Who knows?, Cambridge: Polity

Oakley, A, 2009, 'Fallacies of fact and fiction', *Feminism and Psychology* 19, 1, 118–22

Parsons, T, 1952, *The social system*, Glencoe: The Free Press

Rich, A, 1974, Toward a woman-centered university, in A Rich, *On lies, secrets and silence*, pp 126–55, New York: WW Norton & Company, reprinted 1979

Woolf, V, 1938, with *A room of one's own* and *Three guineas*, Oxford: Oxford University Press, reprinted 1992

Wootton, B, 1950, *Testament for social science*, London: George Allen & Unwin

Wootton, B, 1967, *In a world I never made*, p 278, London: George Allen & Unwin

THIRTEEN

From accidental to ambitious sociology

Linsey McGoey

Linsey McGoey is senior lecturer in sociology at the University of Essex and co-director of the Centre for Economic Sociology and Innovation (CRESI). She is editor of *An introduction to the sociology of ignorance: Essays on the limits of knowing* (Routledge, 2014). With Matthias Gross, she is co-editor of the *Routledge handbook of ignorance studies* (Routledge, 2015). From 2011 to 2013, she served as a steering committee member for the World Health Organization's programme, Women's Health and Children's Health: Human Rights and Evidence of Impact.

It was either in Lima or Cusco that I found a novel that would change my life. The novel, *The real life of Alejandro Mayta,* was by Mario Vargas Llosa. It was not one of his best.

Anyone who has ever spent time backpacking will recall the makeshift libraries in every hostel corner, the books swapped so many times that their pages start to lose their heft, growing thinner than Rizla paper.

Crammed behind the ubiquitous copies of *The beach* or *Siddhartha* you could usually count on at least one book that you hadn't already read.

I picked up Llosa's book three months into a six-month visit to South America, at that moment when living out of your backpack for months on end, perfecting the art of a nicely rolled cigarette, befriending other travellers who looked exactly like yourself – mostly white, mostly middle-class, mostly educated on our parents' dime – begins to wear on your conscience.

It began to dawn on me that I might not emerge from South America as I had expected: fully bilingual in Spanish; a rookie writer for a leading North American daily newspaper; a Martha Gellhorn in training.

I was 24 years old and I was failing at the only career I ever wanted – to be a freelance journalist.

Things in South America started off well. Somehow, within a week of arriving in Quito, I had managed to land a 'job' as an unpaid freelance photographer for Narco News, an online news bulletin dedicated to exposing the social and economic devastation wreaked by the US war on drugs.

I was assigned to shadow a petite, chain-smoking Bolivian journalist named Luis who had been ferried from La Paz to Quito to cover the run-up to the election of Lucio Gutiérrez, Ecuador's president from January 2003 to April 2005.

Luis was a small, spirited, excessively candid man. "How tall are you?" He fired at me when we first met, in a bar in Quito, having been put in touch with each other by the publisher of Narco News.

"5'10," I replied.

He shook his head. "That's too tall."

"How old?" He asked next.

"24."

He shook his head again. "That's too young."

"To be a journalist," he added, looking me up and down with clinical detachment. "Give yourself at least ten years."

"But I'm here now," I pointed out.

"That's true," he conceded, with unconcealed disappointment.

"How's your Spanish?" he asked, in Spanish. I shook my head uncomprehendingly. I was intending to learn while there, I explained.

He laughed. For a long time. Then he ordered another beer for himself and, without asking, a Coca-Cola for me, as if he was chaperoning a minor.

I spent two weeks trailing Luis as he interviewed a dizzying number of high-placed indigenous leaders who had been central to Gutiérrez's campaign, taking photos while Luis and his informants seemed to kill themselves with laughter every time I moved across the room.

"What's so funny?" I asked finally.

"You," he replied. "They ask me where you're from, and I say, 'Who, her? My giant Gringa assistant in the corner?' I explain that you're a Canadian – and that you can't speak a single word of Spanish. It cracks them up every time."

Luis returned to La Paz after two weeks, but not before bustling me inside a building where I was to photograph a "very, very important man". With his penchant for the dramatic, Luis refused to elaborate further until we were a few yards away from the man himself.

"You'll never guess who it is," Luis whispered.

"Lucio Gutiérrez."

Luis looked crestfallen. "That's right," he admitted. "I've taught you well. He's the new *president*."

A week or two later, after travelling from Ecuador to Peru, I received an email from the publisher of Narco News. Sadly, he was not able to offer me a formal position on Narco News' internship program. Blankly, I stared at the computer screen. I was being fired from an unpaid internship. I couldn't even keep a job as a volunteer.

On the topic of failure, a comment by the writer Howard Jacobson has always struck me as apropos: 'It starts early.'

My early failures as a freelance journalist, struggling to write articles on South American political uprisings (I sold a total of two articles in six months) prompted a career rethink. I had, on occasion, thought fleetingly of going to graduate school – but where?

I had heard that the MSc in international relations at the London School of Economics was the very best programme for international studies in the world. And I knew that I didn't have the grades for it.

The nice thing about failure is that it engenders shrewdness. Working, or failing to work, for Narco News had been a sobering experience. Sheer enthusiasm was not enough: I needed to master the art of calculation. Looking at LSE entry requirements, I saw that only one out of every 15 or so applicants were admitted to study international relations. One out every four applicants, on the other hand, made it into the anthropology department.

There were other departments that were as competitive – or as uncompetitive – as anthropology. But that week, I happened to be reading *The real life of Alejandro Mayta*. And one of the characters was an anthropologist. It was a silly, arbitrary, romantic decision – but if you can't make a romantic decision while living in Peru, fired from an online news bulletin with the word 'Narco' in its title, then when can you?

I've since lost my copy of Llosa's book. A review in *The New York Times* notes that it centres on the fictional story of Mayta, 'a little-known Trotskyist' who tries in vain to lead an uprising in the Andes against a military junta in 1950s Peru. Mayta is described as something of a conflicted soul, 'a screwed-up idealist, a victim of the factionalism and in-fighting of the Left'.

Ah, yes. The novel was even better preparation for a career in academia than I realised at the time.

I think it was halfway through my MSc in social anthropology that I read Michael Taussig's *The devil and commodity fetishism in South America* (1980). Perhaps the book should have evoked nostalgia for when I was physically close to the regions that Taussig writes about – but it didn't. It *was* inspirational, but in a cerebral, less visceral way. Taussig's writing managed to strike a perfect balance between compelling imagery and stark factual analysis that, to me, is what the very best sociology or anthropology does. It must strive for factual accuracy in a way that fiction cannot and need not emulate. And yet that doesn't mean sociology must lose its sense of poetry or imagination.

C Wright Mills's work offers a compelling description of the paradox of sociology; the uneasy balance of creativity and cool analysis that good sociological writing can aspire to.

As C Wright Mills puts it, the value of sociology

> is the capacity to shift from one perspective to another – from the political to the psychological; from examination of a single family to comparative assessment of the national budgets of the world; from the theological school to the military establishment; from considerations of an oil industry to studies of contemporary poetry. It is the capacity to range from the most impersonal and remote transformations to the most intimate features of the human self – and to see the relations between the two. (Mills, 2000 [1959]: 7)

A task as ambitious as C Wright Mills' demands as much humility as it does hubris. It demands constant grasping after a form of understanding that is forever out of reach. Ambitious sociology is rooted in the obligation to acknowledge the limits of knowledge while constantly striving to transcend those limits. To 'fail better,' as Samuel Beckett once suggested.

I haven't been a sociologist for very long. I finished my PhD six years ago and I've been employed as a lecturer for about three years. At a few serendipitous and particularly arduous times during those years, I have written something of which I have been especially proud.

The first is an article titled 'On the will to ignorance in bureaucracy'. It was written in the second-last year of my PhD and published in the journal *Economy and Society* (McGoey, 2007). I remember late evenings reading over a long day's work, and then rising early in the mornings to scribble ideas that had come during half-conscious moments in the night. I spent weeks crafting each sentence of that 9,000-word article. And they have never felt like wasted weeks. A few years later, I felt a similar sense of complete, joyful immersion while writing the introduction to a special journal issue that I had edited, also on the topic of ignorance.

Perhaps to feel particularly proud of two essays isn't much. But to me it feels like an okay start. Both articles led to unexpected collaborations with inspiring scholars based throughout the world. Both articles forced me to rework and rework fleeting thoughts until I felt I was conveying an insight without wasting too much of my reader's time with jargon or unneeded obtrusiveness. The articles helped me to feel contented and privileged to have chanced upon this accidental career, this immersion in a profession in which I did not expect to find myself.

And yet there's that word – privilege – which worries me. C Wright Mills wrote as eloquently about power, about privilege, as he did about the sociological imagination: 'By the powerful we mean, of course, those who are able to realize their will, even if others resist it.' (Mills, 1956: 9).

When it comes to the problem of privilege, perhaps it's not enough to feel contented or appeased by earlier work. Perhaps what's needed is not satisfaction but continual doubt. At the very least, doubt leads to difficult but necessary questions. What makes for a valuable career? What separates sociology from other academic disciplines, or academia from other professions?

I've always been uncomfortable with 'disciplinary jingoism', the tendency to see your own discipline as superior to other disciplines. I've often struggled to understand what really separates the objectives of a journalist, or a fiction writer, or a sociologist. Foucault famously called his analyses 'fictions'. As he commented, 'I am well aware that I have never written anything but *fictions*. I do not mean to say, however, that truth is therefore absent.' (Foucault 1980: 193).

Often the quote is treated scornfully – as evidence of the extreme relativism of his approach. But I've always found the quote inspiring. And I take from it the belief that emphasising the distinctions between different types of writers is not particularly helpful. What is useful is to embrace the common elements of different fields; to celebrate what unites them, rather than divorces them.

One thing journalists, sociologists and fiction writers share is the ability, even the obligation, to communicate the stories of those who, for whatever reasons, have had their own voices silenced or threatened. We have the opportunity, even the duty to speak truth to power – to expose and to condemn the ways that 'social systems' privilege the ability of some to realise their own will at the expense of others.

I doubt that I have managed to do this enough – to challenge the very privileges from which I've benefited. In fact, I would say that at different times of my career, it's been implied that a sociologist's job is *not* to take positions or to pass judgement. The job of the sociologist is to describe, not to prescribe. How very wrong that seems to me – as wrong as my Bolivian friend Luis' admonishment to try and write something "in ten years".

Over the past decade, I've shifted from an accidental sociologist to an ambitious one – even if that only means 'failing better'. Failure may start early. Failure may be endemic to many of our efforts. But, to rephrase Foucault, that doesn't mean that success is therefore absent.

References

Foucault, M, 1980, *Power/knowledge: Selective interviews and other writings 1972-1977*, C Gordon (ed), New York, NY: Pantheon Press

McGoey, L, 2007, On the will to ignorance in bureaucracy, *Economy and Society*, 36, 2, 212–35

Mills, CW, 1956, *The power elite*, Oxford and New York: Oxford University Press

Mills, CW, 2000 [1959], *The sociological imagination*, Oxford and New York: Oxford University Press

Taussig, M, 1980, *The devil and commodity fetishism in South America*, Chapel Hill, NC: University of North Carolina Press

FOURTEEN

Sociographer by design? Boundary crossings and interdisciplinarity

Yvonne Robinson

Yvonne Robinson is a senior research fellow in the Weeks Centre
for Social and Policy Research at London South Bank University.
A geographer by background, Yvonne's research interests include
children and young people, education, race, ethnicity and the arts.
Yvonne has successfully undertaken research and evaluation for
the Economic and Social Research Council and a number of UK
government departments, producing articles and reports on excluded
and vulnerable groups as well as arts-based research methodologies as
a means for understanding marginalised group experiences. Yvonne is
currently involved in a project exploring the impact of young people's
participation in Arts Award.

The possibilities presented by sociology have for me rested upon an idea of what geography is not or is lacking. This may seem controversial ground as talking honestly about the limits of geography in relation to sociology immediately sets up a binary opposition between the disciplines. In some ways, this kind of thinking is a red herring because, being a geographer, I fully subscribe to the idea that 'where things happen is critical to knowing *how* and *why* they happen' (Warf and Arias, 2009, 18) – a narrative that puts space first. But thinking about why geography has sometimes not been enough it is possible to reflect on how sociology has come to matter to me, both personally and professionally. This chapter seeks to develop these thoughts, reflecting on the various insights I have gleaned from sociology as a geographer working across disciplines. Being asked to contribute to this exciting collection of essays on sociologist's tales, prompted me to think again about my motivations for starting an academic career as a social researcher. My reasons, especially in retrospect, point to an interest in societal issues and a belief that knowledge formed about this should be of benefit beyond the academy. Focusing on my career to date, I aim to show how crossing boundaries between disciplines reinvents, as well as sustains, disciplinary identity, and for me, has proved a wonderful gateway through which to open up connections to new spaces and working environments.

Sociology: an outsider's perspective

As someone looking in from outside, sociology has always had a broad practical and hands-on appeal, a reputation for dealing with real-world 'bread and butter' issues that have everyday resonance and applicability. This is something I had considered before undertaking my first degree in human geography. Back then (some 20 years ago now) geography, on the street and in the pub, had a negative popular image, and as I have come to find out perception is sometimes as important as, or more important than the reality of the matter. The reality of this hit me again very recently when at a friend's party. I got into conversation about what I do for a living and ended up trying (and I fear failing) to move the conversation away from the tired image of an old fashioned and uninspiring school geography conjured up.

But sociology has always had more popular appeal than geography. You only have to visit the BSA's website to learn of the growing popularity of the discipline. At degree level, studying sociology can bring about 'personal enrichment' while encouraging students to 'see the world in new and interesting ways', skills highly relevant to 'a range of employers' (www.britsoc.co.uk/WhatIsSociology/studyingsoc. aspx). As a sociologist, you can also expect to feel more at home in the media spotlight as experts from the field, perhaps more than any other discipline, are regularly invited to give their perspective on TV news items and comment on the current stories making the headlines. It is easy to see the logic in this: these are the stories that form the basis of everyday research in sociology as researchers attempt to gain deeper insight into the issues shaping our social world. And arguably, it is this idea of defining and informing public, everyday life that is one of the unique selling points of sociology, possibly resonating with students wanting to progress professionally and academically in the discipline.

As a new student of human geography it was the discipline's interaction with sociology, albeit foregrounded by a spatial perspective, which appealed to me. I remembered this when undertaking doctoral research into the 'cultural geographies of community theatre', and as part of my studies I eagerly imported ideas from sociology. One scholar whose work I considered particularly relevant was the German sociologist, Ferdinand Tönnies, whose distinctions between social groups *gemeinschaft* and *gesellschaft*, helped to crystallise my thinking on what the 'community' of community theatre might mean. At the time, my borrowings from sociology had led some students to hotly debate the absence of 'great forefathers' (and I would add 'mothers') in geography, and I had been frustrated at how the argument had panned out. I could not pretend to share in the sense of frustration the discussion had generated among the students when for me more difficult and pressing issues facing the discipline were apparently overlooked or ignored.

For example, I have always struggled with the enduring whiteness of geography (Bonnet 1996; Shaw, 2006) and its failure to get to grips with gender inequities within the discipline (McDowell, 1993). To some extent, I realise that this is in part a reflection of wider inequalities in society more generally, but nevertheless such inequity reinforces my feelings of not belonging. People come to academia through a variety of routes and through their own experiences. If, as in my case, that experience is as a black woman – an experience othered by normative expectations of what academics generally, and geographers in particular, look like; an image of 'who I am not' – it is perhaps understandable that one would have doubts about 'fitting in' or go somewhere else where they felt they more easily could. Admittedly there are also challenges for sociology in this regard but by and large my 'fit' with the discipline is a much more comfortable one – at least in terms of being better represented by people like me. And I think it would be a mistake for prospective research students to overlook the importance of this, and of finding a department and research centre where they are valued and feel very much a part of the picture.

Ultimately what counts is the ability to ask your own questions and make decisions based on your own needs – whether pragmatic or emotive. Making time to reflect on personal ambitions, expectations and motivations will be integral to any decision to pursue sociology (and for that matter, any profession) and achieving individual goals. As I am neither a sociologist nor student of sociology by training, I can only advise on the opportunities sociology has afforded me, particularly in regard to enhancing understandings of my own subject. However, I also recognise that the thinking and doing of sociology varies for different people so building on personal and professional interests and experiences will be important in drawing balanced conclusions about the discipline.

Sociology: making connections – opening doors

In the last few years my own interests in sociology have grown as I have looked for new insights through my research and writing. Robin Longhurst's assertion that 'disciplinary boundaries are not straightjackets' (1997, 495), struck a chord again with me recently, and I continue to respond to this rallying call almost two decades on to look beyond perspectives normally available. Interdisciplinarity for me now – as it has always been – is about opening up, rather than closing down new ways of thinking about geography. But much more than this it has helped free up what academia and being an academic can mean in the context of often fixed and routine representations of the academy. This has been important to me for precisely the reasons mentioned previously but also because of the particular pathway I have taken into the academy. It is a route that could be described as a fairly traditional one – that is, formal education, followed by further then higher education – although in the 'non-traditional' sense of being a 'first generation' graduate with very little social or cultural capital. My journey to the academy has also been diverted. Twice stopping to pursue what promised to be a budding career in acting, I took two, one-year largely unsuccessful gaps, before tentatively taking up doctoral study. Perhaps because I had always envisaged life as a performer, my 'role' as an academic has been one sometimes awkwardly inhabited, and I have struggled to feel 'in place' in academic space.

Having said this, my work now within the Weeks Centre for Social and Policy Research has helped me more comfortably inhabit the sometimes difficult space of academia. I have learned through experience that it is crucial to find a space and working environment in which you are supported and given the freedom to pursue academic and research interests. In preparation for writing this chapter, I contemplated my various moves as a researcher through various departments and organisations over the past ten years. I reflected that after moving from the geography department at UCL on completion of my PhD, I have subsequently worked as a social scientific researcher, and nearly always with or among sociologists. The Weeks Centre in particular has been really stimulating for me, and I have been encouraged to use insights from geography as well as my arts background to develop interdisciplinary research (see for example, Robinson, 2008). Far from compromising my professional identity as a geographer, joining the multidisciplinary team at the Weeks Centre has provided opportunities for me to engage substantively with sociological perspectives while putting geographical skills into practice. Sociology then, if you like, has allowed me to lay claim to geography's unique body of knowledge and skills, and reignited my sense of 'disciplinary belonging'.

This would be my personal claim to sociology. But it's a claim that's based on my own unique experience and background – gendered, raced and academic identity. The reality is, any decision to pursue a career in sociology will involve balancing a range of personal priorities and interests as well as careful reflection on the opportunities, benefits and challenges a career in sociology could bring. It is not enough to base decisions on secondhand experience, however substantial; instead, choose sociology for what it means to you, as a real, viable option and sustainable career.

Perhaps I have always been a 'sociographer' by design. In such a role I am able to explore the interface between sociology and geography, and plan and conduct research that is interdisciplinary in its focus. I think it is important to try and make these links from where you are so as to foster new ways of working that encourage innovation and creativity. I have always felt more comfortable conducting research that is grounded in the wider community, and which facilitates opportunities for experiential as well as expert knowledge. It so happens that sociology is, by and large, the space in which I can do this. Talking honestly, as I have tried to do, has not been about setting up binaries between sociology and geography but instead highlighting the importance of disciplinary identity and belonging, and how this can be found by crossing disciplinary borders and looking beyond your own discipline.

References

Bonnett, A, 2000, White identities: Historical and international perspectives, London: Longman

Longhurst, R, 1997, (Dis)embodied geographies, *Progress in Human Geography* 21, 4, 486–501

McDowell, L, 1993, Space, place and gender relations, *Progress in Human Geography* 17, 2, 305–18

Robinson, Y, 2008, Harry and Susie get married?: A performative approach to data collection, *Forum Qualitative Sozialforschung/Forum: Qualitative Social Research*, 9, 2, Art 47, http://nbn-resolving.de/urn:nbn:de:0114-fqs0802478

Shaw, W, 2006, Decolonising geographies of whiteness, Antipode 38, 851–69

Warf, B, Arias, S, 2009, The spatial turn: Interdisciplinary perspectives, London: Routledge

FIFTEEN

'I am a sociologist'; but what exactly is a sociologist and how do you become one?

Claire Maxwell

Claire Maxwell is a reader of sociology of education at University College London. Her work engages with the concept of agency and examines how privilege, agency and affect are mutually constituted. She is interested in the spaces of private and elite education and how families, schools and young women shape and unsettle the processes through which class and gender privilege may be reproduced. She also has a long-standing commitment to research on sexuality education and gender-related violence prevention work in schools.

It was only a little later on in my pathway into and through the Academy that I began to situate myself firmly and with some degree of confidence as a sociologist. It was, and still is to a large extent, a discipline which I do not feel I have the full measure of – not having had a traditional grounding in the subject via my studies. It is also a discipline whose boundaries (as perhaps many other disciplines in the social sciences) feel very fluid. I continue to attempt to find an identity for myself as an academic, and as someone who wishes to contribute to a specific 'field', while navigating the complicated, unwritten hierarchies and rules of the Academy (Hey, 2004). At the same time, I am having to find ways to cope with the uncertainty the university sector as a whole is experiencing, with particular universities and certain disciplines experiencing even greater levels of insecurity. Will there be a future for me, and for many others like me who wish to see ourselves as sociologists – as people who seek to understand the social, the operation of power, and the ways institutions shape relations?

I had never heard of 'sociology' until it became an option module in my third year at university, where I was studying politics, philosophy and economics (the only truly broadly social science degree available at Oxford). I cannot really articulate what or why – but I enjoyed this module more than any other module on the entire degree course. It was interesting, it was accessible, and I was the only one at my college wanting to do it – so I had one-to-one tuition. It was a very brief engagement with classic social stratification theories on the organisation of social and labour relations and the means of production through a historical review of industrialisation in Europe and North America. It was only eight one-hour sessions, but it shaped what I did next in important ways. I realised that politics and development economics were not my real passion. Rather, it was to understand further how institutions and the organisation of the broader economy shaped social relations.

I continued onto a master's – with a focus on the social, but also with a view to securing a professional qualification – which took an 'applied social studies' approach to training social workers. On this degree I was introduced to psychology, social policy, sociology (this time – again, quite a short, rather traditional take on sociology through a focus on deviance, group behaviours, gender roles and so forth), but also the importance of drawing on an evidence-base for practice and how broader theories from within social work facilitated further understandings of how people develop and live within families and broader institutions. My Master's thesis and my initial PhD work focused on rape and sexual violence, and took a largely psychological focus (mainly because this was the first kind of literature I initially found). However, I then read *The male in the head* (1998) by Janet Holland, Caroline Ramazanoglu, Sue Sharpe, Rachel Thomson – and the direction my PhD needed to take became clear. This is when I began to read more sociologically-informed theory on gender and sexuality and my engagement with sociology and a desire to enter academia started in earnest.

Throughout my undergraduate and postgraduate training I had never been based in a sociology department, which is why I never received a basic, traditional induction into the discipline or, until relatively recently, have felt able to position myself as a sociologist. In order to do so – you need other 'sociologists' to position yourself in relation to and alongside. In my first seven years working in a university, I was in a multi-disciplinary research unit, where even those in my small team saw themselves variously as anthropologists, social workers or educationists. It is only through the development of my own research interests that I have been able to move towards understanding myself as a sociologist. Yet, the fact that I was based at a university specialising in education, now the Faculty of Education at UCL, – adds a further complicating dimension to my identity as a sociologist. My interest in education stems largely from an interest in young people, their relationships with others, and the spaces that shape them. Schools (and education) therefore usually play a significant role in their lives. While part of my current work – on private education – clearly aligns me with the field of 'sociology of education', my other interests in the concepts of agency, affect, privilege and what it means to be elite move me into more broadly sociological fields.

Given my role at my current university – I have sought to position myself as a sociologist of education – the best of both worlds? Well, at least in my university context perhaps. But when I consider whether I might want to move elsewhere in the future and where and in what guise that would be, I am left with this uncomfortable quandary – would I want to move to a sociology department or an education department? I have concluded for the time being, that this would depend in part on what roles there were available, and crucially what my research focus at the time of application was. I suspect my interests will always straddle sociology and education.

But how important is it to be able to define yourself as a something within the Academy (Clegg, 2008)? Does it matter; and if it does – why and how? The desire for recognition makes the constitution of (a legitimate) identity important (Honneth, 1995; McNay, 2008; Hey, 2013). Within higher education we are largely recognised for our contributions to the knowledges shaping our understanding of a field, an issue. At present, it appears as if much of this value is assigned through publications and securing research grants. The question then becomes – what journals should I publish in, how many publications do I need, how do I promote my work and try to ensure it becomes cited (again, and again, and again!)? The journals we seek to publish in have the effect of shaping us, our identity, our recognition. What if a paper is rejected by a journal – does it mean your work is not sociological enough, not engaging with the appropriate (depth) of theoretical ideas popular in the field at that moment in time? Are you a sociologist who engages largely with, in and through theory? Is your empirical work foregrounded or does the data largely play a support role in driving your careful thinking about concepts? These are all questions I find myself constantly reflecting on and navigating when attempting to identify who I am in the Academy and what kind of a 'sociologist' I am.

Many of these questions appear to be driven by an anxiety evoked through the uncertain times we are in, my own desire to name myself and be named by others, but also the numerous possibilities that exist for sociologists to enter the Academy and develop their own 'niche'. This is of course also hugely exciting – the possibilities for so-called cross-disciplinary thinking and working, the lack of necessity to fully name oneself and stick to a fixed identity, of being able to morph to a certain extent to fit a role we see advertised or wish to create.

For me being a sociologist is about drawing on the empirical to make sense of and extend theory – in relation to questions about how societies and institutions function, how individuals, families, groups, communities experience and understand themselves and others, their biographies, their belonging and their becomings. It is about the micro-, meso- and macro-levels and how these intersect. Sociology is a hugely eclectic discipline, where colleagues draw on a wide variety of influences to find different (and better?) ways to understand what is being observed, narrated to them, and felt (by them and others). I see sociologists as identifying, recording, challenging, bringing new insights to bear on the small, almost imperceptible flows of affect between people, objects, moments, while also seeking to understand to the workings of institutions or particular spaces that shape material, affective, social, economic, political relations, and similarly interested in examining country-level and global concerns. 'Old' and 'newer' theories come in and out of vogue, and there are moments in fields or sub-fields where particular conceptual assemblages appear to be 'in favour'. Where you align yourself does have an impact on how you might identify yourself, and to which group of academics you start to be seen as connected. This is important in facilitating the development of fields of enquiry, and enabling through critical and usually constructive dialogue to reach towards exciting ways of making sense of the empirical. Yet, when groups of academics cluster around a set of theoretical ideas or seek to occupy particular fields, it can have the effect of marginalising certain perspectives and even the person offering such alternative understandings – a less positive aspect of the experience of being in the Academy (Hey, 2004).

My experience suggests that it is important to publish in journals and books which have value in your fields – so I seek to get papers accepted in sociology and education journals, as well as those publications which straddle both. It is also useful to try and become involved in conferences and professional associations linked to your field – to support networking, get a sense of the wider field (the British Sociological Association's *Network* magazine, for instance, is also great for this!) and to hopefully contribute to the development of our discipline in small but important ways. These steps should support you to navigate that never-ending journey of positioning yourself and establishing your 'credentials'.

Hugely supportive for my journey into and through the Academy has been a small handful of usually more senior colleagues from whom I have learnt so much about analysis, writing and teaching, but who have also been willing to make time for me to reflect on my experiences and answer questions about particular pathways I might take and how to decide which opportunities to take up and which ones I should try and create for myself! I, in turn, hope I can be that kind of colleague for others in some small way. If your department does not have a system for facilitating these kinds of support, perhaps your PhD supervisor or even external examiner might initially play such a role. Otherwise, seek out colleagues you have met, who seem generous in spirit and 'wise', and ask for a little of their time.

Biographies and political/ideological position are, I would argue, deeply embedded in the identity of a sociologist (Hey, 2004, 2013; Clegg, 2008). The demand for, and desire to contribute to, social justice efforts seems to strongly shape the research areas prioritised by many colleagues. Some of the most exciting work on social class, what it means to 'be a woman', not wanting to confirm to heteronormative discourses and so forth, come from scholars whose own experiences of being marginalised have fuelled their desire to look underneath these processes. My own research interests have been motivated by outrage (sexual violence, the experiences of women in intimate relationships), but also professional experiences (understanding teenage pregnancy, the concept of vulnerability in shaping agency within intimate, sexual relationships), but also a fascination with the Other (a private education, elite families). However, a more strategic focus on 'gaps in the literature', the identification of potential niches in the field have also motivated the decision of what to research and what kind of a sociologist to become. The desire to identify a niche, a space currently unoccupied to fill up and make tracks in is closely linked to my perception of what the 'rules of the game' in the Academy are and are an attempt to have a go at playing this game. Finding a way to align the instrumental with the affective are ultimately what has shaped my emerging career as a sociologist. What keeps me going despite times of uncertainty is the regard I have for the work that teachers and researchers do in the Academy and the wish to be 'one of them'. However, beyond that, it is the immense pleasure derived from the craft (Hey, 2004, 2013) – to undertake ethical research and produce new understandings through writing.

References

Clegg, S, 2008, Academic identities under threat?, *British Educational Research Journal* 34, 3, 329–45

Hey, V, 2004, Perverse pleasures: Identity work and the paradoxes of greedy institutions, *Journal of International Women's Studies* 5, 3, 33–43

Hey, V, 2013, Privilege, agency and affect in the academy: Who do you think you are?, in C Maxwell, P Aggleton (eds) *Privilege, agency and affect*, pp 106–213, Basingstoke: Palgrave Macmillan

Holland, J, Ramazanoglu, C, Sharpe, S, Thomson, R, 1998, *The male in the head: Young people, heterosexuality and power*, London: The Tufnell Press

Honneth, A, 1995, *The struggle for recognition: The moral grammar of social conflicts*, Cambridge: Polity

McNay, L, 2008, *Beyond recognition*, Cambridge: Polity

SIXTEEN

Sociology:
from committing to being?

Paul Hodkinson

Paul Hodkinson is reader in sociology at the University of Surrey.
Following completion of his undergraduate degree and PhD at the
University of Birmingham he worked for four years at the University
of Northampton prior to moving to Surrey in 2003. His research and
writing have focused on subcultural theory, the social significance
of social networking sites, theories and understandings of media,
ageing youth cultures and experiences of targeted victimisation
among alternative music scene participants. He is author of *Goth:
Identity, style and subculture* (Berg, 2002) and *Media, culture and society*
(SAGE, 2011). He is also co-editor, with Wolfgang Deicke, of *Youth
cultures: Scenes, subcultures and tribes* (Routledge, 2007) and, with Andy
Bennett, of *Ageing and youth cultures* (Berg, 2012). He is co-editor of
Sociological Research Online.

My first encounters with sociology were thoroughly tied up with what felt like a broader setting free of my identity. The chance to study the subject for the first time motivated what was to become a somewhat life-shaping decision to leave my rural town comprehensive at 16 and study A-levels at Plymouth College of Further Education. I didn't really know what sociology was at the time but was taken by the idea of debating questions relating to education, religion, families, criminal behaviour and the like. It appealed to my developing interest in Politics (with a capital P) and contrasted with the more traditional offerings at school. It felt like something I could identify with as well as study. Conveniently, as it turned out, college also enabled a much-needed break from school itself, and the peers with whom I had negotiated – not particularly successfully – my early teens.

I'm not sure whether A-level sociology was quite what I expected – there was some politics in there, but the finer-grained analysis of different elements of the social world introduced all manner of questions that hadn't occurred to me before. Centred, inevitably, on an early edition of Haralambos (a much maligned text that I actually rather admire), classes offered a mix of open debate and structure – and although the syllabus was limited, there was ample encouragement to think critically and question everything, as it seemed (Haralambos and Holborn, 1991). Looking back, this fitted perfectly with a developing (and fairly pretentious) sense of myself as 'alternative', both culturally and politically. Yet among this embrace of opposition and difference, the incessant practicing of exam answers in class was helping me to write and argue in an organised and coherent way, a rather less romantic but equally essential ingredient for any sociology career.

If my first encounters with sociology were orthodox, then disciplinary parameters became altogether more complex during my undergraduate degree in Media, Culture and Society at the wonderful Centre for Contemporary Cultural Studies at Birmingham. Staff at the Centre had generated a uniquely fertile and supportive atmosphere of learning, their passion and commitment for their work and its broader significance transferring itself to students with an intensity I'm not sure I've seen before or since. Still, it was not until half way through my second year that I began to transform from an enthusiastic but inconsistent undergraduate to a would-be scholar. I specifically remember getting my first genuinely high mark – for an essay on Marx and alienation – as something of a watershed moment. I also did well in a subsequent project on Foucault's *The history of sexuality* (1978), a book whose deconstruction of normally unquestioned categories probably inspired me more than any other text at this early stage. The achievement of high marks and positive feedback provided me with the confidence and drive to read more extensively and – in spite of the chasms in my knowledge – to feel that I could contribute and argue rather than regurgitate. Becoming a 'real' academic still seemed a distant prospect but it felt like something had clicked.

Yet the place of sociology in all this was unclear, and, even more so, the notion of actually *being* a sociologist. At Birmingham the emphasis was on the interdisciplinarity of cultural studies, the degree combining sociological features with various aspects of the social sciences, arts and humanities. Was I on the road to becoming a sociologist, then, or something different? The ambiguity persisted during my PhD studies. Enabled by the good fortune of being offered a teaching-based studentship in another Birmingham department, my project comprised an ethnographic study of goth subculture. For a time, I regarded myself as a budding cultural studies scholar, until one day at a popular music studies conference, I found myself publicly labelled a sociologist during a conference session in which I had rather brazenly (and clumsily) questioned the value of textual analysis of music as compared to empirical studies of the producers and listeners. I had, it seems, 'committed sociology', to coin a phrase. I wasn't sure I concurred with the label at the time, but gradually became more reconciled to it. I was increasingly arguing from what felt like an empirical, sociological perspective, against understandings of youth cultures derived from theoretically driven cultural analysis including, ironically, the seminal work of the Birmingham CCCS on post-war subcultures (for example, Hall and Jefferson, 1976). At the same time, my encounters with different forms of cultural studies were increasingly leading me to conclude that the 'version' of this discipline that had been conveyed at Birmingham was rather more 'sociological' – at least in some respects – than in cultural studies departments elsewhere, something reflected, possibly, in the Centre's eventual renaming as the Department of Cultural Studies and Sociology.

Yet, as all good sociologists (and cultural studies scholars) will tell you, the labels we come to identify with also reflect the ways in which we find ourselves positioned, including within the institutions in which we work. And so my identity as a sociologist of culture and media was further cemented at the University of Northampton, where I took up my first academic job, as a lecturer in sociology within the School of Social Studies, contributing – alongside a separate Cultural Studies School rooted in the arts – to degree programmes in media and popular culture. I had dreamed of becoming a lecturer at Birmingham and, after a couple of years at Northampton, was shortlisted for a lectureship there, only to narrowly miss out. As it turned out, it was a lucky escape because, in 2002, the Department of Cultural Studies and Sociology at Birmingham was, unforgivably, closed down.

For all my horror at the closure of the CCCS and, with it, the ending of that particular personal dream, I was also discovering the value of developing my perspective, experience and knowledge in pastures new. Providing an ideal environment for my first post as a sociologist of media and culture, Northampton enabled me to learn about the intricacies of academic life at a high quality teaching-intensive institution with an able and supportive set of colleagues. Opportunities to develop my approaches to teaching and learning, both individually and with others, were ample. I learned about the importance of being able to teach far outside my main areas of expertise – and about how this could broaden my knowledge. I built up a substantial portfolio of lectures that would serve well for a number of years. And I learned about course design, academic administration and, of course, some of the internal politics and diplomacy that universities involve. Finally, I started to learn how important it is to continue to find at least some time to write and research, even when writing 2–3 new lectures a week.

For it was the publication of a book based upon my PhD (Hodkinson, 2002) – alongside the teaching experience I had gained – that opened the door to my move, four years later, to the Department of Sociology at the University of Surrey, where I have now worked just over a (gulp) decade. As at Northampton, my primary orientation, both in research and teaching, was the sociology of culture and media, which suited me perfectly. But the sense of *being* a sociologist became stronger at Surrey. Partly this reflects the clarity and strength of the identification with the discipline among colleagues but increasing pressure to gain publications and prestige within the discipline itself – not least as a result of the alignment of subject groupings within external assessment exercises – also played a role.

Speaking of which, as a high performing research department, Sociology at Surrey also opened my eyes fully to the pressures and realities of research and writing in a national higher education context increasingly driven by publication targets and research income. It has taken time and some anxiety to adjust. I had published a well-received book and some chapters for edited books were in the pipeline when I joined Surrey, but regularly publishing journal articles was to become something of a struggle. My first journal submission took a hammering from reviewers and was rejected outright. I later published a revised and much-improved version of the paper elsewhere (Hodkinson, 2005), something that provided a valuable lesson in itself. My next two journal papers, though, also required more review iterations and anxiety than would have been ideal. While I later was to learn that such processes are perfectly normal, it remained the case that I wasn't really producing as many journal articles as would have been ideal.

This was partly because I had thrown myself enthusiastically into various aspects of course delivery and administration at Surrey as well as organising external conferences, seminars, journal special editions and the like. But feeling relatively at the centre of things provided crucial fulfilment, enjoyment and motivation for my developing career so I don't regret it. I might have been more astute, however, with respect to the number of book chapters published in my early career. All appeared in well-received collections, helping to bring my work to a broader audience and strengthen professional relationships and networks, but, in light of the importance of RAE/REF in the UK, at least one of them probably ought to have filled a slot in the journal papers section of my publications list instead. The warm glow generated by an invitation can make it hard to say 'No', but learning when to do so can be important.

A further issue was that, having exhausted publication possibilities from my PhD, I found myself with little new research about which to write. I became somewhat locked into a cycle whereby I would write a research grant application, get turned down and then write another. The editing of an anthology (Hodkinson and Deicke 2007), writing of further book chapters (for example, Hodkinson, 2006; Hodkinson, 2008) and, eventually, a text book (Hodkinson, 2011a) helped maintain a healthy looking publications list on the whole. But the relative paucity of journal articles and the research bids cycle were interconnected in the sense that I had slightly lost my focus, for a few years, on what – for me at least – is as fundamental to being a sociologist as anything, which is going out, doing social research and writing about it.

And so it was that the solution to one of the stuttering elements of my developing career was to design a small project, buy a digital recorder and go out and interview people. The immense fulfilment that this generated has prompted me to reflect on how sad it is that, in externally funded sociology, principal- and co-investigators rarely get to do much hands-on research. I've therefore made the most of what makes me tick as a sociologist, both in this and another more recent piece of collaborative research funded by a small (though invaluable) internal Surrey grant – at the same time as continuing to try, try, try again with those research bids, of course. Most significantly from the point of view of contributing to my department's well-being, my 'unfunded' research has contributed to the publication of a relatively healthy number of journal articles in the last few years (for example, Hodkinson, 2011b; Garland and Hodkinson, 2014) with, hopefully, more in the pipeline. The lesson here? Do prioritise external funding but don't wait around forever for it to come through. Sociologists, at least in my case, need to keep doing research and the approval of research councils and the like is not – I hope – a prerequisite for doing so.

As well as carrying out and writing up research, the last few years have been dominated by greater administrative and decision making responsibilities – most notably as deputy head of department but also as co-editor of the journal, *Sociological Research Online*. I've also begun to come to terms, slightly grudgingly, with the notion of not being quite so young, new or naïve as I was – and that can carry its own pressures. In terms of location, I have been lucky enough to have the occasional possibility to move, and there's little doubt that sometimes a new position can reinvigorate drive, imagination and ideas, but I'm happy to have stayed at Surrey on both a personal and career level. Like everywhere, we have had our share of pressures and strains, but I continue to find Sociology at Surrey an inspiring place to be and, most importantly, a friendly, collegial and supportive community amidst an increasingly challenging broader environment. Such things are easily taken for granted.

There's a great deal more I could have included in this short piece. Being taken by surprise at media interest in my work at various points – and managing the various challenges this can bring – is one example, though I'm not sure I've really worked out how to do so effectively. In terms of the substance of my sociology, I might have reflected more, perhaps, on the connections between elements of my research and my personal identities and affiliations, most notably with respect to music and style subcultures, which have seldom been too far from my interests both in work and leisure time. The benefits and complexities of 'insider research' are something I've dwelt upon in detail elsewhere (Hodkinson, 2005). Of greater importance here, though, is the broader point that, from my days as a precocious A-level student, I've felt fortunate that life within and outside work seem to have informed one another so fruitfully. And I imagine this is probably so, in one sense or another, for many sociologists. It's one of the reasons why, in spite of ongoing insecurities, uncertainties and everyday pressures, I continue to feel lucky that I get to be one.

References

Foucault, M, 1978, *The history of sexuality: Volume 1*, London: Allen Lane

Garland, J, Hodkinson, P, 2014, 'F★★king freak! What the hell do you think you look like?' Experiences of targeted victimisation among goths and developing notions of hate crime, *British Journal of Criminology*, 54, 4, 613–31

Hall, S, Jefferson, T, 1976, *Resistance through rituals: Youth subcultures in post-war Britain*, London: Hutchinson

Haralambos, M, Holborne, M, 1991, *Sociology: Themes and perspectives*, 3rd edn, London: HarperCollins

Hodkinson, P, 2002, *Goth: Identity, style and subculture*, Oxford: Berg

Hodkinson, P, 2005, Insider Research in the study of youth cultures, *Journal of Youth Studies* 8, 2, 131–49

Hodkinson, P, 2006, Subcultural blogging, in A Bruns, Y Jacobs (eds) *Uses of blogs*, New York: Peter Lang

Hodkinson, P, 2008, Grounded theory and inductive research, in N Gilbert (ed) *Researching social life*, 3rd edn, London: SAGE

Hodkinson, P, 2011a, *Media, culture and society: An introduction*, London: SAGE

Hodkinson, P, 2011b, 'Ageing in a spectacular "youth culture": Continuity, change and community amongst older goths, *British Journal of Sociology*, 62, 2, 262–82

Hodkinson, P, Deicke, W (eds), 2007, *Youth cultures: Scenes, subcultures and tribes*, New York: Routledge

SEVENTEEN

Drift, opportunity and commitment: the shaping of a professional career

John Scott

John Scott is an honorary professor at Copenhagen University. He began his career at Strathclyde University and has held professorships at Plymouth, Leicester and Essex universities. His most recent books include *Conceptualising the social world* (Cambridge University Press, 2011), *Objectivity and subjectivity in social research* (with Gayle Letherby and Malcolm Williams, SAGE, 2013), and *Envisioning sociology: Victor Branford, Patrick Geddes, and the quest for social reconstruction* (SUNY Press, 2013). He is a fellow of the British Academy and was awarded a CBE for services to social science.

My studies in sociology began in 1968 at Kingston College of Technology (now Kingston University), from where I graduated in 1971. This was a heady time to enter the social sciences, which were undergoing a major transformation the consequences of which we are still working through. There had been a huge expansion of student intake to sociology, which was beginning to slow down by the early 1970s. New theoretical approaches from the US and, especially, from France and Germany were making themselves felt within a sociological tradition that still owed a great deal to Parsonian structural functionalism. Newly recruited lecturers and their students were embracing these new and radical theoretical perspectives and were increasingly stressing the links between theoretical critique and practical action. It was an exciting time to begin an academic career.

Discussions of education and achievement often stress the importance of hard work, rational choice, and careful planning. Studies in the sociology of education have shown the far greater importance of social background and conditions, of opportunity, and of educational practices. This was certainly true in my case. I did not come from an academic background but had supportive, and relatively well-off, parents. My entry into an academic career, however, was also a matter of drift in which I rather blindly took advantage of the opportunities available to me. I had never been especially academic at school and never had any idea of what I wanted to do in life. My first steps towards academic study arose simply from my interests in the various subjects available to me at school.

My favourite school subject had always been geography. Its focus on the real world and its contemporary condition appealed to me more than the abstractions of science or the literary texts studied in English, and so I applied to study geography at university. Fate intervened and I performed badly at A-level. I got a tolerable pass in geography, failed French and scraped a pass in mathematics. The pass in mathematics remains a matter of surprise to me. The course was divided into two papers. One was in 'pure mathematics' (in which I achieved a princely 18 per cent in the mocks) and the other was in 'statistics' (in which I got 92 per cent). Averaging out of these two must have got me my pass. The only reason I got 92 per cent in statistics was that they gave us the formulas on a printed sheet, so it was just a matter of adding up and multiplying. This is, perhaps, why I have never felt daunted by mathematics and eventually made some contributions to social network analysis. A continuing concern has been to summarise and explain mathematical procedures rather than simply to 'do' the mathematics.

Having no idea what to do after school, I opted to stay on in the sixth form to try to improve my A-levels. I decided to retake geography, but felt there was no chance of improving in my other subjects. Through geography I had become aware of economics and so decided to study it, although it was a subject that my school did not teach. I went to a very traditional grammar school that praised such pupils as Brian May, who had gone on to study astronomy at Imperial College – I'm not sure how the school felt when he gave it all up to become the lead guitarist in Queen! Anyway, the school did not teach economics and had given up on me, so it allowed me to try to teach myself the subject.

It was at this time that I discovered that I actually liked academic work. Free from the restrictions of formal teaching I found that I could enjoy reading and writing about things that interested me. I decided to re-apply for a degree and, having been rejected by universities, I tried the local college at Kingston. Browsing through their courses in economics I came across a sheet listing a degree in sociology, which I had never heard of. (It wasn't then an A-level subject.) Sociology seemed to combine the bits of geography and economics that I liked, so I applied for it and to my surprise they accepted me.

Sociology at Kingston was a life-changing experience. I encountered great and committed teachers who opened-up whole new areas and I rapidly decided that this was how I wanted to spend my life. The degree was very wide-ranging. An external degree of London University, it included courses on theory and methods, comparative social institutions, and modern Britain, together with courses in ethics and social philosophy, economics, statistics and social policy. During the second year we added options in such subjects as political sociology, criminology, sociology of religion and industrial sociology.

It was hard-going, but all the parts fitted together well and I acquired a good, rounded knowledge of sociology. The degree would not, perhaps, be regarded as so 'rounded' these days, as it was before the important changes of the 1970s that introduced feminist theories and an awareness of gender. It gave nevertheless a comprehensive and wide-ranging approach to sociology. The limited opportunities for specialisation and choice of options meant that students were given a view of how societies had to be seen as wholes that are greater than their parts and that the various parts fit together into particular patterns of integration and contradiction. This orientation has always remained with me and is something that I later emphasised in my presidential address to the BSA (Scott, 2005) and in my book *Conceptualising the social world* (Scott, 2011). It has also given me a continuing interest in all aspects of the subject and a desire to read beyond my particular specialisms. This is partly a matter of sheer interest and enjoyment, but it has also had consequences for my work. I have often found that reading and discussing work in other areas can generate insights for my work and that those working in other areas face similar theoretical and methodological issues from which I can learn.

I became involved in the BSA as an undergraduate. I joined the Association in 1971 in order to attend its annual conference, which was being held on deviance – the hot topic of the day. At the conference I saw and heard those who, until then, I had only read about in my textbooks: the high point was an evening meeting of a study group, when I sat next to Howard Becker and contributed to the discussion that he led. I can't remember what I said: it was obviously far less memorable than the occasion itself.

This was great preparation for beginning a research degree. I was accepted for a PhD at the LSE, and I got a permanent lectureship a year later. That was in 1972, just about the last time that it was possible for someone without a PhD and with only a year of research behind them to get any kind of academic job. My job was at the University of Strathclyde, in Glasgow, and I began, at last, to teach the subject that I had been studying. I was determined to try to learn from the negative experiences that I had at school and hoped to emulate those who had inspired me at college.

I have continued to enjoy teaching and researching in sociology. From Strathclyde I moved to Leicester and then to Essex, probably the strongest social science university in the UK and the best department of sociology in the country. Towards the end of my career I decided to take up the offer of a post at the University of Plymouth, hoping that I could contribute to the development of the subject in an institution that was quite different from the more traditional universities in which I had worked. Again, circumstances intervened and the changing context of higher education finance meant that Plymouth sociology experienced contraction rather than growth. Managerial issues at the university, which hit sociology especially hard, led me to resign my emeritus professorship in protest and to give some solidarity to my colleagues who were made redundant or put under huge pressure.

In all that I have done over the years I have tried to recapture something of the excitement of my student days: the years when I began to enjoy academic study, discovered sociology, and decided that that was the path I wanted to follow. In studying sociology I also began to better understand myself and the social world around me. Two of the first books that I read were Peter Berger's *Invitation to sociology* (Berger, 1963) and C Wright Mills's *The sociological imagination* (Mills, 1959).

These gave me a new insight into my own life and the larger events and conditions that I had read about in my studies of economics and geography. I became aware that everyday encounters had an intrinsic connection with larger events of historical significance and that these are, in turn, both shaped by and shape social structures. I was able, for example, to reflect on my own educational biography and to see the ways in which my identification with sociology arose from the specific historical expansion of sociology in the 1960s and the structural context of a selective, class-based educational system. My professional identity was a product of both my generation and my circumstances.

The very idea of social structure was a quite novel object of understanding that I had simply not previously encountered. I came to understand how the things that we and others do are conditioned by factors that operate 'behind our backs' and of which we are unaware, but that are, nevertheless, real. I was completely convinced of the need to approach these issues analytically, whether through the work of writers such as Karl Marx in his materialist understanding of economic and class structures or through the more culturally focused arguments of Talcott Parsons. I never accepted the view that Parsons's work was inherently and inescapably conservative: its analytical stance offered the possibility of a radical structural analysis that could connect directly with the concerns of those who investigated conflict and power. It was the arguments of David Lockwood and then Alvin Gouldner that convinced me of the possibility of linking these ideas together into a compelling framework of social understanding.

I was also attracted by the idea of studying the 'science of society', which was how we unselfconsciously described sociology at the time. Having come into sociology straight from a very conventional boys' grammar school I was not aware of any great discrepancy between everyday practical concerns and academic study. It seemed self-evidently possible to study the social world as objectively as any other phenomenon. The idea that a 'scientific' understanding of the social world could be achieved and could produce a true account of events did not seem at all problematic. Parsons and Marx seemed to provide concepts that could be used to provide the kinds of objective explanatory accounts that I had found – or thought that I had found – in economics and the illuminating empirical descriptions that I had found in regional geography.

The year 1968 was, however, a period of unprecedented student radicalism. While those of us living in the outer suburbs of Greater London had generally thought that the 'swinging sixties' must have been happening elsewhere, the dramatic events of 1968 could not but affect even the most conventional students at a college of technology. I became aware of the importance of the critical perspective offered by sociology, of the ways in which political differences can shape our perceptions of the world, and of the ways in which we construct explanations of social differences and inequalities. This awareness lay behind my attraction to the sociology of deviance, where Howard Becker was developing the idea of the inescapable need to identify with top dogs or underdogs according to your values and political standpoint. I moved towards a position in which the value-relatedness and socially bound character of sociological knowledge had to be combined with the rational discourse and methods stressed by the advocates of social 'science'.

It was some years before a gendered perspective on this became apparent. However, it was the papers presented at the 1974 conference on 'Social Divisions and Society', held in Aberdeen, that launched a massively important intellectual debate that opened the eyes of many men to the importance of gender as a social division. It also had implications for the BSA, whose meetings were marked by disputes over the role of women in the sociological profession and led to the high-profile departure of some men from the association in the face of what they saw as a concerted feminist 'attack' and politicisation of the subject. Intellectually and professionally there was to be no turning back.

For me personally, the importance of the social standpoint taken on knowledge and the implications of this for perspectival yet objective knowledge was something that figured centrally in my thought thereafter. I was able to develop this in a book on *Objectivity and subjectivity in social research* (Letherby et al, 2013), written with Gayle Letherby and Malcolm Williams in the form of a 'trialogue'. We aimed to show that situated subjectivity and rational objectivity were two sides of the same complex process. Sociological understanding involves the melded appreciation of how one's own embodied and embedded standpoint must be combined with the equally partial perspectives of others and subjected to critical appraisal in order to achieve a more comprehensive – and so more objective – account of the world.

My own research in sociology was largely focused on issues of class and power related to economic and political development. I studied 'elites' and upper classes, initially in the context of Scottish society and the challenge posed by the development of the North Sea oil industry, and later for Britain as a whole and its relationship to elites in the United States, continental Europe and the Far East. The key outcomes of this work were my initial book *Corporations, classes and capitalism* (Scott,

1979) and its later revision *Corporate business and capitalist classes* (Scott, 1997), together with *Who rules Britain?* (Scott, 1991a) and more general contributions to social stratification (Scott, 1996) and power (Scott, 2001). The research was also the basis on which I developed a number of contributions to research methodology (Scott, 1990; 1991b). This area of research interest reflected my upbringing in a Labour-voting, middle-class family. Sociology had given me the analytical tools that I needed to explore the issues with which I and my family had been particularly concerned.

My orientation towards whole societies and the fact that I worked on the interdisciplinary boundaries with economics and political science led me to examine the disciplinary boundaries that exist within the social sciences. I came to accept a much-modified version of Auguste Comte's view that sociology is the most general of the social sciences and that other social sciences can be seen as, in many respects, sub-divisions of sociology. In my Presidential address to the BSA Conference (Scott, 2005) I sought to defend the holistic character of sociology without denying the importance of interdisciplinary work: which might better be seen as 'inter-specialism' work. Different social scientists might work from differing standpoints and with different concepts, but they are to be seen as engaged in a common intellectual endeavour of social understanding. No one theoretical standpoint is likely to provide all the answers to sociologically interesting questions. There should be no false claims to completion or to the exclusive priority of one's own preferred approach. Nor should there be any denigration of the theoretical perspectives of others. We are involved in a common intellectual endeavour that must involve mutual respect and tolerance and a willingness to discuss and debate theoretical differences, rather than to resort to arguments by fiat.

I have always seen an involvement in the British Sociological Association as an integral aspect of my commitment to the sociological profession. While there is an understandable tendency, reinforced by institutional pressure, to identify with one's specialism, this should not be at the expense of identification with the discipline as a whole. All sociologists should be members of the Association and should contribute to its work on behalf of the discipline. The work done by the Association is often invisible and so is unfairly under-rated by members and non-members alike. I have spent a great part of the latter half of my career as a member of its Executive or Council and I have been editor of its newsletter *Network*, general secretary, treasurer, chairperson and president. Through the BSA I have been able to participate in other activities central to the discipline. These have included a committee on the 'benchmarking': of sociology degree schemes, the Teaching Quality Assessment exercise, the Research Assessment Exercise, and the Research Excellence Framework. In all these roles I have sought to apply my view of the subject as a holistic yet diverse intellectual activity and to defend its character in the face of its critics. It was great to feel that peer recognition of this work led in 2013 to the award of a CBE 'for services to social science'.

There is little of importance that I would change in my career. Of course, there are many things that I would prefer not to have happened: principally the cuts in sociology in the 1980s and subsequently that led to many departmental closures and job losses. I have been fortunate in avoiding the disasters faced by many colleagues. However, sociology teaches the importance of recognising the unintended consequences of action. If anything could have been changed, what other, unanticipated and undesirable changes might then have happened? In terms of my own discovery of this exciting subject and the ways in which my knowledge and understanding of it have unfolded during my career I would want to change nothing at all.

It is important to be very careful about offering advice to others. One's own experiences – reflecting one's particular history and structural circumstances – are rarely a satisfactory guide for those entering the profession at a different time and under different circumstances. I was fortunate to gain a first permanent job in 1972, having completed only one year of my PhD, and no such opportunities are available today. An established post comes – if at all – only after the completion of a PhD, the production of a number of publications, and a series of temporary and short-term appointments. My only advice to those now entering the profession would be to follow your personal preferences as best you can and not to aim at immediate fame and fortune. These may arise – though perhaps not the fortune – as a result of the unintended consequences of your actions as you negotiate your way through the particular structure of opportunities that you encounter. It is impossible to know whether our actions will lead to the long-term goals that we pursue and we cannot predict the future. That is both a key insight of sociology and one of its greatest limitations. Both the insight and the limitation are to be embraced.

References

Berger, PL, 1963, *Invitation to sociology: A humanistic perspective*, Harmondsworth: Penguin, 1966

Letherby, G, Scott, J, Williams, M, 2013, *Objectivity and subjectivity in social research*, London: SAGE

Mills, CW, 1959, *The sociological imagination*, Harmondsworth: Penguin

Scott, J, 1979, *Corporations, classes and capitalism,* 1st edn, London: Hutchinson

Scott, J, 1990, *A matter of record: Documentary sources in social research*, Cambridge: Polity

Scott, J, 1991a, *Who rules Britain?,* Cambridge: Polity

Scott, J, 1991b, *Social network analysis*, London: SAGE

Scott, J, 1996, *Stratification and power: Structures of class, status and command*, Cambridge: Polity

Scott, J, 1997, *Corporate business and capitalist classes*, Oxford: Oxford University Press

Scott, J, 2001, *Power*, Cambridge: Polity

Scott, J, 2005, Sociology and its others: Reflections on disciplinary specialisation and fragmentation, *Sociological Research Online* 10, 1

Scott, J, 2011, *Conceptualising the social world: Principles of socilogical analysis*, Cambridge: Cambridge University Press

EIGHTEEN

A passion for empirical sociology

Eileen Green

Eileen Green is professor emerita of sociology at Teesside University.
Her research interests include gender, work and leisure, sociology
of the digital and working with disadvantaged communities. Her
books include *Virtual gender: Technology, consumption and identity* (2001,
Routledge), *Youth, risk and leisure: Constructing identities in everyday life*
(2004, Palgrave) and *Gender, health and information technologies in context*
(2009, Palgrave Macmillan). She is currently vice chair of the British
Sociological Association and became an elected academician of the
Academy of Social Sciences in 2001.

Like many women academics before me, I regularly cross discipline boundaries, but I am primarily a sociologist. Faced with the question 'What kind of sociology do I do?' The answer is interdisciplinary, action research. That is what excites me.

How long have I thought of myself as a sociologist? It has probably been since I became a full-time postgraduate student on the MA in sociology at Essex University in 1974. In fact my interest in sociology goes much further back. It began with an irritation at the 'university speak' my sociologist boyfriend engaged in with his mates at informal get-togethers in the late 1960s/early 1970s. Denied a similar route into higher education by my failure to thrive at a catholic convent school in Berkshire, I left school aged 16, searching the local paper for jobs. Dental nursing attracted me, proving to be a good choice in terms of both geographical mobility and the field work context for my first piece of empirical research. I moved to London amid the excitement of the 1960s joining a temping agency and working my way around dental practices in the city for two years. By the age of 20 I realised that my salvation lay in higher education, but without A-levels I was fortunate to scrape a place on a teacher training course. The enlightened curriculum gave students the opportunity to choose a main subject and sociology was on offer. Specialising in sociology as a primary teacher was unusual; excited by the prospect of doing my own piece of mini research, I embarked upon a qualitative study of dental nurses' experiences of work. Working for two-week periods at different dental practices I recruited my sample, and recorded my participant observation notes on a notepad in the ladies' lavatory. Research ethics aside, my work mates assumed I had a weak bladder. It was a defining moment and I still have the handwritten record of a wildly over ambitious project which persuaded me that dental nursing was a boring, dead end job.

Three years of primary school teaching followed in East London. However, the confines of a staffroom populated by married women teachers who shopped for dinner in their lunch break, and a head near retirement who was unimpressed by child-centred education and sociology, dampened my interest in teaching. I yearned for the excitement of ideas. My sociological imagination had been ignited by my first brush with research and I enrolled on a part-time Council for National Academic Awards (CNAA) degree in the sociology of education at the soon to be Middlesex Polytechnic at Ponders End. As post war baby boomers, my generation took advantage of the expansion of higher education and social science. The women among us witnessed our male contemporaries entering research/lecturing jobs while enrolled as post-graduates (Westoby et al, 1976; Platt, 2000). Girlfriends and wives became nurses, social workers or school teachers, the majority leaving their jobs to become full-time mothers or return part time.

Graduating in 1974 with a 2:1 and a keen interest in (Marxist) sociology imparted by lecturers who would soon rise up the managerial ladder in the fledgling polytechnics, I applied for a place on the MA in sociology at Essex University. Successful at gaining one of the two ESRC grants held by the Sociology department, I also secured the luxury of a married women's top-up grant the same year, granting me a financial independence. Essex university campus designed as egalitarianism in concrete towers, was a hotbed of political activism; diversions from study included rent strikes and student sit-ins which made news during a long hot summer of social change. I was entranced. In retrospect, the final ingredient in becoming an academic was to separate from a husband by then well established in the same field. Severe financial cutbacks to HE in the mid-1970s reduced the possibility of academic jobs for those of us graduating then, but my teacher-training background and urgent desire to leave London, secured me a job in a college of education. My flight north to Sheffield introduced me to the women's movement and chip butties at the station cafe, as I began teaching sociology to trainee teachers mainstreaming in domestic science. Fortunately for me, the end of my temporary contract coincided with the major reorganisation of HE, which amalgamated colleges of education with local polytechnics and I was offered a permanent job in the Sociology department at Sheffield City Polytechnic.

The late 1970s and early 1980s found me reading sociology texts a week ahead of my students, as I realised that my own sociology tutors had fed me a diet of mainly Marxist sociology. Lectures on the founding fathers had me hastily mugging up on Weber and Durkheim,[1] while able to debate the intricacies of Gramsci versus Althusser and Poulantzas. I still owe a debt to the Middlesex tutors who introduced me to the complexities of Marxist debate via a grey print journal entitled *Theoretical Practice* (Althusser et al, 1973)[2] but I cursed them for their political proclivities as I struggled with a CNAA approved curriculum. Once I found my teaching legs I became interested in the development of sociology across the public sector, joining the CNAA Social Studies Board (1984–87). In 1986 it was with an overwhelming sense of nostalgia that, I walked the corridors of my old college, then part of Roehampton Institute, as a specialist adviser/assessor for sociology and part of the national quality assessment process imposed upon universities by the Higher Education Funding Council for England (HEFCE). During that week I learned that Roehampton is famous for its long line of women heads and professors, among them my benefactress.

Empirical research became my passion

By this time I had consolidated a new relationship and given birth to a son. I was soon to learn the importance of gaining a mentor. A supportive woman colleague encouraged me to pursue my interest in empirical research and I gained my first funded research grant in 1980, which financed a qualitative study of part-time women workers in the Sheffield steel industry. Juggling motherhood of a two-year-old with a full-time teaching post which included supervising my first research assistant, caused chortles of amusement among my male colleagues who raced past me for promotion as directors of large social science degree programmes. 'We don't do research in polytechnics,' they crowed. Sustained by close women colleagues and enlightened by feminist politics, the next ten years in a stable job enabled me to develop my interest in the sociology of women's work and leisure alongside developing one of the first MAs in women's studies in the UK, but not before I had been at the forefront of a campaign for the first Sheffield Polytechnic nursery. Showing off my six months' pregnant bump, a colleague and I convinced the sceptical, male principal that women staff wanted to return to work full time. Few HE institutions in the UK had nursery provision at that time, baby boomer women had to do it for themselves, which in our case included developing and leading an arm's length nursery management committee. The summer of 1983 was spent writing my first successful ESRC grant proposal on women and leisure, which culminated in a first book (Green, Hebron and Woodward, 1990). This consolidated my interest in feminist sociology, leisure and gender theory. The networking opportunities presented by convening a BSA study group on leisure built my confidence and enlarged my ambitions, leading to a period of sustained work with the Leisure Studies Association, which I chaired between 1998 and 2001. The project on women's leisure changed my working life. Suddenly the research was high profile and I belatedly realised how small was the proportion of polytechnic staff who were successful at gaining research council funds. Trips to international conferences and invitations to address public bodies followed, but the time pressure took its toll on my personal life and I became a lone parent. My ex-partner moved close by enabling us to share childcare and minimise disruption to our son's life, as we struggled to keep two academic careers afloat.

I was hooked on empirical research, the more interdisciplinary the better. I had developed an intellectual identity as a socialist feminist sociologist which was to sustain me through many more research projects. In 1987 I directed a project on gender and information technology funded by an ESRC/SERC grant[3] which honed both my skills in action research and the rigours of managing a research team. I am not sure that I would recommend this type of 'learning on the job' approach, or indeed that it would even be possible these days, but I grabbed the opportunities that opened up on a number of mostly external fronts. I learned the lesson echoed by many an academic, that your work and skills are often more appreciated by external audiences than by those in your own institution, let alone your own department. However, the late 1980s was also the time of a new relationship and another child for me, bestowing again both pleasures and the pressures of time. I took the minimum maternity leave and carted my baby daughter to numerous conferences since I was still heavily involved in research.

The 1980s also marked a pivotal point in my career, teaching women's studies at postgraduate level encouraged me to develop my ideas about feminist theory and contribute to the 'gender turn' in sociology which was to have a major impact upon British sociology. The MA in women's studies gave me a platform and the international networks from which to develop a Polytechnic Centre for Women's Studies. I was director for its four-year life span, which gave me the base to develop a BA in women's studies and be the contractor for an ERASMUS contract which established the European Women's Studies Network (WISE); and to host one of the conferences which launched the Women's Studies Network UK in 1989. Such developments were followed by the establishment of specialist women's/gender studies journals (for example, the *Journal of Gender Studies* (1995) and *Feminist Theory* (2000)).

Management or research?

In 1992 the major reorganisation of higher education institutions brought about a sharpening of competition at both institutional level and between academics, especially in research. With the movement back into traditional subject boundaries, the Centre for Women's Studies became marginalised, as did women's studies teaching across most institutions. Deeply involved in defending the profile of sociology in the new regime, I immersed myself in an ever-expanding set of managerial responsibilities including becoming head of Sociology from 1994 to 1996. Flattened management hierarchies and a devolved budget ate up my time for research and presented me with a steep learning curve as I became 'part of the establishment'. Re-entering the mainstream of sociology, I began to be perceived as a threat, whereas previously I had been sidelined in the women's studies ghetto. Taking on a management role during a period characterised by increased pressure on universities, especially the post-1992 variety, to bring in external funds and to gear their objectives to meet the requirements of industry and commerce, presented me with an increasingly demoralised staff group. My sympathies lay more often with them than the newly entrepreneurial face of senior management, besides which I missed doing research. Most academics still get to a 'career moment' when they are faced with management responsibilities which threaten to eclipse their research time, unless they are fortunate enough to have some time protected by their potential REF status.

I made the decision to maintain my research profile and applied for a readership. Despite a track record in gaining external research funds and publishing, my sideways move into women's studies with its attendant feminist politics was to cost me dearly in promotion terms. I was deemed to lack the necessary form of leadership skills for such a post and my application was blocked. No matter how strong my external profile, I needed the formal backing of my line manager with whom I had sparred once too often. A hard lesson learned at this juncture was to avoid confrontation with the boss! It took me over a year to negotiate this obstacle, but I persisted. Having gained the support of a sympathetic senior male colleague, who joined me in a series of staff development sessions with my head of department, I demonstrated the required leadership skills.

Moving on

Finally in receipt of the coveted readership, I became acutely aware of the impossible tensions between maintaining a research active profile and being a good manager. My network of female friends and colleagues were a strong source of support and identification, many forged as part of the Through the Glass Ceiling Group for women in higher education. The latter gave me the courage to aim for a chair and my own research centre, but I needed to move institutions. Sometimes it is better to simply move on. I was successful at gaining a chair in sociology at Teesside University in 1996, in a post which promised a reduced teaching load and negligible management responsibilities in return for establishing a new social science research centre. As founding director of the Centre for Social and Policy Studies a year later, I was under pressure to bring in research funds to establish what was to become a self-sustaining unit. The first large grant came in the same year to fund a three-year action research project on Young People and Risk on Teesside.[4] My love of interdisciplinary research and extensive networks of collaboration proved invaluable, leading to many exciting partnership projects across a range of national and international boundaries and topics.

What helped me?

Reflecting upon what helped me to discover and then consolidate doing the kind of research and sociology that I enjoy, are indisputably an extensive set of collaborators both inside and beyond the academy. Many of them, acquired as a result of the socialist feminist politics and activism which hampered my early promotion attempts, now supported me; becoming co-collaborators and ultimately close friends. I was active in trade union politics early in my career, joining the NATFHE women's group in the 1970s which fought for university-based childcare. These primarily local networks of like-minded feminists provided critical domestic and childcare support when my children were small, but more importantly were a touchstone for finding my way into an academic career that sustained me. Having joined the British Sociological Association as a postgraduate in 1974, my activities within the organisation ranged from an exciting time as part of the Women's Caucus led by Sheila Allen and Hilary Rose in the 1970s, to becoming convenor of the Sociology of Leisure Study Group from 1983 to 1986 and subsequently a BSA trustee in 2008. The BSA has undoubtedly been a key part of maintaining my identity as a sociologist.

Conclusion

Do I have advice for other would be sociologists? I am sure there are easier routes than the one that I have taken, although the pressures on early career people are as great as they were 40 years ago, albeit different. One important point to bear in mind is to have faith in the kind of sociology and/or research that you want to pursue and try not to get deflected into areas deemed appropriate by the academy; easier said than done, of course.

Thinking about what I might have done differently, I could have heeded the advice of senior women to try and work my way around the obstacles to forging my own path in sociology, rather than taking on institutional battles which were doomed to failure, due to my lack of status and power. In other words I could have tried to be more strategic and play a long game. More personally, two ill-fated relationships to other social scientists taught me to avoid academics as life partners. It is difficult to manage academic competition at both work and home. Or maybe I finally learned the art of compromise. As a professor emerita of sociology at Teesside University since 2011, I have ample time and opportunity to choose my sociological activities these days. I have enough research data to sustain me for another 40 years but not content to only do 'armchair research', I have just taken on the role of vice chair of the British Sociological Association. I never could resist a challenge and the next few years will certainly provide that in terms of fighting to sustain sociology as a discipline in UK universities.

Notes

[1] *Discovering sociology: Studies in sociological theory and method* by John Rex, 1973, published by Routledge and Kegan Paul, was to become an invaluable companion during this period of my career.

[2] This publication is probably a classic of its time and a collectors' item, as it is almost certainly out of print.

[3] *Gendered by design? Information technology and office systems*, Eileen Green, Jenny Owen and Den Pain, 1993, published by Taylor and Francis, was one of the outcomes from this project.

[4] *Youth, risk and leisure: Constructing identities in everyday life*, W Mitchell, R Bunton, E Green (eds), 2004, published by Palgrave, was an outcome from this project.

References

Althusser, L, 1971, *Lenin and philosophy and other essays*, London: New Left Books

Althusser, L, Balibar, E, Cutler, A, Lecourt, D, Gane, M, 1973, *Theoretical Practice*, Issue 7/8, January, London: Theoretical Practice

Gramsci, A,1977, *Antonio Gramsci: Selections from political writings 1910–1920*, London: Lawrence and Wishart

Green, E, Hebron, S, Woodward, D, 1990, *Women's leisure, what leisure?*, Basingstoke: Macmillan

Moore, P, 1987, University financing 1979–86, *Higher Education Quarterly* 41, 25–42

Platt, J, 2000, Women in the British sociological labour market, 1960–1995, *Sociological Research Online* 4, 4

Rex, J, 1973 *Discovering sociology: Social studies in theory and method*, London: Routledge and Kegan Paul

Westoby, A, Webster, D and Williams, G, 1976, *Social scientists at work*, Guilford: Society for Research into Higher Education

NINETEEN

Me, myself and sociology

Gayle Letherby

Following degrees and part-time teaching at Staffordshire, Letherby
moved to Coventry University in 1994 as lecturer in sociology
and left in 2005 as reader in the sociology of gender and deputy
director of the Centre for Social Justice. Since then she has worked at
Plymouth University where she is professor of sociology and director
of the Institute of Health and Community. Her research and writing
interests include reproductive and non/parental identities, travel and
transport, working and learning in higher education and all things
methodological.

This is not the first time that I have written about myself within my academic writings. Indeed, anyone interested in my work, should they want to, could easily discover many of the significant biographical events of my life, both personally and career wise. I came to higher education later than many and began my first degree in the late 1980s when I was 28. Following A-levels (I was lucky to get the two I did considering the amount of bunking off I did during sixth form) I studied to be a nursery nurse and then worked for six years, first in a postnatal ward of a large city hospital, next in a university day nursery and finally as a private nanny. Following 15 or so months of attempting pregnancy and a miscarriage at 16 weeks I felt unable to work with children for a while and took some typing jobs to fill my days and earn some money. Bored and un-stretched intellectually I went to my local FE college to see what evening courses were on offer and there began my love affair with all things sociological. I couldn't get enough of studying or of sociology and the effect it had on the way that I felt about the world and my place within it. The class was on a Monday and there were two TV programmes on later in the evening; one following a couple through their first year of marriage and another focusing on individuals who had survived in difficult circumstances. I'd rush home to catch them, watching them with new, enlightened eyes. This was the start of the development of my 'sociological imagination' (Mills, 1959). In this first year of sociological study I also became much more interested in the experience and consequences of personal politics and my exploration of and relationship to feminism also began at this time. A year later I began my BA Sociology at North Staffordshire Polytechnic (now Staffordshire University).

From the very first day I knew that I wanted to find out more about areas and concerns that I felt were misunderstood and under-researched and planned for my final undergraduate research project to concentrate on women's experience of miscarriage. My auto/biographical focus continued into my doctoral career where I focused on the status and experience of 'infertility' and 'involuntary childlessness' (which I write in single quotation marks to highlight the problems of definition). As a postgraduate student I also began to write with others about methodological issues and about working and learning in HE. Collaborative work continues to be important to me and is something that I would recommend to postgraduates and early career academics. This type of working is not an easy option, not least because it can be challenging when collaborators do not agree, but shared responsibility is a motivator and working together is often a learning experience for all involved. Alongside these academic developments I joined the British

Sociological Association and as a postgraduate member I went to a BSA summer school, became co-convener of the Human Reproduction Study Group, co-organised a BSA Family Studies group day conference, and joined the then Equality of the Sexes Committee. Throughout my career I've continued my involvement with the BSA and value very much the support and friendship I receive from sociological colleagues and from those in the BSA office in Durham. At conferences and other events I've learnt new things and received helpful critical comments on my own work; on committees, task groups and editorial boards I've found role models to follow and received valuable advice about the academic job.

My life has not turned out the way I thought it might that afternoon in school when having failed my maths O-level I was told by the visiting careers adviser, 'Well, that's university out for you, then.' At the time I didn't mind as all I wanted to do was to work with children, in preparation for the ones I fully expected to later mother. To my knowledge I have only been pregnant the once. My research has given me the time and opportunity to reflect on my life – not only in the areas of reproductive and non/parental identity but also in relation to travel and transport mobility and working and learning in higher education – in ways that most people are not able to. My work in the academy has also provided me with alternative sources of gratification as researcher, as writer, as teacher, as supervisor, as mentor. When I first meet first year undergraduates or begin teaching on a module new to me I often tell students that in order to do well at sociology one of the most important things to be is nosy. Nosiness has certainly worked for me. When receiving feedback from my readership application I was told that the reviewers felt that I needed to specialise more if I wanted to 'make professor'. I thought about this for a while but decided that there was nothing I wanted to give up so decided to carry on working in a variety of areas but still attempt promotion. When I was offered my professorship at Plymouth I was told that it was my eclectic approach that got me the job. Evidence, I guess, that you can please some of the people some of the time.

Although I feel no need to apologise to colleagues about my background and my route into academia I do sometimes feel the need to play down my achievements outside of the institution. For example, in order not to feel like I'm 'showing off', I tell taxi-drivers and acquaintances at the gym that I teach and I do not talk much about my publications and promotions with my extended family of origin and at school reunions. So, although I feel comfortable being a professional woman at work, I perceive the expectations of my family and friends of early years to be more embedded in a traditional female working-class frame and/or perceive that my professional status will mark me as an outsider and someone who has 'got above herself'. For a few years after achieving my doctorate and a similar length of time after becoming a professor I used my new 'labels' in public. I usually now describe myself as 'Ms' outside of the academy. Yet, I support and defend anyone's right to use the titles they have worked for, particularly given the assumptions and prejudice that persist about those who historically might not have had the opportunity. While on trains or at conferences I'm still sometimes asked 'What are you studying?' and/ or 'What is the focus of your PhD?' and my two 'favourite' title stories are (1) when telling the market researcher that my title was Dr she wrote down 'Mrs Doctor' and (2) when picking up a delivery from an electrical shop I was told, 'But that's for Professor Letherby.'

As noted above sociology, specifically feminist and auto/biographical approaches and writings, have provided me with the opportunity to critically engage with issues that are central to my own life and to the lives of others with whom I share personal and professional experiences. This is both a privilege and a responsibility that I take very seriously and something that I continue to defend as vital to the sociological project. My academic work has (quite rightly) been subject to debate and criticism by others. But, I would argue, sometimes unjustly so, when I have engaged with the auto/biographical. Work which draws on and celebrates the experiential is described by some as 'un-academic', as 'sensational journalism' (Rothman, 1986, 53). On different occasions my own work has been described as 'sickly self-indulgent and gross self-advertisement', and as 'self-dramatising rubbish'. Eric Mykhalovskiy (1996) whose auto/biographical writing has been similarly criticised argues that working in this way challenges the traditional academic orthodoxy and perhaps attack is for some the best form of defence. Working in a new area and/or with a new approach is exciting but can be intellectually and emotionally dangerous (Lee-Treweek and Linkogle, 2000) and would be much harder without encouragement and supportive critique from others working similarly. Like others (including members of the BSA Auto/Biography Study Group who have supported me along the way) I suggest that critical auto/biographical sociological study – either focusing on one, several or many lives – highlights the need to liberate the individual from individualism. Such an approach demonstrates how individuals are social selves. This is important because a focus on the individual can contribute to the understanding of the general (Mills, 1959; Okely, 1992; Stanley, 1993; Evans, 1997; Erben, 1998). I appreciate that it's easier to make a case or take a stand about something having achieved a certain level of status, once one has a publishing track record, but academic vulnerability never goes away.

One of my first publications was an article on miscarriage, following my undergraduate research, published in a feminist journal. The reviews were positive and encouraging and I adhered to all but one of the recommendations. In discussing my motivation and approach I had briefly outlined my personal experience and one reviewer wrote: 'I would advise the author to think carefully about such disclosures as I have known such information to be used against colleagues in the past.' I have been lucky that my career has taken place at a time where there has been a space for the 'auto/biographical I' (Stanley, 1993) and I have received enough support and encouragement not to be put off by the critique. I also believe in what I do as thoroughly sociological, both substantively, methodologically and epistemologically. For many years I have been interested in the relationship between the research process and product/the knowing/doing relationship and I have argued for a position I call theorised subjectivity, which requires the constant, critical interrogation of our personhood – both intellectual and personal – within the production of the knowledge. It starts by recognising the value as in worth (rather than moral value) – both positive and negative – of the subjective (Letherby, 2003; 2013). This helps me, and I hope other researchers, to reflect meaningfully on the research experience and to take responsibility for the 'knowledge' I/we produce. And yet, as I say, vulnerability remains; recently I was asked to write a chapter focusing on my feminist auto/biographical approach. In this piece I reviewed the work of others, included reference to my own and wrote a little about a new direction that my work is taking. I have for the past couple of years been both writing and drawing on fiction for use in teaching and research and believe that reading fiction can be 'meaningful' and 'meaning making for students' (Lackey, 1994) and that fiction encourages emotional engagement and empathy with others (for example, see Frank, 2000). After explaining my justification for it I included a very short (200 words) piece of fiction that I've written but was told by the book's editor to take this out as it was 'surplus' to my argument. I think this is a shame as performative methods and approaches not only engage our bodies but our minds as well (Douglas and Carless, 2013) and they also have the potential for engagement and impact well beyond our discipline boundaries.

Nearing the end of this piece I realise that I could have approached it differently. I could have written about the way that academia has changed over the past 20 years and the effect of this on my, on colleagues and on student's experience. I have written about this elsewhere (for example, Letherby and Shiels, 2001; Letherby, 2006; Cotterill et al, 2007). My conclusion though would have been the same. Overall, despite, or perhaps because of challenges along the way, my experience within the academy has been a positive one and I am grateful for the opportunities I have had to work with such interesting people throughout my career. If I am ever ambivalent about my place in higher education, which I sometimes am, I am never, ever ambivalent about my status as a sociologist. My first encounter with sociology stimulated and excited me and helped me to understand and explain many of the things that were important to me and to others with whom I share identities and experiences. It still does and I feel sure it always will.

References

Cotterill, P, Jackson, S, Letherby, G (eds), 2007, *Challenges and negotiations for women in higher education,* The Netherlands: Springer

Douglas, K, Carless, D, 2013, An invitation to performative research, *Methodological Innovations Online* 8, 1, 53–64

Erben, M, 1998, Biography and research method, in M Erben (ed) *Biography and education: A reader*, London: Falmer

Evans, M, 1997, *Introducing contemporary feminist thought*, Cambridge: Polity

Frank, K, 2000, 'The management of hunger': Using fiction in writing anthropology, *Qualitative Inquiry*, 6, 4, 474–88

Lackey, C, 1994, Social science as fiction: writing sociological short stories to learn about social issues, *Teaching sociology*, 22, 166–73

Lee-Treweek, G, Linkogle, S (eds), 2000, *Danger in the field: Risk and ethics in social research*, Routledge: London

Letherby, G, 2003, *Feminist research in theory and practice*, Buckingham: Open University

Letherby, G, 2006, Between the devil and the deep blue sea: Developing professional and academic skills and building an inclusive research culture in a climate of defensive evaluation, in D Jary, R Jones (eds) *Widening participation in higher education: Issues, research and resources for the social sciences and beyond,* Birmingham: C-SAP

Letherby, G, 2013, Theorised subjectivity, in G Letherby, J Scott, M Williams (eds) *Objectivity and subjectivity in social research*, London: SAGE

Letherby, G, Shiels, J, 2001, Isn't he good, but can we take her seriously?, in P Anderson, J Williams (eds) *Identity and difference in higher education*, pp 121–32, London: Ashgate

Mills, CW, 1959, *The sociological imagination*, London: Penguin

Mykhalovskiy, E, 1996, Reconsidering table talk: Critical thoughts on the relationship between sociology, autobiography and self-indulgence, *Qualitative Sociology* 19, 1, 131–51

Okely, J, 1992, Anthropology and autobiography: Participatory experience and embodied knowledge, in J Okely, H Callaway (eds) *Anthropology and autobiography*, pp 1–28, London: Routledge

Rothman, BK (1986) *The tentative pregnancy: Prenatal diagnosis and the future of motherhood*, New York: Viking

Stanley, L, 1993, On auto/biography in sociology, *Sociology* 27, 1, 41–52

TWENTY

Turning to the psychosocial: drawing on sociology to address societal issues

Ann Phoenix

Ann Phoenix is a professor of psychosocial research at the Thomas
Coram Research Unit, Institute of Education, University College
London where, from 2007-13, she was the co-director. She co-directs
the Childhood Wellbeing Research Centre, funded by the Department
for Education, and is the principal investigator on NOVELLA
(Narratives of Varied Everyday Lives and Linked Approaches), an
ESRC National Centre for Research Methods node. Her research
focuses on racialised and gendered identities and experiences; mixed-
parentage; masculinities; consumption; young people and their parents;
non-normative childhoods and the transition to motherhood.

What is sociology to me?

One of the reasons that sociology is an attractive discipline is that it allows us to ask and answer questions about the nature of society and people's social experiences. It illuminates commonalities and differences between social groups. It is sociology that helps us to understand social inequalities of various kinds, the social processes by which they occur and, therefore, how inequalities can be addressed. For me, it is the study of the interplay of social divisions and structures that makes sociology a vital and central social science discipline.

My awakening to the importance of a sociological framing of issues came from a perhaps unusual source. In 1976, when I was an undergraduate studying psychology at the University of St Andrews, Jack Tizard, Peter Moss and Jane Perry at the then fairly new Thomas Coram Research Unit, published *All our children: Pre-school services in a changing society*. This was not a sociological text. However, it contextualised pre-school services by tracing the history of pre-school provision and by examining inequalities in the provision of early child education and care. Tizard and his colleagues recognised that the ways in which society makes provision for young children is driven (at least partly) by the ways in which children and families are conceptualised. Furthermore, the resulting structures have an impact on the everyday practices and lives of parents and children, offering clear evidence that social structures and processes are central to personal lives. It was not that this book, by itself, changed my mindset, but it helped to crystallise my understanding that my interests in the processes that produce racialised, gendered and social class differences were not 'just' personal, political and of interest to those who considered themselves directly affected. They were also of academic interest.

Not long after this, I encountered Peter Berger and Thomas Luckmann's (1966) book, *The social construction of reality*. The title encapsulated their thesis that the social order is an ongoing human production rather than naturally occurring. The idea that reality is socially constructed is now familiar to many social researchers, but it was much less evident at the time that I encountered this book, more than ten years after its first publication. The idea had an impact on my work on women who became mothers before they were 20 years old, which was published in 1991 as *Young mothers?* The question mark in the title signalled that the very notion of 'young motherhood' is a social construction in that it carries the connotation that they are too young to be mothers, an idea that arises in particular historical periods, in particular places and is highly value laden.

My increasing engagement with social constructionism as an epistemology results from the theoretical sophistication of sociological thought. Sociology is a theoretically-rich discipline, with theories that explain how aspects of the social world are related and provide perspectives that guide sociological research. Since societies are complex, it is not surprising that sociological theory is also complex and that this theoretical complexity produces debate and negotiation about the nature of (aspects of) society and how it is changing. This dynamic theoretical interchange makes sociology exciting in that it enables both the shifting of disciplinary boundaries in the production of new knowledge ('eureka' moments) and more organic changes to understanding through creative reformulations and transformations to knowledge (Moran, 2011).

The development of notions of social positioning (Davies and Harré, 1990) can be seen as a taking forward of some aspects of social constructionism. It also arises from a eureka moment in that Davies and Harré's conceptualisation of how people take up or refuse positions in interactions arose from the ways in which they came to understand a particular set of their interactions as inflected by gender relations. The example they selected for analysis arises from an argument following the unsuccessful search, in a strange country, for medicine for Davies, who was not feeling well. It arose because Harré (a man given the pseudonym Sano in the paper) said 'I'm sorry to have dragged you all this way when you're not well'. His choice of words surprised Davies (a woman called Enfermada in the paper) who replied 'You didn't drag me, I chose to come.' As they explain in the paper, this led to heated debate:

> Both speakers are committed to a pre-existing idea of themselves that they had prior to the interchange, Enfermada as a feminist and Sano as one who wishes to fulfil socially mandatory obligations. They are also both committed to their hearing of the interchange. Their protests are each aimed at sustaining these definitions and as such have strong emotional loading.

The mutual offence that their exchange generated led Davies and Harré to see the episode as illustrative of the importance of recognising multiple levels of positioning, particularly in relation to gender differences and feminist politics. Their paper gives insights into sociological issues of how social positioning and societal narratives influence the ways in which people think, feel and act. While relatively little sociological research claims to be about the everyday, this is one example of sociology's engagement with the mundane and of how everyday examples can generate theory and give insights into individual agency as well as social structures, processes and inequalities.

Why sociology?

The University of St Andrews, where I did my undergraduate degree, had no sociology or anthropology at the time and, while I had not intended to study psychology, the Scottish system of doing three subjects at a general level in the first year and taking two of these to 'special' level in the second year, fuelled and sustained my interest in psychology. So why am I telling a sociologist's tale?

The basic answer is that sociology foregrounds societal issues that are central to understanding people and relationality. Its substantive concerns complement those foregrounded in psychology. For all the research areas in which I work (for example, consumption, gender, racialisation, motherhood and social identities) sociological and psychological theory and research have provided invaluable insights. Both disciplines contribute to the understanding of how we understand the nature, sources and limits of knowledge (epistemology) and how we think about what human beings are like (ontology). At the time that I studied psychology in the mid-1970s, ontological understandings of children were shifting in exciting ways that were encapsulated in the title of Martin Richards's (1974) groundbreaking developmental psychology text, *The integration of a child into a social world*. This brought together several examples of innovative research on (usually) mothers and very young children that showed that children's cognitive development is fuelled by their social relationships and development. The ontological insight that children are inherently social and that their cognitive sophistication is best demonstrated in social contexts also generated epistemological insights that knowledge is relationally produced. This text and the research and theory it stimulated contributed to my readiness to take up both a 'social constructionist' epistemology and positioning theory.

Exciting as were the developments in social developmental psychology, they left a gap in the conceptualisation of the social that is exemplified in the psychological division of social processes into social and societal. Psychological work frequently focuses on the interpersonal as social and leaves the societal as unexamined social context. Yet, areas such as gender, racialisation and motherhood can only partially be understood interpersonally. This is not to minimise the central importance of the interpersonal, but to recognise that, as the psychologist Urie Bronfenbrenner (1979) suggested, the interpersonal is part of nested systems that operate at micro-, meso-, exo- and macro-levels over time (the chronosystem). Bronfenbrenner's Ecological Systems Theory, parallels Nira Yuval-Davis's (2006; 2012) conceptualisation of social divisions as operating at different levels and so requiring different levels of analysis, which include the national, institutional, intersubjective, representational and subjective constructions of identities. For me, a holistic understanding of the participants in my research requires both analyses of the meanings they make of their social relations and interactions as well as their social positioning (including in social structures that may or may not be represented in their accounts).

Both psychology and sociology recognise the importance of addressing individual and social processes. However, both have frequently treated individual and society (psychology) or structure and agency (sociology) as binaries rather than as simultaneous and nested systems (Hollway et al, 2007). In order to take a holistic view of people as social beings, it seemed to me that each of the two disciplines should ideally follow Sandra Harding's (2008) suggestion (produced in relation to standpoint theory in feminist work), to ask each other's questions. It is not surprising then that sociology became central to my work and thinking. It is because I hold both kinds of questions as equally central and crucial to understanding the social world that I subscribe to the burgeoning field of psychosocial studies where, in different ways, researchers are attempting to treat the psychological and social as equally important and to analyse them as the simultaneous processes they are (see for example, the special issue of *Feminist Review*, edited by Irene Gedalof and Nirmal Puwar that responds to Avtar Brah's (1999) groundbreaking paper, 'The scent of memory').

What advice would you give to someone starting out in a career in sociology?

My point of entry into sociological work and research led me to highlight four issues that early career sociologists might find useful to consider as they forge their careers. The first is to recognise that no one discipline can provide all the tools, insights and methodologies necessary to studying all the questions that fall within its remit. The current widespread espousing of interdisciplinary work is, therefore, to be applauded. In practice, however, this is more easily said than done because it is extremely difficult to apply informed, critically engaged and sceptical evaluative stances in disciplines to which researchers are outsiders. The question of how to do interdisciplinary work that is credible both to sociologists and to other disciplines without years of further study is, therefore, a difficult one. This dilemma can, at least partially, be resolved by discussing ideas with people from other disciplines and conducting collaborative work.

The second is the importance of paying as much attention to methodology as to substantive areas and, in doing so, to avoid methodological dogma, both at the level of specific method and in terms of whether quantitative or qualitative analyses are conducted. In my experience, much can be gained from methodological eclecticism and attention to methodological innovations while simultaneously attending to epistemological consistency. One crucial reason for this is that developments within sociology both require, and stem from, methodological developments. As with the interdisciplinary point above, methodological expansion is much assisted by collaboration, both with peers and with those more senior and junior than oneself, who help to keep the discipline and individual sociologists themselves vibrant and dynamic. Equally important, sociologists at all stages of their careers benefit from staff development courses, something that many employers will fund.

The third issue that an early career sociologist might find useful to bear in mind is that people are agents in that they make decisions and negotiate their actions and accounts. However, their agency is constrained and/or enabled by how they are positioned in social structures. This is an old issue in sociology, often referred to as the agency/structure debate. It has become commonplace over the last 30 years to view agency and structure are inextricably linked. However, it is difficult to design research studies that recognise that agency and structure operate simultaneously and affect each other (Lewis, 2013; Lutz et al, 2011; Yuval-Davis, 2012). An important sociological question continues to be, therefore, how agency is constrained by structure and/or how structure is produced and operates through people who are, to some extent, agents (Mizen and Ofosu-Kusi, 2013; Phoenix, 2011).

The final issue relates to orientation to work and career. I would suggest that it is invaluable to accept a range of invitations to write or speak about one's research. For me, being willing to do this has generated a network of people in various countries with whom I share research interests and who have facilitated numerous publishing opportunities for me. This strategy has to go hand in hand with clarity about which pieces of work are feasible and practicable (since such opportunities are unlikely to be part of anyone's everyday responsibilities). Even this is, however, slightly less straightforward and self-evident than first appears in that, when I have found myself overstretched and tied to administrative detail, opportunities to write and speak have enabled me to keep up my publications and to develop new analytical and research ideas.

In my career, I have had the privilege and good luck of being able to work in several areas that I have found fascinating and considered consequential. However, with the current competition for research money, many researchers have to switch between short-term research projects in which they may have limited interest. My wish is that everyone will be able to experience sustained involvement in areas to which they are committed and on which they can build their reputations. For that reason, it is important that early career researchers attempt to be proactive about getting their own research money and/ or carving out time to publish in areas in which they wish to build expertise and become known. Accepting invitations is one way of accomplishing this.

Looking back on your career, what would you have done differently?

One of the features of narrative theory I very much like is its recognition that the past changes as the present and potential future shift. From my current vantage point, there is nothing about my career that I would do differently. At the time, there were things that seemed less propitious than others. However, a holistic perspective allows me to see that a job I did not like gave me invaluable teaching experience and colleagues worth their weight in gold. I would have liked to be better versed in classic sociological theories and to have attended more of the courses and talks that I found interesting. Yet, in the absence of an ability to make time elastic, this was not possible without giving up other important commitments. Similarly, while my work–life balance too often privileged work, this is an area that needs continual negotiation and rebalancing at different transition points in the life course.

References

Berger, P, Luckmann, T, 1966, *The social construction of reality: A treatise in the sociology of knowledge*, Garden City, NY: Anchor Books

Brah, A, 1999, The scent of memory: Strangers, our own, and others, *Feminist Review* 6, 4–26

Bronfenbrenner, U, 1979, *The ecology of human development: Experiments by nature and design*, Cambridge, MA: Harvard University Press

Davies, B, Harré, R, 1990, Positioning: The discursive production of selves, *Journal for the Theory of Social Behavior* 20, 43–63, www.massey.ac.nz/~alock/position/position.htm

Gedalof, I, Puwar, N, 2012, Recalling 'The scent of memory': Celebrating 100 issues of *Feminist Review, Feminist Review* 100, 1–5

Harding, S, 2008, *Sciences from below: Feminisms, postcolonialities and modernities*, Durham, NC: Duke University Press

Hollway, W, Lucey, H, Phoenix, A (eds), 2007, *Social psychology matters,* London: Open University Press

Lewis, G, 2013, Unsafe travel: Experiencing intersectionality and feminist displacements, *Signs: A journal of women and culture* 38, 4, 869–92

Lutz, H, Herrera Vivar, MT, Supik, L (eds), 2011, *Framing intersectionality: Debates on a multi-faceted concept in gender studies*, Farnham: Ashgate

Moran, S, 2011, Metaphor foundations in creativity research: Boundary vs organism, *Journal of Creative Behavior* 43, 1, 1–28

Mizen, P, Ofosu-Kusi, Y, 2013, Agency as vulnerabilty: Accounting for children's movement to the streets of Accra, Ghana, *The Sociological Review* 61, 363–82

Phoenix, A, 1991, *Young Mothers?*, Cambridge: Polity

Phoenix, A, 2011, Youth, research and doing intersectionality, in R Leiprecht (ed) *Diversitätsbewusste Soziale Arbeit*, Schwalbach: Wochenschau Verlag

Richards, M (ed), 1974, *The integration of a child into a social world*, Cambridge: Cambridge University Press

Tizard, J, Moss, P, Perry, J, 1976, *All our children: Pre-school services in a changing society*, London: Temple Smith/New Society

Yuval-Davis, N, 2006, Intersectionality and feminist politics, *European Journal of Women's Studies* 13, 3, 193–209

Yuval-Davis, N, 2012, *The politics of belonging: Intersectional contestations*, London: SAGE

Part 3
How does one become a sociologist?

TWENTY-ONE

A long haul

Berry Mayall

Berry Mayall is professor of childhood studies at the Institute of Education, University of London. She has worked since the 1980s on the sociology of childhood and has published widely.

My engagement with sociology is interlinked with my personal history, and so the two have to be described together. I graduated in English (literature) in 1958. No careers advice was offered, beyond directing 'girls' into secretarial or teaching work. I tried various avenues and had a memorable experience at the BBC. I applied for a job as trainee drama director and when I got to the interview, they said, 'We thought we would ask you to come along, because we wondered why you applied: we don't take women.'

The social and political climate for women, whether or not graduates, in the 1950s and 1960s was dire. Woman's destiny was marriage and children, and when some of my cohort got married on the last day of the last term at university, we fellow graduates thought that was success. Commentators at the time, proclaimed that women must and would spend 15 to 20 years bringing up their two or three children, but that after that there was plenty of time for them to take up or resume their careers (for example, Titmuss, 1958). There were a few dissenting voices – women mostly, arguing that it was a waste of education (paid for by the state) not to use women's education and skills (Banks and Banks, 1956) and in 1949 governmental concern about shortages of 'manpower' led to a Royal Commission on Population Report which argued that measures be introduced to allow women to combine motherhood with paid work (see Myrdal and Klein, 1956: 196). Later – in 1964 – the government relaxed its rules on not expanding nursery places, provided the new nursery place would release a woman to resume her job as a teacher.

After some false starts, however, I took the traditional course and from 1959 taught in girls' grammar schools (this is just before comprehensivisation came in). Then after marriage and child, I taught very part-time for the Inner London Education Authority (ILEA) in a further education college. By the late 1960s, however, ILEA decided that all its teachers, however experienced, must do a training course, and word in the staff room was that it was excruciatingly boring. So I cast around. Maybe there was something else I could do.

I signed up to do a programme that would give me a further degree and social work training – at the LSE. There was not only a grant, there was an element of subsistence, for me, a married woman! Once accepted, that summer of 1969 we had to do some social work 'placements' to give us an idea of what social work entailed, and its variety. Then in the first year of study we worked for a diploma in social administration, following undergraduate courses in sociology, psychology, economics and theories of the welfare state. Then I worked for nearly two years as a social worker in the children's department of Tower Hamlets, in a department established to help children who could never go home. Then I did the second – very long year – at the LSE, with academic training for the MSc alongside two and then three days and finally four days a week over the year as a social worker at the London Hospital, ending up in the children's ward. So I also qualified as a social worker. The whole enterprise lasted from the summer of 1969 to the autumn 1973.

I think, looking back, that the LSE offered a very well balanced course; we tussled with the academic subjects, and were able to link them up with our practical experiences out in the 'field'. Psychology was a mixed bag – it included ideas about perception, alongside Harry Harlow's maternally deprived monkeys and, of course the immensely influential John Bowlby (for example, 1953). We argued with the economics tutor's view that we are all economic men who seek their own advantage. But sociology allowed us to think about the social, economic and political situation of the people with whom we worked. In my case, with my interest in children, it was my first encounter with how macro approaches to the workings of society could be seen as relevant to thinking about children. Like many other students, I found and still find C Wright Mills's *The sociological imagination* an inspiring read.

In the autumn of 1973, I applied for two jobs – both part-time, since I still had 24-hour a day responsibility for a child. I was turned down for the social work job, but accepted at the Institute of Education to work with Jack Tizard, an eminent psychologist, who was acutely aware of the range of social conditions in which children grew up and the gross inequalities of opportunity for children. At the new Thomas Coram Research Unit, we were to interview every mother of an under-five in the local area, to ask them what life was like with their child, and what daycare provision they would like. A childcare centre was established in the Coram Foundation's building, to offer responsive, flexible care. We also had a comparison site in west London, again with a new nursery provided. Healthcare services were to be integral to the daycare provision.

This was the era – which lasted until the Labour government came in in 1997 – when successive UK governments refused to take responsibility for the provision of daycare; by the mid-1960s women had set up playgroups to (partially) fill this gap; and there was also the long-established childminding system, whereby women, mostly untrained and living in poor housing, looked after other people's children. I asked if we could do a sub-study of childminding, and the

Department of Health funded it, first a pilot and then a bigger study (Mayall and Petrie, 1983).

It was this encounter with the whole daycare field, and in particular with the perspectives of women on living and working with children, which encouraged me to think about children from a social constructionist point of view. Notably we found that mothers thought of children as people, from the word go. Childminders and nursery nurses thought of children as objects of management. A later study, with health visitors, found that the child was a project, to be socialised within developmental norms. When I wrote up my PhD in 1980 – on childminding (Mayall, 1981), I was able to draw on a large literature (much of it from the USA) on how children are differently conceptualised in varying times and places. American sociologists were also telling us that functionalism (where children are socialised into social norms) did not adequately account for what observably happened in real life; which was that people were social agents, who, through interaction, made a difference to social relations and to how people are understood. Notably interactionists (Goffman, Becker), were opening the door to thinking of children as active, contributing social agents, a point that linked in with newly fashionable psychological ideas, about how children contribute to learning (Vygotsky), and in particular through their first relations at home with parents and siblings (Dunn, 1984; 1988). Barbara Tizard and Martin Hughes (1984) wrote a perceptive book on how children learn through discussing day-to-day topics with their mothers. So it would be fair to say that my encounter with sociology was interlinked initially with my personal experiences, in work with mothers and children.

I am, however, missing out, so far, the important social movement that also took place while I had total responsibility, unhappily, for my daughter: feminism. I remember reading in the *Guardian* about the first women's lib conference held in Oxford in 1970 and the demands for the liberation of women from social motherhood. There should be 24-hour nurseries. And there must also be an equal division of responsibility between men and women for the care of children. This hugely important movement is described in other chapters in this book. But at the time, influenced by Bowlby, and seeing no prospect of my totally unreconstructed husband making any change in his use of time, I think I rather devalued the importance of the feminist movement. Indeed in the 1950s and 1960s, as was later explained, women had no theory to account for their guilt, depression, anger, resentment; each carried these burdens on her own (Segal, 1990).

It was during the 1980s, however, that the movement to reconceptualise childhood began to take off in England, and it was led by social anthropologists – Judith Ennew and Jean La Fontaine. I think it must have been their studies of other societies that led them to sympathise with the social constructionist viewpoint and of course to point to the contributions that children in most societies make to the division of labour. I went to some of these meetings and read their work and began to make links with European sociologists' work, for they were adopting a much more structural approach to childhood – thinking about the concept of children's work and about the social status of childhood (for example, Qvortrup, 1985). I started the first UK seminar group on childhood in 1990, and that helped UK people to meet and discuss their work.

My sociological empirical research work on childhood took off thanks to the Institute of Education. In 1990 they offered to underwrite half the salary, for six years, of three members of staff. This meant that I could do a pilot study without external funding, to establish first that I had something to say and second, that social research with children was possible (for one of my research proposals had been turned down on the grounds that no useful data could be collected with under-12s). So in the 1990s, I carried out four studies with children, focusing on the intersections of home and primary school, from the point of view of children. Much of the later funding came from the ESRC (Some of this work is written about in my 2002 book).

We have been asked to reflect on certain questions. Here are some notes. This narrative has, I hope, made clear how personal history is interlinked with social and political history. I cannot simply say that I would have done things differently – for it was not then in my power. Doing a degree in English Literature was what I wanted to do at the time, and not something I would have wanted to forego. And at the time (1950s) sociology was only just getting going in UK universities – bright young Oxbridge types with classics degrees headed for Leicester.

Looking back on my own journey, I do think it was important to have experience of real world dilemmas faced by people, and these experiences have been important to me in trying to come to terms with sociological ideas. So I would generally suggest to people that they should work in a variety of jobs before settling (if they do) into academia. It is great to see that our students on our MA in the sociology of childhood and children's rights do mostly take this view and indeed come to our sociological discussions with valuable insights from the real world.

As I have often remarked, I see the sociology of childhood as a political enterprise – a view that is not universally held. I think analysis of children's social status leads us to understand not only the rights but the wrongs of childhood. I want to see the social and political status of childhood improved, with fair distribution of national resources to children. The dominant discipline regarding children is still developmental psychology and though its disciples may be politically oriented and want to improve the social condition of childhood, the underlying concepts of the discipline – emphasising the journey to adult competence that children make – are a bit of a stumbling block to consideration of the social status of childhood. By contrast, interlinkages of sociological ideas with respect for children's rights, fit well together.

References

Banks, JA, Banks, OL, 1956, Employment of sociology and anthropology graduates 1952 and 1954, *British Journal of Sociology* 7, 46–51

Bowlby, J, 1953, *Child care and the growth of love*, Harmondsworth: Penguin

Dunn, J, 1984, *Sisters and brothers*, London: Fontana

Dunn, J, 1988, *The beginnings of social understanding,* Oxford: Blackwells

Mayall, B, 1981, Childminding as a service for working mothers and their children aged under two years, PhD thesis, University of London

Mayall, B, 2002, *Towards a sociology for childhood*, Buckingham: Open University Press

Mayall, B, 2013, *A history of the sociology of childhood*, London: Institute of Education

Mayall, B, Petrie, P, 1983, *Childminding and day nurseries: What kind of care,* London: Heinemann

Mills, C Wright, 1959, *The sociological imagination*, Oxford: Oxford University Press, 1967

Myrdal, A, Klein, V, 1956, *Women's two roles: Home and work*, London: Routledge and Kegan Paul

Qvortrup, J, 1985, Placing children in the division of labour, in P Close, R Collins (eds) *Family and economy in modern society*, London: Macmillan

Segal, L, 1990, *Slow motion: Changing men, changing masculinities*, London: Virago

Titmuss, RM, 1958, The position of women, in RM Titmuss (ed) *Essays on the welfare state*, London: Unwin University Books, Paper first given as the Millicent Fawcett Lecture at Bedford College, London University in 1952

Tizard, B, Hughes, M, 1984, *Young children learning: Talking and thinking at home and at school*, London: Fontana

TWENTY-TWO

Putting sociology to work in the NHS

Jocelyn Cornwell in conversation with Mark Doidge

Jocelyn Cornwell is the founder and director of The Point of Care Foundation, a charity that aims to help healthcare organisations improve the experiences of patients and staff. Previously, Jocelyn worked in healthcare regulation at national level, as an NHS manager and in research at the Open University. She is the author of *Hard-earned lives: Accounts of health and illness from East London* (Tavistock, 1984).

Mark: Okay, so the first question then is, can you tell me how it is you became a sociologist? A bit about your background in your career?

Jocelyn: I went to Cambridge University where you could take two different subjects as an undergraduate. I did history part one and social and political science. I was involved in the women's movement, in the early 1970s and in the socialist society and was very interested in politics.

I left in 1976 and my first job was doing a survey of outpatient departments in London teaching hospitals, which was a complete dead end! [Laughter] Very, very, very dull. I spent my days in clinics getting patients to complete questionnaires. Computing was in its infancy and you would punch the data into cards. Anyway, the survey was run from a department called Community Medicine (these days it would be called Public Health) and fortunately for me the head of the department told me about a master's degree in sociology applied to medicine at Bedford College, London University. At the end of the master's, and on the strength of it, I applied successfully to do a PhD in East London.

I had read a letter to the *British Medical Journal* by a bunch of A&E consultants who were insisting that the problem with their department at the London Hospital was that local people 'misused' it. Working-class people had, what they described as, a 'fatalistic approach' to their health which made them incapable of using services appropriately: the doctors claimed their patients were leaving health problems too late and then turning up as emergencies.

I thought it was an outrageous letter, but it was enough to stimulate me to think "Well, why do people use the A&E department as they do?" Initially, I was going to do a comparison of beliefs in the working-class community – which was a famous community sociologically because of Young and Willmott's (1957) work on family and community in East London in the 1950s – with the beliefs of people from Bangladesh. But I was persuaded by my supervisor that would be far too big a project so I did an ethnographic study of families and social networks in Bethnal Green and Hackney. I was supervised at Queen Mary College by a geographer, Professor David Smith, and had an external supervisor, an anthropologist in Bristol called Vieda Skultans. I finished, got it published as a book called *Hard earned lives: Accounts of health and illness in East London*, which has become a standard text for many courses.

I had never thought I would be an academic. In fact, I knew that I didn't want to be an academic. I never thought twice about what I was going to do ever, actually, but instead did the next thing that interested me. I had been teaching in a medical school and working as a counsellor for the Pregnancy Advisory Service. I wasn't making much money and I applied for various jobs. I had liked the topic of my PhD. I liked working in London and I liked East London health politics. I tried unsuccessfully to get a job in a CHC, a community health council.

Instead I got a research fellowship at the Open University – initially as a contract researcher and I also taught for them as a tutor on a good multi-disciplinary course called Health and Disease (U205).

After two years I realised that I would have to apply for research money on topics that really I didn't care that much about and that this wasn't for me at all. I didn't want it enough to be an academic and had no idea how to get from contract research into a tenured job.

I have been incredibly lucky really. In those days, in the 1980s, The King's Fund (a London-based health charity) had a tradition of being interested in the development of services. I knew people there and they seconded me for six months to write some papers on older people's care and how to create decentralised management structures that would be much closer to patients and their needs than centralised management. A number of jobs then came up in the NHS, which were, as it were, pre-figured rather than prescribed by the papers I had written. Two health authorities in England – one in Islington, London and one in Devon – advertised jobs for 'locality managers' – decentralised management positions for managers who would be based and working in local neighbourhoods. I did and got one of the five jobs that was going in Islington and did that for three years.

I worked in the NHS in community services as a locality manager for three years and then Margaret Thatcher in the 1980s launched the first radical reform of the health service. The Audit Commission already existed as a national body, whose task had been to audit and do value for money studies in local government. Now with the Thatcher reforms of the NHS in the 1980s, the Audit Commission took on the external audit of the health service and I thought it might be an interesting place to work. They had a brand new directorate called Health Studies, which was going to do value for money studies in the health service.

I applied to be a researcher for this department: it gave me an amazing education and I stayed there for ten years ending up as one of the deputy directors in the health studies directorate. During that time, I did major national public reports on maternity services, district nursing, anaesthesia and a big one, which was politically controversial, on GP fund-holding.

The work was a combination of research, project management and report writing. For every national study you set up an advisory group and because the Commission was a national body, you could very easily get the top people in a particular field to be on the advisory group. You would research the topic in 8–9 study sites – the expenditure, the quality of the service and how it was organised – then write a national report on the opportunities for efficiencies or other gains.

It was the most privileged position within which to bring research and management together. The Audit Commission was very well known in the 1990s. Every major national report we published would be on the front pages of the broad sheets. It was a great place to be and a fantastic education.

Mark: Was that something you were interested in, that combination of management and research?

Jocelyn: Yes, I was really interested in management by then, having been a manager for three years. I was very interested in the organisation of the NHS and it was a good place to be. It taught me a lot about writing accessible reports and many other things.

Then Tony Blair's government got in and you can't imagine my pleasure and excitement when their priority was going to be quality of care, not just money. Part of the Blair reforms was to create the first inspectorate for the health service, which was called the Commission for Health Improvement (CHI). I got invited to go to the Department of Health on secondment to help the civil servants set up the new organisation (CHI), and spent nine months in the Department of Health as a senior civil servant. I would say that was the next best education after my master's degree.

Mark: Really? Why was that?

Jocelyn: Well because it was such an extraordinary environment to be in. Real life, complete bureaucracy and I was attached to the team of civil servants who were taking the legislation of the Health Act through parliament in 1999. My job was to help the civil servants have an idea of how to make things work in practice, to put flesh on the bones of this idea of an organisation and help them to make it a reality. I did everything from choosing the first premises, to being involved in the appointment of the chairman, the chief executive and the commissioners, who were the governing body, to developing the strategy. When the people to run it got appointed, they invited me to carry on my secondment and help them. And then I applied for a job with them and became the deputy chief executive. So by then, it was the year 2000 so 14 years ago. I just thought it was one of those things, you know?

Mark: No strategy?

Jocelyn: There wasn't a strategy but there was a thread: I was always interested in patients. I was always interested in the quality of care. I was always interested in, how do you make it better than it is? I think the fact that I had been well trained and had done a PhD, that I was a sociologist, was relevant, you know, because as you said, it gives you a way of looking at things, which is quite hard to articulate sometimes but just comes very naturally. I think it is partly about understanding power. And the power of ideas and the, sort of, materiality of ideas, you know, making things happen?

In my master's degree, the study of the health professions fascinated me – the kind of vested interest cloaked as altruism [laughter]. I think I have always felt I've been an outsider on the inside and that's actually quite a rare thing to be, I have discovered. In all those environments, you know, as a regulator or as a manager and particularly working with healthcare, which is a very complex environment, very few of the players in that world actually understand each other's point of view or even have the faintest sense that someone might have a different point of view.

Mark: Exactly, yeah. So is it a really useful skill to be an outsider, then, on the inside?

Jocelyn: I think of it as being someone, who is always a liminal person – on the threshold of things. Sometimes it is very uncomfortable, you never feel like you totally belong. But on the other hand, I have come to see that it has been one of the key things that has helped me in my career. Just that ability to not just see things from other people's points of view but bring different types of people together and say, "You have all got something to contribute here. It is not enough to just do it on your own."

That was really what happened and then CHI, the Commission of Health Improvement, was an extraordinary experience because we had to set it up from scratch and it was really in the public eye, as the regulators are now. We were idealistic, the people who set it up. We saw it as being very much for healthcare improvement, and fell foul of the government, who wanted an Ofsted-type inspector. We were abolished after two years so we were the first casualty in a decade of creating new organisations and then abolishing them.

We had two years to set up CHI, then we were abolished and there was two years of handover to the successor organisation during which I became the acting chief executive for the last 18 months. It was very political and very stressful in lots of ways but also very interesting. In 2004, the new incoming organisation wanted none of the directors of the old one to be involved and so we all lost our jobs, one way or another.

I then started to freelance and what I do now comes out of that period. After a while, I realised that I didn't really like being a freelancer – it was a bit like being a contract researcher. You were always doing things other people commissioned you to do.

I wrote the proposal for what I do now, a programme of research and practical actions to try and improve the experience of patients in hospital called the Point of Care.

The King's Fund liked the idea and funded it and I developed a small team. For the last six years, we have worked in healthcare and actually become very well known for our work.

We were ahead of the curve in terms of talking about patients' experience and thinking about compassionate care so when the Mid Staffordshire Public Inquiry Report was published, we were one of the organisations that people have begun to look to as having done interesting practical work on the ground. This year I set up The Point of Care Foundation as an independent charity to continue the work.

Mark: Okay. I am going to move on to the next question: what are your ideas on what sociology has changed? How has sociology contributed or changed your outlook?

Jocelyn: Well, as I say, I feel like it is a bit like what I was born to do or at least, it is how I see the world. I think that the master's degree really shaped me intellectually, actually. I don't know what else to say really except that I feel like it informs the way that I work and the assumptions with which I work. After all that long period of being a manager and then being at the Audit Commission I realised when I wrote the proposal for the Point of Care that it was, in a sense, a bit more like going back to the PhD in that it had to come from me. Since then, in my short biography for when I speak at conferences, I always describe myself as a sociologist.

People need to know this. This is where I come from. I am not a doctor, I am not a nurse, and I am not a manager. I know a lot about the health service but I am a sociologist in it.

Mark: Do you think it has made you a better manager or director or fundraiser or anything like that or do you think it just informs your observations?

Jocelyn: No, I don't actually think it has made me better at those things. I think it might have made the quality of some of the work I have produced better but I don't think it has enabled me to be a manager or to run an organisation – those are things you have to learn how to do, you know. I am a visiting professor at Imperial now. I don't feel the same in academic terms anymore.

I have commissioned a lot of research and I am one of a very large team of people who are applying for research grants to the National Institute for Health Services Research. But I always feel that I must tell people that I am not a real academic anymore. Academic work has moved on so much, just the technology of it has changed so much.

Mark: What way do you think it has changed?

Jocelyn: Well in my day, if you did qualitative work, it was very manual and all done with cards – the way you analysed your data and recorded it and so on. Now, all of that is much easier to automate, the same as literature reviews and producing written work. I mean, I typed my PhD, you know. Every page and then had to get it re-typed by a proper typist.

Nothing like that would happen today I'm sure. It is mostly in the field of doing literature reviews that I feel that I am not a proper academic. There is software to handle references and all of that sort of stuff but I can't be bothered to learn how to use it because I don't need it to do my core job.

Mark: So there is a whole range of skills as being part of a sociologist and academia that has changed.

Jocelyn: Yeah, I think so and likewise I have acquired skills that I suspect most academics wouldn't need to have, in the management of budgets and knowing about employment and how to run an organisation. I don't feel that I am an academic sociologist but I do feel that I am informed and my work is informed by sociological perspective.

Mark: Okay, let's move on. Would you advise someone, say your younger self or someone else, to study sociology now? If so, why and if not, why not? If someone has gone into a career outside of academia, would you advise them to go into academia or do something like you've done?

Jocelyn: It is very personal, isn't it? A lot of my friends are academics. I don't envy them [laughter] I think it is quite testing and quite an unrewarding life, actually, a lot of it unless you are really scholarly in your personality. I think sociology can be very flaky.

I think it's far too easy an option and taught – I imagine – quite badly when I see some sociological research. I think if it is taught well, it is a brilliant topic and so I think I would advise people to look quite carefully at finding a good course and know what they were looking for. I think it is a good topic to study at master's degree level. I think that would be a very valuable thing to do and when people ask my advice about doing a PhD, I say "Are you sure you really want to spend another three to four years of your life doing this?"

I don't think people realise how hard it is and I think it is very tough. I don't think that has changed very much since my day. It seems to me to still be the case.

Mark: Is that just tough intellectually or tough…?

Jocelyn: I think tough personally, existentially. I think people lose their way and the universities are not always very supportive of them.

Mark: What advice would you give to someone attempting to carve out a career in sociology or using sociology?

Jocelyn: I don't know that I am very well placed to do that. I am not close enough to it. I certainly think that it is worth getting some experience of the world outside of academia. The most interesting sociological work for me was doing things like…there was a book by Huw Beynon called *Working for Ford* looking at working in car factories. There is a very interesting group at the Bayswater Institute, who write about organisations and working life and they are mostly people who are placed inside organisations for years.

I am much more interested in that kind of sociology than very theoretical post-modern work. I think there is a whole territory of sociology, which I found increasingly uninteresting, which seemed to be entirely preoccupied with itself and not at all with the world so that was what really helped turn me off it, I think.

Mark: Okay, when you talked about your career, looking back on that, is there something you would have done differently? Would you have done anything different?

Jocelyn: No, not really because I never had a plan and never had an ambition other than to do interesting things. I have loved work and have always had a very interesting working life but it wasn't a plan for working life at all. In fact, every single job I have ever done has never existed before – there was never a locality manager before the locality managers.

The Audit Commission's health studies directorate was entirely new, setting up the Commission for Health Improvement was entirely new. I really liked doing new things, I think. There couldn't be a career where you always want to do new things but that is, in effect, what I have managed to do.

Mark: Okay, excellent. Last question, really. If you could choose one reading or one book that inspired you that you would recommend someone to read to understand your view of sociology or your world, what would you recommend?

Jocelyn: I think *Working for Ford* is a really brilliant book, actually.

Mark: Right, it's on my list! [Laughter] Okay, we will stop there. Thank you very much.

References

Young, M and Willmott, P, 1957, *Family and kinship in East London*, London: Routledge and Kegan Paul

Beynon, H, 1975, *Working for Ford*, Open University

TWENTY-THREE

Clinging to the precipice: travails of a contract researcher in sociology

Mel Bartley

I graduated in sociology and philosophy in 1968, received my MSc in medical sociology in 1972 and PhD in social policy in 1988. I am at present professor emerita of medical sociology at University College London. My research interests are unemployment and health, health inequality, health in the life course and the relationship between research and policy.

My story is one of grim determination and stubbornness in the face of recurring hurdles. I tell it here as a cautionary tale, in part. I am sure I made mistakes, maybe also there was a certain inevitability to my path, but perhaps this story, my story, will resonate with others or will even act as an encouragement. I have been told that the students in my Department at UCL regarded me as an example of 'how a person can do it their own way'. Other early career academics have said they regard me as an example of how to preserve a degree of autonomy. Although all this happened more by accident than design, it is a source of pleasure that my chequered history might be helping some people to follow their own dreams.

My relationship to academic medical sociology has been like a bad affair with an unfaithful lover. I have never been able to get over the fascination of the subject, with its enormous potential for discovery and the improvement of human welfare. As a result, I have clung grimly to the precipice of job insecurity. The amount of work I have had to do just to keep myself from being expelled from academic life has taken over almost my entire existence (if my life's partner were not in the same business I doubt he could tolerate it).

Early influences: discovering medical sociology, 1968–74

The year 1965 was a great one in which to go to university, just in time to graduate into the political upheavals of 1968. I had never heard of sociology, but was advised to change from philosophy and politics by my tutor. She had decided I was destined for academic work and knew that a degree from Reading University might have some chance to open doors in this newer discipline. This change of major subject gave me access to the inspirational teaching of Viola Klein and Salvador Giner (among others) and at their further urging I began to look for ways to remain a sociologist.

As an American citizen I was not eligible for a grant to study further, so I applied for various research assistantships, and somehow managed to land one of these, despite having nothing more to offer than a 2.1 from an obscure university.

It was very hard to make the transition from my friendly, rather sleepy 'red brick' university. I had felt very secure at Reading, being taught by people who were not at the time well known and had plenty of time for their students. It was a great leap from this to the relatively pampered, vain ambition I found around me at my next destination (which I will not name). The research team leader had little or no experience of projects or of fieldwork. We stumbled through questionnaire design, field training and so on. However, I did learn how to deal with IBM cards, and calculate a Chi squared from tabular data (with a calculator, there was no Excel or SPSS in 1969), which has always stood me in good stead.

The search for a second post was very hard, and the difficulty of finding academic jobs was to be a major theme for the rest of my career. I applied for many jobs and went to many interviews. One place that interviewed me was Bedford College, for a research job on something called the Camberwell Study. It seemed to me that the study leader, George Brown, was following an intellectual journey with a kind of single mindedness that rang bells in my head. However, after the interview I was taken aside and told everyone liked me but I was really too young and inexperienced for the post that needed to be filled.

My eventual second post was far less stressful than the first. This was such a positive experience that I decided I did want to do a higher degree. People talk about 'life-changing experiences', and the MSc at Bedford was one of these for me. I was stunned by the idea of 'health inequality' – that a person's position in society could literally influence the length of life and the risk of various diseases.

Political exile: 1974–78

The road from MSc was, however, to prove very indirect. Like many whose parents were caught up as combatants or as victims of bombing, ethnic cleansing, and other aspects of 'total war', in the Second World War, I was brought up to believe one may need to be prepared to sacrifice or even die for a righteous cause. While studying for the MSc and working at a subsequent research job I met many political activists, some of whom were pretty contemptuous of academics. So I left the academy and took various jobs. I learned to type, worked as a receptionist in an NHS hospital and later as a typesetter in a printing works. These experiences had a profound effect on the way I have thought about health inequality to this day. The notion that people in less socially advantaged jobs have arrived there because they were already in poor health has ever since struck me as totally laughable. In such 'routine/unskilled' jobs energy and resilience are in fact at a far higher premium, and the physical strength and endurance required greater. I would love to see any of the academics who put forward the notion of 'health selection' as a cause of health inequality try to survive the conditions my fellow workers experienced for one year, let alone a lifetime of labour.

Like most routine workers, however, I soon found myself spending a lot of time wishing I was not at work at all. It struck me that life is not that long, that one should spend so much of it wishing time away.

A false start: 1978–82

So in 1978 I decided to try and get back into research. I applied for a clerical post on the British Regional Heart Study, a large field study of the causes of heart disease. The most valuable thing about my time at the Royal Free was the friendship and colleagueship of Lucy Carpenter and Derek Cook. They coached me through an Open University course in statistics (MDT241), despite my lamentably weak mathematical background. I also met such rising stars of social epidemiology as John Fox and Michael Marmot. At this point, I could only contemplate people like John and Michael from a great social distance. Michael to this day likes to remind people that I once made his tea.

Sadly, however, after a while things began to fall apart at the Royal Free. At the end of the summer of 1980, the study leader told me I was not to take further part in the research using the BRHS data. At the time of course, still a 'junior' person with no confidence, I assumed everyone had decided I was too stupid to play a useful part. I began to suffer from panic attacks. Fortunately, however, Lucy was a friend of leading psychologists, Dr (now Professor) Marie Johnstone and her husband Derek. They provided me with a great deal of social support, allowed me to 'jump the queue' for relaxation classes in psychiatric out-patients, and even taught me some clever behavioural techniques to be used in the face of harassment and bullying that I remember to this day. Marie advised me to go away and study for a PhD in order to become a legitimate academic rather than an intermittently glorified clerical assistant. I was lucky enough to be considered for a 'linked' ESRC-funded place to study for the PhD with Adrian Sinfield, a world-renowned expert on unemployment, at Edinburgh University.

My PhD work took me far from medical sociology into the world of social policy. It ended up being a case study in the relationship between research and policy in the 1980s debate on unemployment and health, written up as *Authorities and partisans* (Edinburgh University Press, 1992). Any reader of this chapter interested in more detail of this period will now be able to spot which one of the partially anonymised characters in that book is me, so I will not spend more time on it here.

Getting on the precipice: 1988–96

Once I had my shiny new PhD, in 1988, I was excited at the prospect of an academic career in medical sociology. I guess I should have known better than to think the path would now become smooth to a tenured academic post. I spent two years working at the Institute of Education (IoE) on a project on gender differences in health. I had been told that I should really show that I could do quantitative as well as qualitative studies if I wanted an academic career. So I learned to use SPSS and started to learn some more advanced statistics. But more problems started at the end of this grant (of which I was co-holder), in 1991. There just were no jobs around. I applied to stay at IoE and was not even interviewed. I applied for a lectureship in medical sociology at Essex and similarly did not get an interview. In the end I talked myself into a part time job at The King's Fund for one year.

I then acquired a post teaching sociology to *Nursing 2000* students at Goldsmiths' College, for two years in the first instance but with, it seemed, good chances of lasting longer. The work was very interesting, I enjoyed teaching clinical students again, though it was hard, it taught me a lot and I loved the college. However, at the end of the first year the Nursing 2000 student intake nationally was cut by half, and I was made redundant. In any case, I was told, I would need to prove I could raise more research money before being worthy of a proper academic job.

While working at Goldsmiths I had also been collaborating closely with some colleagues at City University. With three other colleagues I applied for a grant to study unemployment and health using the 1958 British Cohort Study, the National Child Development Study (NCDS). Around this time a new post was being recruited at City for a lecturer to help out on the new MSc in social statistics. When I asked about the post I was told that the fact that my PhD was in social policy (I also taught occasional lectures in 'government statistics and policy debates' in the course) created a problem. One of the tenured lecturers in the sociology department had been promised that no-one would be considered for this new post who might 'step on her toes' so now I had learned data analysis, had some research money (my second ESRC grant) but still no job.

With my P45 in my hand, I got a phone call from Ray Fitzpatrick, then at Nuffield College Oxford who wondered if I would like to come and work on a project he had set up. I would have to take a fall in status from Research Fellow to Research Officer, and they could not afford to pay me full time. My colleagues at City agreed to use some of the money from the 'unemployment and health' project to employ me for two days a week and this, with three days at Nuffield, provided full-time employment for another two years (1993–95).

These were very happy years. The project on unemployment and health proved to be even more exciting than I had hoped. At the same time I got involved through Ray with the development of a new social class measure (the ONS-SEC) designed for use in official statistics. During this period I also received another (small) grant from ESRC to work on new census-linked data, again with Ian Plewis. When things go well, there is, for me, nothing that gets close to being as satisfying as research.

By 1995 I had collected quite a few refereed papers using both qualitative and quantitative methods, and three lots of ESRC money. So when a job was advertised at Surrey University – 'senior lecturer in medical sociology to teach research methods' – it did not seem over-ambitious to apply. I was once again not invited for interview. At the last moment, Nuffield College extended my contract for another year, to 1996.

I had been approached about one or two jobs teaching medical students. However, one needs a certain amount of confidence to face their hostility to social science. After 10 years post-PhD without managing to land an academic post, mine was not up to the demand. I had always really wanted just to teach sociology relevant to health – research was a means to an end. But my confidence was now so shattered I could not face teaching.

Was it worth it? 1995–present day

By this time it had finally penetrated my consciousness that it was not possible for me to have a career of the normal kind in academic medical sociology, teaching as well as doing research. I was therefore grateful when in 1996 I was recruited by Michael Marmot on a three-year contract to work on his Whitehall II Study at UCL medical school. This would take me once and for all away from medical sociology into mainstream social epidemiology. I have learned to keep myself going with a series of funded projects by hopping from one bandwagon to the next – greatly helped by the fact that 'health inequality' itself became a bandwagon after 1997. The Whitehall II money was followed by an ESRC Fellowship that enabled me to write a book on health inequality, then an ESRC Research Network and finally an ESRC Centre. In the course of this, UCL agreed my promotion to a personal chair and, I thought, had also agreed to underwrite my salary in the event that I fail to raise more research money. However, the medical school did not approve this, saying that spare HEFC money in my department (Epidemiology) should be used only to finance academics with medical degrees. So I ended my career never having had a HEFC-funded post (even my wages as ESRC Centre director went on the form as 'incurred costs').

Maybe academic social science never was the search for truth and welfare that I fantasised as a student and a young(er) researcher? I feel I have, at times, had to take part in a number of rather boring and unscholarly data-bashing exercises in order to maintain my insecure place in the business. I have found in social epidemiology somewhere I am tolerated rather than an intellectual homeland. But maybe part of my problem has been that I was too slow to wake up to the realities of academe, and clung too hard to my illusions.

Looking back now I have to admit that the lack of security actually goaded me into greater achievements than I ever would have managed in a nice secure lectureship. I am good at research. I am good at promoting teamwork and the free flow of ideas. I would not have applied for an ESRC Research Centre in 2006 if my job had not been (once again) under threat. But it has been fascinating to put together a team of social and biological scientists to work on life-course data just at this time, when so much more data is becoming available. Especially since I am now 'emerita' which means I can carry on writing and discussing without having to fill in too many more forms.

What would I say to those earlier on in their careers in sociology? This will not be popular, but learn to analyse data. Never mind fancy statistics because the next most important thing is to find the people you most like to work with and treasure these relationships (some of them might even be statisticians). Never let an idea be lost, the things you feel frustrated not to be working on are what you will apply for grants to do next, and you can never have too many of these. If you value excitement and autonomy over security, there is still no other job as good as an academic one, but it cannot be all things to all people.

TWENTY-FOUR

The pursuit of a sociological career overseas and the navigation of an outsider perspective

Lara Killick

Lara Killick is an assistant professor in sociology of sport and sport pedagogy and the graduate director of the Health, Exercise and Sciences Department at the University of the Pacific, California. Originally from London, Lara completed all of her education in the UK before moving stateside to take this position. Heavily involved in the BSA throughout her education, Lara was a co-convener of the post-graduate forum from 2005 to 2009 and founded the early career forum with Ruth Lewis in 2009.

As I sat down to brainstorm my thoughts for this chapter, I was reminded of an exercise I recently completed for a 'Faculty Development Center Bootcamp' (Yes, yes, I know many of you reading this just faltered over the spelling of 'center' – bear with me, strange spelling is just one of the many side effects of full immersion into life in the United States). A few weeks into the programme, we were charged with a reflection task: how did we get here and where do we want to go? In both regards, I took a path slightly less travelled. First, a four-year sabbatical between my undergraduate and graduate school experiences, in which I travelled the world and set up my own business, then to the USA to pursue an academic career. I have been asked to reflect on both of these here, particularly the challenges and rewards I have experienced as an overseas early-career sociologist.

Awakening my sociological imagination

I discovered sociology relatively late. A state-educated girl from south-east London, I completed my A-levels in English literature, business studies and physical education and was barely even aware of the discipline that would come to shape so much of my life. The first in my family to attend university, I headed to Durham to earn a BA in 'sport in the community'. The curriculum adopted a broad approach to the study of sport, but sociology was notably absent. My sociological awakening was facilitated by the arrival, in my final year, of Dr Emma Poulton, a sociologist of sport who became my early mentor and dissertation adviser. However, my initial introduction to the subject was short-lived. Struggling to deal with recent life events (death of my boyfriend and my parents' acrimonious divorce), I reached graduation completely burnt out and packed my bags for a two and a half year trip around the world. In part to emotionally re-charge but also to expand my world view beyond Europe and the life I had become so familiar with.

The trip had a profound effect on several elements of my life. Spending 30 months as a perennial cultural outsider fuelled my inherent curiosity about the world around me and piqued my interest in the dynamic power relations and subsequent inequities contained within diverse global societies. Stereotypes were challenged, critical questions were raised and my world view was indelibly altered. Driven by my overseas experiences, I started my own sports coaching company on my return to London. The business blossomed but I became increasingly disillusioned with the self-serving decision making processes of those in power and the deep-rooted systems of oppression, inequality, discrimination and sexism that I encountered. Beyond my recognition at the time, my 'personal troubles' were intersecting with my growing awareness of 'public issues' and I was laying the foundations for a career in applied sociology. I sought clarity, a framework to understand it all and the tools to engender change. In 2004, I dissolved the business and returned to the University of Leicester to complete an MA in the sociology of sport. The journey abruptly escalated. There was no turning back. Suddenly, I had a language to explore, probe and examine the inequities I had seen and experienced during my travels and in the sports industry. I was challenged to think so hard that it hurt. I was hungry for more.

Survival

My MA transitioned into a PhD in the same field but at a different institution. This proved to be a treacherous experience. Beyond the inherent difficulties of completing the thesis itself (the isolation, the emotional labour, the never-ending feelings of fraud/self-critique etc), I also found myself plunged into the politics of academia. Despite the best efforts of my supervisor, I got caught in the crosshairs of long-entrenched power plays between senior faculty members; the ramifications of which had a significant impact on my mental health, self-confidence and personal relationships. It was a torturous time but one that I survived thanks to the significant support of my partner, my mentors and most notably, my network of colleagues from the BSA's post-graduate forum (PGF). The experience armed me with several life lessons that have come to shape my subsequent career trajectory. First, while academia is definitely the career for me, I learnt that the ruthless, pressurised, political and misogynistic environment of a research intensive department is not. This revelation drew my attention to the diversity of higher education institutions and the importance of selecting the correct 'fit' as I transitioned from PhD student to academic faculty. I carefully researched the institutional mission and department dynamics of potential job opportunities and prioritised these factors in my job search. Second, I learnt the value of support networks, especially those situated outside of your immediate work environment. The PGF and BSA more broadly, were integral elements of my support system. They provided valuable perspective on my experiences and offered the emotional and pastoral support needed to survive my destructive PhD environment. I remain a strong advocate for forums in which students/faculty can develop similar networks of support and challenge institutionalised forms of discrimination. Finally, I learnt the importance of a strong and 'present' mentor network, particularly for young female scholars in a male-dominated field. The sage advice and astute insights provided by my supervisor and other key mentors were critical to my wellbeing, my short-term survival and my long-term career development. In hindsight these were valuable lessons to learn so early in my career. While at the time it was a deeply difficult arena to navigate, my experiences became the impetus to pursue a career outside of the UK. Furthermore, the holistic development of my students, the ongoing engagement with systems of oppression and the empowerment of disenfranchised groups have driven my research agenda and become the cornerstones of my academic philosophy.

Making the transition

As my PhD scholarship neared its completion, I started to consider my options. I had long harboured a dream to live abroad and this juncture in my life appeared to be a perfect opportunity to realise this dream. My primary location of choice was the US. During my six-month traverse of the county in 2000/1, I was intrigued by the inherent contradictions I had observed. For example, despite being the so-called 'land of the free', I encountered many residents who were denied basic personal freedoms and existed in a structure that limited their agency. I was fascinated by the principal role of religion, the divisive two-party political system and the abundant stereotypes that surrounded American people. I was curious to experience these elements of US society from a lived perspective; particularly how these paradoxes play out in the fragments of everyday life.

The first challenge was familiarising myself with the US job search process. I needed a cultural guide. I reached out to one of my US friends, Jenn, at the time a junior faculty member at a Californian State university. She directed me towards the American version of jobs. ac.uk[1] and the search began. Truthfully, I had never really considered or explored the subtle variances between the UK and US educational systems. I had a vague sense that they were different and it wasn't long before I encountered a host of unfamiliar words (for example, tenure-track; assistant/associate professor; adjunct faculty), all of which required considerable translation and detailed explanation. My introduction to the US educational system was underway.

I applied and was called to interview for my 'dream job'; a tenure-track faculty position at a small liberal arts institution in California that combined my former life as a coach/educator with my current one as a sociologist. Challenge # 2: The US interview process. Through my PGF colleagues I was aware of the UK higher education interview process; a one-day affair, all the candidates together, a 'job talk' and a relatively brief panel interview. The US version was a different beast altogether. Two full days on campus, individual interviews with over 10 faculty and administration, breakfast, lunch and dinner with the department, minimal sleep and an hour-long teaching episode. A test of endurance as much as anything, but also an extensive insight into US campus life. Well, I 'endured' and a couple of weeks later received a phone call informing me that I got the job and would start that August. My excitement at receiving the job offer combined with my naivety of the system prevented me from engaging in any sort of negotiation around my salary, my benefits or start-up costs. My first missed opportunity, I had much to learn it seemed.

Leaving my family was hard and the initial transition was brutal. I arrived to 100-degree heat and was thrown into the whirlwind of a campus preparing for the new academic year. It all seemed so overwhelming. I was isolated and alone. An outsider the minute I opened my mouth, my accent revealing my foreign status. I wasn't only making the transition from PhD student to faculty but also crossing into a whole new educational system. One I felt ill-equipped to navigate. I was bombarded with unfamiliar terminology (for example, tenure, P&T, GEs, GPA, sophomore) and immersed in a system that felt inherently foreign (for example, grades of 99% being awarded, no cohort system instead classes containing a blend of freshman, juniors and seniors, the size of tuition fees, discerning between State, UC, private and for-profit institutions). I felt like a zoo animal at times, my strange verbiage and accent a source of much hilarity for my students and colleagues. My frustration heightened by the sense that we *should* be speaking the same language, that this culture *should* feel familiar, that communication *shouldn't* be this hard. My cultural references had been completely pulled from under my feet. My students didn't even know what cricket, rugby or netball *were*, let alone their sociogenesis and social significance in the UK. My well-used cadre of sporting case studies were completed stripped of meaning and the names, events and stories offered by my students resonated little with me.

It was a steep learning curve but my outsider status does accord me some advantages. The students revel in the novelty of my accent, they are curious about my life experiences and fascinated by life outside of the US. Under the guise of curiosity, I find myself being able to probe some of their deepest cultural norms and values without them retreating to deep defensive positions. Drawing on my own experiences, I help them explore and consider alternative perspectives and offer a different lens to approach discussions. Making friends has been eased by my outsider status; I stand out in a crowd, my voice marking me as 'different', unique, more easily remembered. Furthermore, drawing on my sociological training has helped me to make sense of these personal lived experiences as an outsider. For example, as I started to exhibit quiet symbols of my heritage at work, a Union Jack postcard on my office door, pictures of London in frames on my wall, I critically reflected on my efforts to retain some connection with the motherland. A flag I had never associated with 'back home' (indeed something I had often considered a symbol of shame, racism and xenophobia) being appropriated as a source of pride, identity and connection with my roots. Somehow I grow simultaneously 'more British' and 'more American' every day.

Four years on, I find myself adapting. The initial frustrations have long since passed replaced by a growing understanding of the complexities of US society. The elements of my life that at first seemed so foreign and overwhelming have become 'normal' and everyday. As with my initial move, I fall back on sociological frameworks to help make sense of my emotions. I contemplate the fluidity of identity, my performance of self, the cultural differences between the US and the UK and my growing affinity for the former, the social desire to 'belong' and the consequences of being considered an 'outsider'.

Closing thoughts

The pursuit of an academic career in the current educational climate is not for the faint hearted. Job opportunities are dwindling; higher education is becoming increasingly 'impact' orientated and the demands placed on faculty members are ever expanding. Neither is the engagement of our sociological imaginations an easy endeavour. It is difficult to 'switch off'. The 'job' follows you wherever you go as that which you study are the very interactions and systems in which you yourself are enmeshed. Your 'laboratory' surrounds you. But, if you commit to the journey you will be rewarded. A life defined by the sociological endeavour is one of intellectual curiosity, commitment to societal change and contains many opportunities to challenge and extend your life experiences. The discipline has provided me with a worldview, language and conceptual tool kit to be able to question, examine, problematise and make sense of both my own lived experiences and the world I am a part of. Sociology has also opened the door for me to experience life in other cultures. Despite the challenges I discussed above, the moments where I regret my decision to move overseas to pursue my career are rare indeed. If you wish to follow a similar path, be prepared to engage in substantial emotional labour and experience times of cultural isolation, frustration and the ongoing negotiation of your own sense of identity. But revel in the 'otherness', use it to develop your awareness of difference and stoke the fire of inquisitiveness. Hone your analytical skills and develop a broader range to your sociological toolbox by immersing yourself in the unfamiliar. Mobilise your different perspective to open a world of possibilities for your students. Your outsider perspective can bring to life endless debates and discussions among those whom you encounter. Enjoy the ride!

Note
[1] The Chronicle of Higher Education, if you are interested, see http://chronicle.com/section/Home/5

TWENTY-FIVE

Tales from the field: applied policy research and the sociological imagination

Carol McNaughton Nicholls

Carol McNaughton Nicholls joined NatCen Social Research in 2008, becoming co-head of Crime and Justice Research, and is now a director at Truth Consulting. Carol has held research grants from the ESRC, European Commission and the Nuffield Foundation, and managed many commissioned research projects for central government departments, including the Ministry of Justice and Department of Health. She is a qualitative research expert, passionate about situating lived experiences within social and cultural contexts and enabling exploration of highly sensitive issues. She is also an editor of the textbook, *Qualitative research practice: A guide for social science students and practitioners*, (SAGE, 2014).

In 1997 I started my degree course at the University of Glasgow. I had a burning interest in the world, and no idea about the way in which academia (or indeed most social institutions) operated. I was accepted to read English Literature. Glasgow University offered a flexible degree course, with students initially taking three subjects and specialising after their second year. At the advice of my director of studies, as my third subject, I took 'sociology', though I was unsure what it was really about.

Starting to engage with this subject it was as if the scales fell from my eyes. Finally the absurd, complex, multi-layered social world around me could be actively scrutinised, rendered visible and better understood. It was a revelation to me that everyday social institutions, practices and behaviours that we take for granted could be understood as socially constructed – knowledge that seemed both utterly obvious yet also exhilarating.

Sociology, was, and is to me about attempting to understand systematically the way societies are organised and how we and others experience life within these social structures and are affected by them. Most sociologists go on to develop particular theoretical or empirical areas of expertise to which they apply their sociological understanding. The ability to conduct social research, generate and interpret data about social phenomena, and communicate clearly the insight this leads to are also key skills of a sociologist.

After my first two years at the University of Glasgow, I went on to specialise in sociology, focusing on feminist theory and criminology, alongside research methods. Wonderful lecturers, such as Michelle Burman, and Paul and Barbara Littlewood informed my passion for sociology. Drawing on the courses I had already completed and at the suggestion of my supervisor, my undergraduate dissertation focused on the policing of sexual assault, interviewing specialist police officers working in Glasgow. So my first piece of advice: find a supervisor whose work you admire and then take their advice.

Following my first degree I went on to complete an MSc in social research at the University of Edinburgh, learning a great deal from my cohort of fellow students, and then a PhD from Glasgow University, focusing on transitions through homelessness. This was research in which I explored lives coloured by traumatic experiences and interpersonal abuse. Indeed it was recognition of this that solidified my research interest: even when conducting research about addiction, homelessness or mental ill health, the narratives of participants often highlighted traumatic experiences such as domestic violence or abuse as a catalyst for these related issues. After working within academia as a research fellow, I have gone on to become a social researcher specialising in qualitative research with a focus on sexual abuse, interpersonal violence or other traumatic experiences. In this position, as an empirical sociologist, I would also assert that sociology should be constructive and transformative. The understanding about the social world that social research provides should be capable of being practically applied – whether through informing social policy, evaluating social programmes, or rendering visible hidden social problems.

I was struck then when reflecting on my career for this chapter, just how much it has come full circle and what a privilege it remains to be leading the research I do. As a senior research director and then co-head of the Crime and Justice team at the National Centre for Social Research (NatCen Social Research), I have specialised, alongside brilliant and supportive colleagues, in leading research projects focusing on different forms of abuse and violence, with survivors, perpetrators and professionals working in the field.

My research has included a varied remit – exploring what is known about the sexual exploitation of boys and young men; identifying appropriate processes for staff in mental health services to ask about and effectively respond to experiences of abuse; and interviewing convicted sexual offenders about their experiences in prison. A research career should be varied – in each research project you work on you will find new connections with other professionals and individuals from whom you can learn and connections you can build upon.

Why did I seek to become a social researcher focusing on this substantive area and qualitative methodology? While completing my degree course I selected a book from a list of important sociological texts, called *Understanding sexual violence: A study of convicted rapists* by Diana Scully (Routledge, 1990). The findings were fascinating, but to me, even more fascinating was the methods chapter. How had the author gained access to her participants, conducted the interviews, analysed the data and dealt with the myriad ethical and legal issues such research brings? These questions are ones I myself and the team of researchers with whom I work, now deal with on a day-to-day basis. Now, every research project brings new questions, challenges and insight. But I remain profoundly connected to the sociological imagination imbued from my early academic studies and thankful that such a path has enabled me this career.

So what advice would I provide to people starting out as sociologists?

As someone who has a fulfilling career in social research, I can only reflect on my own experiences and hope this may be helpful.

First, for those people studying sociology for the first time, enjoy it. Career options following this are diverse. My friends who studied sociology alongside me have entered a range of professions: from academia, to central government, to social work, policy roles in charities or public services such as the NHS. I can only really advise on developing a research career: but sociology is probably one of the most relevant areas of study for those seeking a social research career. For you, I would advise the following:

- *Cast your net wide* I have focused on a range of different substantive issues. I have experienced using many different research methods over the years, from survey interviewing in needle exchanges to qualitative life history interviews in prison. All of this helps hone the craft of research, and make you better informed when designing and planning studies. So if you would like to have a career in research, start gaining real experience now. Find a role assisting with a research project, transcribing interviews, setting up online focus groups, or recruiting participants. These practical skills are always in demand.
- *Engage with the world* Sociologists, I think, are fascinated by society. To be a good sociological researcher you have to be able to engage with the social and cultural world around you, adapt to different circumstances and build rapport with a range of people. Myopia should have no place in social research, but sadly it can. So, I would suggest, have an open but not an empty mind, draw on different theories, and disciplines, imagine new ways of interpreting your data, and develop your own research practice, drawing on what has gone before. And always, put yourself in the position of the participant when you plan, conduct and analyse your research. Treat them and their accounts with respect.
- *Communicate* It is not enough to just understand social issues, to have impact we have to be able to communicate our findings, so publish papers, present findings at seminars, present to your colleagues, talk to practitioners, communicate findings to research participants or involve them in communicating the findings. Conducting research is the first step – communicating it well is another step altogether, but the two are irreducibly linked. We have an ethical obligation to research funders and participants to make sure the research we conduct is genuinely useful.
- After starting out and exploring different facets of the social world, find what you *care deeply about*. Passion for your subject will drive itself. It is not necessarily an easy path to take – competition for research funding is fierce; as is it for research positions, where you may find yourself conducting just as many administrative tasks for each interesting piece of research. But with passion for the subject, it

does not seem like work, it seems like a vocation and each challenge can be overcome. Each researcher has their own area of interest, and it is advisable to find yours through taking the steps outlined above.

- *Carry your skills with you* There are a wide range of professional spheres where the skills you gain can be applied and adapted. An ability to generate sociological insight into how people behave, to obtain and interpret data, and to communicate clearly, I think, will always be valued.

To end, I will reflect on one of the questions I was asked to consider when writing this chapter. What would I have done differently? In terms of my career I would say nothing. I have been lucky enough to obtain an education that imbued in me a passion for social research, to work with many highly intelligent and talented individuals, to carve a career that allows me to focus on research I feel passionate about researching, and over the years, to meet many interesting people, in some *very* interesting situations. I also now teach qualitative research methods and work to support other researchers hone their own craft.

There is one change that I could suggest, however, without sounding overly sentimental. I wish that some of the accounts of human suffering I have heard in the course of my research I had the power to change. From the mother of an abused child, groomed over many months speaking about how it has had an impact on the entire family, to a survivor of rape who feels utterly let down by the sentence received by the perpetrator, to a young person convicted of a sexual offence who is now full of shame, remorse, and fully aware that they have not only deeply affected the life of their victim but also their own, to an older man, homeless for over 20 years, speaking of how he has lived his life 'away to nothing'. These accounts are affecting and powerful, and it can be frustrating at times, wondering how research can really invoke change. But I think we do have to believe that it can. A world without such research could be one where these accounts may go unheard and unexamined. So we need sociology, to be able to critique, examine and understand the society that we live in and the experiences of all those who live alongside us.

However it is not enough just to try to understand, to be truly relevant the sociological imagination should also be used as a force for change. If society is socially constructed, I believe we have the power to affect the way it is constructed, although perhaps modestly – by informing policy and practice, evaluating programmes or informing campaigns focusing on social injustices that have been rendered visible through the sociological imagination.

References

Scully, D, 1990, *Understanding sexual violence: A study of convicted rapists*, London: Harper Collins (1994 reprint, London: Routledge). An evocative methodology chapter brings to life the research process in a fascinating and original study.

Ritchie, J, Lewis, J, McNaughton Nicholls, C, Ormston, R, 2014, *Qualitative research practice: A guide for social science students and researchers*, London: SAGE

TWENTY-SIX

What sociology means to me: exploring, imagining and challenging

Kate Woodthorpe

Kate Woodthorpe is a senior lecturer in sociology in the Department of Social and Policy Sciences at the University of Bath (2010 to date). Prior to this she was a lecturer in health studies in the Faculty of Health and Social Care at the Open University (2008–10), and completed her PhD in the Sociological Studies Department at the University of Sheffield (2003–07). She gained her Bachelor's degree in sociology at Lancaster University (1998–2001) and her Master's degree at the University of Warwick (2002–03). Kate's research examines contemporary death practices, including funeral costs, professional development and cemetery usage. She is currently the director of studies for the sociology and social policy degree programmes at the University of Bath.

What a fantastic opportunity this is, to be able to write about how I feel about sociology and what it has added to my life. Sociology has enormous value as an academic discipline that is based on informed opinion, intelligible theoretical ideas, rigorous research and robust arguments, but we do not often get the chance to shout about it.

For me, being a sociologist is more than spouting hot air. It is about trying to understand *why* things happen, how they could differ, what could change and where. It is about exploration and imagination, challenging systems, people and procedures, and (it is to be hoped) providing solutions or suggestions for the future. It is about not accepting the status quo. It is about finding your own feet, thinking independently and challenging others. It is about contributing to a civilised and inclusive society. Sociology is a discipline bursting with ideas and potential, but sociologists also have too quiet a voice within the public sphere at present, and there is much more to be done to continue to cement the discipline's credibility.

My own path into sociology has been one of good fortune, fortuitous timing, hard work and persistence. Certainly, I have always thought of myself as very lucky that I was introduced to sociology. In the 1990s sociology was not an option of study at school, so when it was suggested by my parents that I consider it as a degree subject I had very little prior knowledge. Having done A-levels in history, politics and economics, first and foremost I knew that I enjoyed learning about *people*. But I also knew that I was not moved by understanding people in terms of them as individuals. Rather, what I liked was understanding what made people get on (or not) together, what made communities cohere or revolt, and what made societies 'work' more broadly. I wanted to learn more about how these intersected with wider belief systems, institutions, cultural expectations and the political economy.

For me then, sociology was a natural 'fit'. Almost from day one of my undergraduate degree at Lancaster University, I felt fortunate to have found an academic discipline that I cared about. During those years, I observed my peers bemoaning a degree that they considered boring and studying topics that they detested, all in the name of getting a 'well paid' job at the end of it. "How odd", I recall thinking, "if they hate [the subject] now, won't they dislike the job they want to get at the end too?" Quite possibly so – from what I have heard a lot of those peers are now working in completely different areas, some well-paid and some not!

Good fortune has also been with me with regard to where I chose to continue my study and then work. Following my undergraduate degree I did a master's at the University of Warwick, which had a different 'feel' in terms of the department and the sociologists working there. It was, I think, really fruitful to see the breadth of sociology by moving between different departments as a student, and to learn how varying parts of the sociological community conceptualised the world around them differently. Most often, this was apparent in the research pursuits of the academics; at the time, while at Lancaster, a lot of the work being done was in relation to gender and technology. The focus and content of undergraduate teaching naturally complemented this. At Warwick, in contrast, the sociological interests of the staff with whom I was engaged were in research methods, health and emotion, making for a varied and intellectually stimulating learning experience.

After that I moved to the University of Sheffield for my doctoral studies and experienced a terrific four years learning how to *do* research and developing my ability to teach. What was most important for me was that the sociologists with and for whom I worked at that point set appropriately high expectations about written work, research conduct and teaching – not so beyond reach that you felt that you could not achieve them, nor too low that you felt as if you were coasting. The department at Sheffield was a nurturing and supportive environment, and for that I am grateful as it was a solid foundation from which to develop my sociological identity.

Becoming a sociologist

Certainly, to anyone considering a sociological career in academia I would encourage you to expose yourself to as many people, ideas and institutional cultures as possible. I would also extend this to include working with non-academics; over the last two years I have worked with commercial organisations and it has been an informative experience of learning how different organisations operate. Priorities, speed and ethos can be so varied, and when working in a single institution it is tempting to focus on the day-to-day requirements of the job.

In that way, to sustain a sociological career – especially in the early days – it is a case of being on your own case and reminding yourself to 'think big'. For me, this was about actively using the probation experience at the University of Bath to create a research and teaching strategy that had coherence and continuity. By reminding myself of the bigger picture through the required probationary review process, I was able to generate a sense of where I was going. This may be easier said than done, but as a discipline sociology is expansive enough to enable you to find your place within it and keep evolving.

Having said that, it is important that when thinking big you do not neglect the 'small stuff'. Personally, when it comes to the everyday work of 'being' an academic sociologist, I find research that is both intellectually stimulating in terms of providing insight into how society and all its components work, while at the same time being well written and engaging, a real joy and inspiration. Certainly, there have been a few key books and articles that have intellectually nourished me at key points in my sociological career so far. On occasions when I have been up against deadlines with marking, or frustrated trying to get a paper published or finding time to work on a bid, discovering and engaging in such pieces of work has kept my sociological spirit going. These do not necessarily have to be recently published either, a recent case for me would be a colleague's recommendation of Finch and Mason's (2000) work on inheritance in the book *Passing on*, which is to my mind research that is both academically rigorous while also being a genuinely interesting account of how families manage assets when someone dies.

In bringing together the big thinking and small stuff, I also find inspiration in meeting people whose work I have read and realising that they are human and are nice people! Going to the BSA conference has been a great way to meet others, but it takes time and resources to be able to go year after year, and to get to know people. In that way, I would advise those considering a sociological career to be mindful of short-term gains and the long-term task of building up a profile and network. This longer-term strategy takes persistence and energy, and while it is fulfilling it can also be accompanied by moments of doubt and uncertainty. There is an element of being willing to put yourself 'out there' with this job; with your peers at conferences, with your submissions to journals (always being aware that you could face a disappointing rejection), and with what can feel like speculative bids for research funding. I was once told that to cultivate an academic career developing a 'rhino hide' could be quite helpful. For those lucky enough to have a rhino hide already then this may be more straightforward than for others who need to craft a suitably thick(er) one. Ultimately, the depth of that hide depends on the individual and, as I have been advised, the type of academic one wants to be.

Back to good fortune, though, and I can say that my current departmental colleagues are a helpful everyday inspiration, particularly in meetings where they remind me that behind the administrative requirements of the job there is a real desire for making a difference through research and teaching. The snippets of passion that can shine through when debating how units are taught and assessed, which journals we submit papers to, and how we structure our research themes, can be genuinely uplifting and provide timely reminders about why sociology matters. It's a discipline aiming to document and challenge people, to further society, and for that I am grateful that it exists.

Starting out: what the future may hold

If I could be remembered for one thing in my academic career it would be for passing on this gratitude for the potential of sociological thought to students. As a discipline sociology has an enormous capacity to make a difference and the people who are working in this area right now can, should, and do make a tremendous contribution to society. But those of us lucky enough to be working in this field, and those hoping to enter it, need to be conscious of the future. The currency of knowledge and speed in which it is produced is changing and sociologists need to be clear about what they can contribute to this.

My concerns for the future of sociology are twofold. First, the education system from which I benefited is changing beyond recognition. Although it has only been 15 years since I started my undergraduate degree, the freedom with which I was encouraged to learn is being slowly eroded as a result of the complex interplay of political, social and economic forces. While I was encouraged to explore, be creative, to think for myself and take risks in my assessments, I see students now who are increasingly instrumental in their activities and work, focused on their degree marks and employability. This is not to their detriment necessarily, as it is a product of determination and ambition; and of course it may be isolated to a particular type of student who attends a certain type of university. Without doubt, I see students studying exceptionally hard and wanting to 'do' something with their life. And they are rightly concerned about the graduate market, debts, the financial commitment they are making by doing a degree, and how attractive they will be to employers. But it is with sadness that I observe how for some these concerns now outweigh the valuable skills that can be developed and nurtured while at university, and in particular when studying a subject such as sociology. The ability to think, challenge and take risks is giving way to instrumentalism and self-interest.

My second concern is the role that sociologists perform in the public sphere more broadly. Currently, there remains considerable scope to have a bigger presence as a body of informed people who provide insight, explanations and recommendations about future change. To my mind, getting sociology out there is about hard work and persistence. The challenge for individuals is, I think, to navigate the path of meeting all the other requirements of the academic job and maintaining a sense of integrity as a credible source of knowledge, ensuring that one does not morph into an impulsive social commentator or mouthpiece for someone else. This is no mean feat, but there is much work to do to promote sociological viewpoints – even if these are contested by others within the discipline. Debate and progress are at the heart of sociology, and this needs to be reflected in the public sphere, as much as publications and research funding bids. I have been lucky in feeling the goodwill towards sociologists, and I hope that others have experienced, and will continue to experience, this.

So, at the time of writing this piece, overall I feel hopeful about the future for sociology, chiefly as a product of the hard work of the colleagues I see around me. Through their research, their teaching, their engagement with others, networking and so on, I anticipate and trust that the sociological community will thrive, fostering the next generation of sociologists both through teaching sociology students, and developing career young scholars.

Reference

Finch, J, Mason, J, 2000, *Passing on: Kinship and inheritance in England*, London: Routledge

TWENTY-SEVEN

Social science which engages with the real world

Anthony Heath in conversation with Andrea Scott

Anthony Heath, CBE, FBA is professor of sociology at the Institute for Social Change, University of Manchester, and emeritus professor at the Department of Sociology, University of Oxford. His research interests cover social stratification and mobility, ethnicity, electoral behaviour, social and political attitudes, national identity and social cohesion. He has published many books and over a hundred scientific papers. His most recent book, *The political integration of ethnic minorities in Britain*, was published by OUP in September 2013. He is currently leading a team designing a module of questions on attitudes to immigration for the European Social Survey. Anthony has carried out work for many government and international bodies, including work for UNDP in Bosnia and Herzegovina on social capital and human development and for OECD on racial discrimination.
He was awarded a CBE for services to social science in the 2013 Birthday Honours List.

Andrea: First, can you tell me how it is that you came to be a sociologist?

Anthony: Partly by accident. I studied classics first of all in Cambridge and quite enjoyed classics but wanted to engage a bit more with the contemporary world. Then I switched to economics, partly because I wasn't allowed to switch to psychology because I didn't have enough natural sciences for the Cambridge psychology degree. I moved to economics hoping it would be about understanding the real world and I discovered that it wasn't really; it was all about abstract models. It also required a great deal of mathematics, which I didn't have – my maths simply wasn't good enough compared with the really professional economists. At that time, one of the lecturers was John Goldthorpe and he taught a couple of sociology papers as part of the economics degree. John Goldthorpe, David Lockwood and Philip Abrams were all at Cambridge at that time in the economics faculty and although it was primarily an economics degree, they gave various lectures on different aspects of sociology.

I then realised that sociology, at least in the way John Goldthorpe taught it, was concerned with the real world and that sociology had something interesting to say. I didn't know anything about sociology until I went to these lectures. I thought, "Well actually, I can do this" because it didn't require advanced mathematics and it was what I was looking for, so I more or less stayed a sociologist from then on.

Andrea: Was there something in particular that you were really interested in from the perspective of the real world?

Anthony: Yes, I had one particular interest. At the time, between leaving school and going to university, I worked as a supply teacher in a northern secondary modern school and that was a bit of an eye opener. I also joined a running club up in the North East, where many of the other athletes were miners from the local pits and my regular training partners both worked down the pit.

I realised, in a way I hadn't before, that there were huge social inequalities in Britain and that the working class weren't the frightening people that my rather nice middle-class background had led me to suppose, but they were sharp and intelligent and certainly just as good (or often better) athletes than I was. So, I became interested in social class inequalities. This was in Hartlepool. I went to school in Liverpool and then my dad got a promotion that took him over to Hartlepool and I ran for Burn Road Harriers, which was the Hartlepool running club and the people from the pits were mainly from Blackhall Rocks and Easington.

Andrea: So after you got this interest for sociology, you went to study it and then you went to teach it – is that how your career took off?

Anthony: Yes, but there was the odd hiccup. I actually first worked in the civil service, because I wasn't quite sure what class of degree I was going to get, so I thought "I need a job" and an academic career was going to be difficult to break into unless you got a first, which was very, very rare at that time in economics, so I applied for the civil service and got in. I had a year in the civil service working in the treasury, which I found very interesting but slightly frustrating.

I thought I would never quite fit into this civil service and they gave me unpaid leave to go back to Cambridge and do a doctorate so I was able to keep my options open. I could have gone back to the civil service but the doctorate went well and in those days, you could get jobs even before you had finished, so I already had a fellowship and a teaching post before I had finished my doctorate. I just felt slightly more at home in the academic world than in the civil service. I wasn't quite conformist enough for the civil service and the academic life gives you that freedom to be a bit more critical. I think it was part of the critical nature of sociology that I found appealing and I have no regrets at all. I have had a very lucky career and I have seen all kinds of things outside the academic world so it worked out well.

Andrea: What does sociology mean to you?

Anthony: On the whole, I would like to take an inclusive approach to most things and so there is the sort of sociology that I do, but there are also a lot of very interesting sorts of sociology that other people do that is different from what I do so, in a way, I say, "Sociology is whatever sociologists do." I know best the kind of things that I do, fairly quantitative work but not very high tech, based on analysis of large-scale survey data, so that is what I do. Looking at issues of inequality, class inequality, gender inequality, ethnic inequalities more recently, but I think those are core issues in sociology.

I try to read a bit more widely. I work with a wide variety of people, both qualitative and quantitative. I have also worked with political scientists and lawyers, so in a sense, from working with lawyers and political scientists, you get a sense of where sociology stops and they are doing something else; the political scientists are interested in the operation of political institutions and arrangements, so the impact of electoral systems on vote shares, which I have had to read about, but that is not, to me, sociology.

I find it easier to say what sociology is not, but there are an awful lot of different things that sociology is and I think that is possibly a strength of sociology that it is quite a broad-church and that different approaches can give you different insights. Although I don't do discourse analysis or narrative analysis, I don't do it myself but great insights can come from that kind of work, often ones that one can then test in one's quantitative work. People like Stan Cohen and Steve Ball, who are very qualitative sociologists and I find their work extremely interesting and stimulating, sometimes more interesting and much more readable than the quantitative work.

Andrea: Have your ideas on what sociology is changed over the course of your career?

Anthony: Well, I am not sure; certainly with some things. When I started my career, many concepts hadn't been developed or discovered. I started work in the mid-1960s, so Bourdieu's work or Coleman's work on social capital, cultural capital and so on, those hadn't been thought of at that time and I would very much embrace these as core elements of sociology, although I think I had always seen social relationships as being central to sociology and that is what makes it different from, say, economics, which takes a very individualistic approach and tends to ignore social interaction and the way people relate to each other.

I was probably already prepared for those kinds of development because they fitted in with my conception of sociology but then the conception develops into the life of this work by James Coleman and I think social capital is absolutely central to an awful lot of sociology but also cultural capital and the work on identities, which I probably was more aware of because that had been an important part of the Chicago School of symbolic interactionism, which I came across certainly in the 1960s, probably from Philip Abrams' lectures, but of course it goes back much earlier. Yes, my ideas about sociology have been evolving all the time in the light of the new work that has been going on.

Andrea: In terms of your personal experience, has there been anything that has surprised you, made you feel alienated or even more drawn to sociology?

Anthony: I have never found (well, after my years of doing my doctorate research) I never found issues of abstract grand theory, particularly interesting. I think probably some of the abstract Marxism that was very fashionable in the 1970s, I found pretty opaque and pointless because it didn't seem to connect – it goes back to my original reason for wanting to do sociology, understanding the real world, so when things get too remote from the real world and particularly in jargon that I don't understand, often because I haven't made the effort to understand, it should be said, I tended to be a bit put off, so I never got very excited by all of the work of the French Marxists of Poulantzas or Althusser. Indeed I never had any time for Ralph Miliband's work because I just couldn't see where it was going and how it was actually going to help and address real world issues, for example, the disadvantages that coalminers experienced. It is the things that didn't connect with the real world, or my experience of the real world, which was a pretty limited one, which put me off. So I don't have much time for structure–agency debates because I can't see how they would help me try to grapple with the real world issues of which there are so many pressing issues of social justice that I suppose I get a bit, not irritated, but I couldn't quite see the point of them.

When there are such important world issues of inequality and injustice, why are we spending time, a bit like medieval theologians, arguing about abstruse matters of philosophy? So, yes, there have been things that I have not been excited by and, at times, particular things like theories of the state became quite dominant and I felt a bit alienated by some of those debates. But when they weren't so remote, I did find other Marxists like John Westergaard who did tackle real world issues really interesting.

Andrea: Would you advise somebody, say your younger self, to study sociology, looking back?

Anthony: I think so. I think my younger self would have been very happy and really would have thought it a wonderful dream to have gone on and done all of this work subsequently and I think there are huge challenges in contemporary society, not just in Britain but also worldwide challenges. I think that it needs sociologists and I suppose I was a little bit hesitant because I was going into sociology at a time when it was, in Britain, developing quite fast and there were opportunities.

I might say to my younger self now that possibly it might be a more difficult context because you don't walk straight from a doctorate into a tenured job. I had a lot of insecurity as a young post-doc. It seemed a great success to get your post-doc but then a couple of years later you are worrying about how to get onto the next position. I would be a little bit cautious in my advice to a young person because I think the career opportunities are not as good as they have been in the past, but the excitement is still there and the challenges. In a sense, the challenges make it even more important that people work on them so I wouldn't dissuade anybody, but I would just warn them.

I think some realism that the academic career is not the easiest is needed. You also need to be open minded because there are quite a lot of interesting research careers that people can move into but you need to equip yourself so that you can get a job, so yes, I think a bit of realism about what you need.

Andrea: Are there any skills, other than a doctorate or post-doc that young people wanting to go into sociology now need to have? What would those be with regards to additional skills?

Anthony: To have a successful academic career, you have got to be able to write well. You have got to enjoy writing because if you are struggling (and some of my contemporaries were extremely clever but they found it very, very difficult to write it down) and so if you can't write well on schedule and actually be prepared to send it off then you don't want an academic career because it will be frustrating.

It is not just because of publish or perish in the RAE and the REF and so on. I just think to get the most out of an academic career, you do need to write. Further to an academic career, you also need to enjoy teaching and I know you can certainly have a research career without teaching but I always say that if you want an academic career in the university and you don't enjoy teaching then again, it is not going to be satisfying for you and it certainly won't be satisfying for your students.

In teaching skills, what you need to learn is that an enthusiasm for young people and teaching them is important. I think those would be the first things and then there are the more technical issues about skills and, you know, the further, more sociological skillset, where I would think it is important to be fairly broad. I think it is important to have quantitative skills because an awful lot of the work is quantitative and you won't be able to read the quantitative work or similarly in jobs and certainly in applied work if you are not quantitative, but luckily, we don't have to be that quantitative in sociology, definitely in my time, you don't have to be a mathematician.

Another thing that is important when thinking about the whole span of a career and you go on learning is to be open minded rather than just learning one trick and sticking with it. I have seen people who had just learnt one trick early in their careers and have stayed with that one trick. It can be very successful but again, advising a young person, I would say to be more rounded and because technically, methodologically and substantively things have changed very fast.

Therefore, in order to pursue when it is changing really fast, you have got to be continually developing yourself and your skillset rather than thinking, "Right, now I have learned the techniques to be a good sociologist." They might be the techniques good for the next five years but you already need to be thinking about the techniques that may be different in order to maintain the career.

Andrea: Looking back on your career, is there anything that you would have done differently?

Anthony: Yes, I should have spent a year or more in the States and I didn't really have the self-confidence or courage to go off and actually I thought of going early on in my career and just trying to get experience. I even tried to fix up a trip to, I think it might have been Berkeley or one of the west coast places, but my then professor wasn't particularly supportive and it sort of fizzled out. I later had a chance to go to The Center for Advanced Study in the Behavioral Sciences at Stanford University and that was another missed opportunity although it was more for family reasons that I didn't go. I think it would have been very helpful to have gone to the States because, I think, American sociology is very big and very, very good and has very high professional standards. They are a bit insular but I am sure that I would have learnt a lot very fast if I had had a year of immersion in a good American university.

I think that was a mistake, not to have gone to the States. I am sure I made lots of other mistakes but that is the big strategic one where definitely I should have tried harder to go. Although, I have been quite lucky, things have worked out. I was very lucky to be involved, and I started off being really theoretical drawing on my economic background and I found my feet when I was invited to join Chelly Halsey and John Ridge on the Nuffield College social mobility study and that is when I realised that this is what I enjoy doing.

So, that was great. Yes, that was a good move, a lucky move. I think on the whole, I would like to have learned more statistics earlier on. I always felt I sort of struggled a bit and I would benefit from having more maths. I would also benefit from having better languages, but you can't do everything. I think possibly I didn't take sufficient advantage of some opportunities.

I think my advice for a young person would be to take advantage of the opportunities and be critically aware of them – so probably be a bit adventurous. I think it has worked out well so I shouldn't belittle myself too much but possibly I stayed too long in Oxford; it might have been, again, a good idea to move to different intellectual environments, meet a different range of people, tackle other issues, but I have been very lucky.

Andrea: Is a sociology career more luck than design?

Anthony: Yes, I don't think I had any grand design and some of the things I was most pleased with were almost wholly luck although some of it, in any career, is just being in the right place at the right time so it was luck getting into the Nuffield mobility study. If John Ridge and Chelly had been, sort of, keen to keep it to themselves, they could have left me out, they had no need of me and I had no particular skill but I acquired the skills as a result of working with them so I was very lucky to be invited.

I was very, very lucky at a later stage when one of the criticisms of the social mobility study was that it was only on men and I thought, "Actually, if this is a fair criticism then we ought to look at women, gender differences and how these things play out," so I thought that it would be nice to try and do some of the same things but with a representative example of women as well as men.

I discovered the British election surveys because they were of course representative surveys and some of my colleagues who had worked on the electoral surveys kindly ran a few cross-tabs so I that could look at gender differences and then we decided that we would try and put in a bid to run the next election survey and I would be the sociology expert along with a political science colleague.

Unfortunately, he became ill and I thought that I would have a go anyway and I think it was Clive Payne, who said, "Oh, if you are going to put in a bid to do with the election survey, why don't you talk to Roger Jowell, he is very good and would be keen to run the fieldwork side." Again, it was luck that I met Roger and we got on extremely well, we saw things in similar ways so that was a wonderful collaboration, and I hugely enjoyed working with Roger and with John Curtice – and that was pretty much luck.

Again, with John, I think it was Kenneth Macdonald who said, "Oh, we have got this bright young doctoral student, who might need a job. Why don't you think about employing him as your research assistant on the study?" So there was a lot of luck about getting into the election survey, working with Roger and working with John. That was great but I became a political scientist and I ran the British election surveys from 1983 to 1997 and that was all totally unplanned but very stimulating and I am very glad to have had that chance to work with Roger and John.

References

Ball, S, 1981, *Beachside Comprehensive: A case-study of secondary schooling*, Cambridge: Cambridge University Press

Cohen, S 1972, *Folk Devils and Moral Panics*, London: MacGibbon and Kee

Coleman, J, 1988, Social capital in the creation of human capital, *American Journal of Sociology*, 94: S95–120

Halsey, H, Heath, AF and Ridge, JM 1980 *Origins and Destinations: Family, Class and Education in Modern Britain*, Oxford: Oxford University Press

Heath, A, Jowell, R and Curtice, J, 1985, *How Britain Votes*, Oxford: Pergamon Press

Mead, GH, 1934 *Mind, Self and Society*, Chicago: University of Chicago Press

Westergaard, J and Resler, H, 1975, *Class in a Capitalist Society: A Study of Contemporary Britain*, London: Heinemann

TWENTY-EIGHT

A sporting chance?
Notes on an ongoing career in the sociology of sport

Richard Giulianotti

© Jonathan Long

Richard Giulianotti graduated with a first-class MA (Hons) degree in sociology in 1989 from the University of Aberdeen, where he was also awarded a MLitt in social research methods (1993) and PhD (1996). He was employed at the University of Aberdeen from 1990 to 2006, and then moved to Durham University. In 2011 he took up his current post as professor of sociology in the School of Sport, Exercise and Health Sciences at Loughborough University. He is also professor II at Telemark University College, Norway. His main research interests are in sport, globalisation, development and peace, crime and deviance, and migration.

What is sociology to you?

The simple answer is the study of societies, in terms of all their key dimensions: historical, social, economic, cultural and political. For more depth and detail, rather inevitably, I would draw on C Wright Mills (1959), to highlight four key aspects of the discipline. First, with C Wright Mills, the 'sociological imagination' is marked by the capacity 'to translate personal troubles into public issues' – in other words, you become more able to understand individual experiences and events with respect to deeper social processes and structures. Second, the sociological imagination is not the exclusive terrain of trained sociologists, but evident in much everyday critical reflection and comment by individuals and social groups. Third, the sociological imagination should also harbour a critical standpoint on power relations, and a political and emancipatory focus, underpinned by a commitment to social justice. Fourth, I would add a further point on the sociological *imagination*: the sociologist needs to bring creativity, innovation and imagination to bear on how the issue at hand or research problem is to be identified, studied and explained.

In recent decades, as a subject, sociology has become increasingly complex and diverse in three main ways: first, in its interdisciplinary qualities, as boundaries become more blurred and impractical with other disciplines and sub-disciplines, such as anthropology, criminology, cultural studies, economics, education, geography, law, philosophy, political science, psychology and social policy; second, in the dazzling plurality of theories, methods and substantive fields of inquiry that are spread across the sociological spectrum; and third, as globalisation processes have intensified, so sociology has become an increasingly transnational discipline that is focused on increasingly 'glocal' social phenomena.

Why study sociology?

To give a sociological answer, this is perhaps driven by a mix of socialisation, contextual influences, resource allocation and (minor) risk-taking. In my own case, I had a long-standing curiosity and interest in many of the themes and issues addressed by the discipline, notably regarding social inequalities, social justice and cultural movements. Growing up, I had the benefit of being socialised around plenty of family and friends (notably around different youth subcultures) who adopted a healthy scepticism and criticism towards all sorts of social issues. I started university at Aberdeen in the mid–1980s as a law student, but did not enjoy it, so took what appeared to be a significant career risk by resolving to study whatever was of most interest. (It's worth noting that if a student loan/fees system had been in place, I would probably have acted differently.) After dabbling in different social sciences, I moved into an undergraduate MA in sociology at Aberdeen where I had the benefit of some inspiring teachers, particularly Mike Hepworth and Chris Wright, and a terrific diversity of stimulating subjects, which included consumer culture, the body, youth cultures, crime and deviance, political sociology, the welfare state, nationalism/ ethnicity and migration (inspiring a dissertation on a very local topic: Italian families in north-east Scotland). I enjoyed the wide range of theoretical debates which sought to explain the major social changes of the time, notably neo-Marxist approaches, cultural studies, critical theory and postmodernist/poststructuralist theories. There was a good mix of mature and younger students, and great opportunities to debate issues and throw around ideas.

My first degree allowed me to develop plans for a PhD on a subject – football fan subcultures – that appealed to me in two main senses: first, sport in general was an area of major interest; second, there were pretty obvious differences between the then main sociological paradigms on these subcultures and what I had observed among these groups at first hand. Although for the PhD I had an offer from Oxford and an opening at Salford, I stayed at Aberdeen when full research project funding was put in place: backed by great support and guidance from Norman Bonney and Mike Hepworth, I led on the successful writing of a one-year research bid to the university, followed by three-year and six-month awards from the ESRC, to investigate Scottish football fan groups and youth subcultures, and then Irish football fans.[1] In my first month of paid employment as a sociologist, I was conducting fieldwork at the 1990 football World Cup in Italy with Scotland fans, which led to a paper in *Sociological Review* a year later (Giulianotti, 1991). The research grants saw me through my postgraduate training and into a first permanent post at Aberdeen in 1995.

In retrospect, I have no doubts that staying in Aberdeen was a correct decision in regard to developing my research. The department under the leadership of Steve Bruce was very much research-led, and there was plenty of scope to teach in areas that were of significant research interest. One potential challenge faced in Aberdeen was that I was the only specialist in the sociology of sport. On the other hand, this apparent isolation encouraged me to locate research on sport within a wider social and cultural context, to build links with other research fields (such as the sociology of crime and deviance), to work more with diverse overarching social theories, and in particular to develop research connections and partnerships with more colleagues at other institutions in the UK and overseas. Latterly, Roland Robertson joined our sociology at Aberdeen and it was a terrific surprise to find that he had a major interest in sport (particularly football), and indeed regarded this as an increasingly important field of study. I have since had a lot of fun working with Roland on the interrelations between football/sport and globalisation, which has resulted in two books, many articles and a two-year ESRC research grant.[2]

Why 'be' a sociologist: what does that mean?

Sociology is such a diverse subject that it is impossible to insist on a set range of personal characteristics or focus areas: you might be interested in quantified social trends, small-scale social groups or promoting political transformations. Whatever your interest, I would agree with Wright Mills, Sennett and others who see sociological practice as a craft, requiring creativity, continuous cultivation and a commitment to producing good work. There is also an important interplay between the sociologist and the wider social milieu. On one hand, the sociologist brings the discipline, its craft and its questions into whatever activity is undertaken whether inside or outside formal research or teaching; in somewhat clichéd terms, the sociologist never 'switches off' entirely. I am no different to other sociologists at sport events, who have missed plenty of highlight moments on the field of play due to watching spectators or police–spectator interaction – usually to the bemusement and irritation of our fellow attendees. On the other hand, it is also important for sociologists to appreciate that they will bring something of their distinctive, broader environments and backgrounds into the discipline. To put that point in a transnational context, there's a glocalisation process going on here: the global phenomenon (the discipline of sociology) is interpreted, adapted, and recreated by local and national actors in a diversity of ways. I would be disappointed to see 'difference' being undermined and for the discipline to become more formally standardised than it already is.

What advice would you give to someone starting out in a career in sociology?

My first bit of advice to young academics would be to pick a subject area that interests them the most, so that they are able to engage fully with the discipline and do their best work. Their main aim should be to demonstrate their capacity as independent scholars, in terms of undertaking original and imaginative research and analysis that has clear 'added value' in being distinctive and different to what has been previously produced. So I would strongly encourage young academics to be creative in the problems and issues that are identified, the questions that are asked, and the theory and methods that are brought to bear. That creativity has to be driven by a commitment to say something fresh, to avoid reproducing what has gone before, including in the arguments or the approaches of the young academic's research supervisors or mentors. Creative work might take many forms, such as the innovative application of particular research methods, or the use of new theories within a particular area of research (such as sport), or the study of a new substantive issue or an under-examined social group. I would encourage young academics to engage critically and creatively with a variety of theoretical approaches. Single theoretical paradigms are fine so long as the resultant work is genuinely new and original, rather than going over well-trodden ground or saying pretty much what your mentors and supervisors would say if they addressed the issue. It is more interesting and imaginative to engage with a mix of theories to examine and explain a particular social phenomenon. Young academics should also make the most of their data; at times they may otherwise underestimate the quality and originality of what they have discovered and generated. In terms of writing papers and grant applications, young academics might want to keep in mind three different academic audiences: first, the specialists in their specific research area, with whom they will likely have the most everyday contact; second, research methodologists, who will assess the robustness of the methods of the paper and grant bid – a key factor on which the submission will stand or fall; and third, mainstream social scientists, who are crucial audiences and referees for mainstream journals and for grant applications, and who are perhaps best reached if the paper or grant application shows how this work is relevant to them, with a focus or findings that may be transferred into other research fields. In my own case, I have sought to do this in articles that I have written or co-written on sport-related themes, which have been published in mainstream journals, such as *British Journal of Sociology* and *Sociology* (Giulianotti, 1991; Giulianotti and Robertson, 2004; 2007a; 2012; Giulianotti et al, 2014). A final point would be to encourage young academics to be outward looking and to cross boundaries; to engage with difference (as we often lecture our students). This means talking to sociologists who ask different questions, apply different methods and utilise different theories; it means engaging fully with scholars from other disciplines, whether in the social sciences or beyond; and it involves spending time at conferences with academics from other national and cultural contexts, and from whom you can learn a great deal.

Looking back on your career, what would you have done differently?

Some of my career decisions might be queried, but I doubt that I would act any differently in hindsight. First, switching degrees from law to sociology was a big risk, particularly for the first family member to go to university, and with the New Right in its pomp; but looking back, the move seems more than justifiable in personal if not economic terms. Second, I might also have moved much earlier from my home-town university as a student or academic, but as I noted earlier, throughout that period in Aberdeen, excellent research openings kept falling into place. Third, since my first degree, my specialist research field has been in sport, and like most academics at different career stages, I have had opportunities to move into other specialist subject areas. Criminology has been the obvious option, following early research on football hooliganism and youth subcultures, and later ESRC-funded research into policing and security in sport, including London 2012.[3] Moreover, this is a subject area that has expanded massively in the UK over the past two decades. In sociology, the other research fields of interest have been migration (through prior work on Italian families, and on UK and Irish expatriates in North America and Australasia), and globalisation studies (since developing extensive collaborative work with Roland Robertson, a world expert in this field). However, while I would expect to remain focused primarily on sport, there remain plenty of opportunities to continue to dip into these other research fields in future.

In regard to writing, on reflection there were times at the start of my publishing career when I might have softened my language and tone when engaging critically with other work, and also produced more conventional ethnographic work during my early studies. At this time also, I was involved in producing a lot of edited collections; today, this may not always look like the best CV-building strategy, but these books were fun to do (particularly when working with old friends like Gary Armstrong and Gerry Finn), they opened up a lot of new ground at the time, and helped to build up my international contacts and reputation (see Armstrong and Giulianotti, 1997; 2004; Finn and Giulianotti, 2000). Elsewhere, in my first monograph – *Football: A sociology of the global game* (Polity, 1999) – I might have worked more closely with globalisation theory, which has since become a major research interest. It would be nice to have the opportunity to rectify that omission in future through a fully revised version of the book.

Notes

[1] The ESRC award reference numbers are R000232910 and R000221343.

[2] See Giulianotti and Robertson (2004, 2007a, 2007b, 2009, 2012). The ESRC award reference number, for the project on Scottish football and globalisation with Roland Robertson, is R000239833.

[3] The ESRC award reference for this project is ES/I/0005424/1.

References

Armstrong, G, Giulianotti, R (eds), 1997, *Entering the field: New perspectives on world football*, Oxford: Berg

Armstrong, G, Giulianotti, R (eds), 2004, *Football in Africa*, Basingstoke: Palgrave/Macmillan

Finn, GPT, Giulianotti, R (eds), 2000, *Football culture: Local conflicts, global visions*, London: Frank Cass

Giulianotti, R, 1991, Scotland's Tartan Army in Italy: The case for the carnivalesque, *Sociological Review* 39, 3, 503–27

Giulianotti, R, 1999, *Football: A sociology of the global game*, Cambridge: Polity

Giulianotti, R, Robertson, R, 2004, The globalization of football: A study in the 'glocalization' of the serious life, *British Journal of Sociology* 55, 4, 545–68

Giulianotti, R, Robertson, R, 2007a, Forms of glocalization: Globalization and the migration strategies of Scottish football fans in North America, *Sociology* 41, 1, 133–52

Giulianotti, R, Robertson, R (eds), 2007b, *Globalization and sport*, Oxford: Blackwell

Giulianotti, R, Robertson, R, 2009, *Globalization and football*, London: Theory, Culture and Society, SAGE

Giulianotti, R, Robertson, R, 2012, Mapping the global football field: A sociological model of transnational forces within the world game, *British Journal of Sociology* 63, 2, 33–58

Giulianotti, R, Armstrong, G Hales, G, Hobbs, D, 2014, Global sport mega-events and the politics of mobility: The case of the London 2012 Olympic Games, *British Journal of Sociology*, forthcoming, DOI: 10.1111/1468-4446.12103

Mills, CW, 1959, *The sociological imagination*, Oxford: Oxford University Press

TWENTY-NINE

Sociology: involvement and detachment

Robert Mears

Rob Mears gained a sociology degree from University of Leicester in 1973, an MSc in medical sociology from Bedford College, London and a PhD from Leicester. He is currently professor of sociology and dean of the School of Society, Enterprise and Environment at Bath Spa University. He chaired the QAA National Benchmark Panel in Sociology, was chair of the Sociology Advisory Panel at the HEA National Subject Centre at Birmingham University, and was chair of the British Sociological Association between 2008 and 2011.

Why did I study sociology? Reconstructing motives after decades is always risky, but I am sure that one thing that drew me to sociology as a teenager was its novelty. Its absence from the school curriculum gave the discipline a certain cachet – it smacked of the 'underground' and all that was challenging about social movements in the 1960s. In the sixth form of a boy's grammar school in 1968, we were enthralled by events in Paris and elsewhere, and excited by the prospect of widespread radical change outside the conventional leftist mould. These radical social movements appeared to offer the prospect of a world turned on its head and sociology seemed bound up with this. At school a geography master persuaded a few of us to subscribe to *New Society.* It seems astonishing now that a social science magazine had a weekly readership of 60,000. Its popularity in the 1960s was evidence of, 'the crystallization of a distinctive interest in gleaning knowledge of social life and social relationships in areas that had hitherto been ignored,' (Savage, 2010, 113). *New Society* showed that the 'everyday' could be a legitimate subject of interest and the institutions that I imagined I was rebelling against – family, school, work – could be objects of systematic study. My curiosity was cemented when I read the Jackson and Marsden classic, *Education and the working class* (1965). Here was a study that echoed my experiences and a discipline that helped to explain life as a working-class grammar school boy and the complex interactions between home, school, parental values and intergenerational mobility. I went to Leicester University to study sociology with no idea that it housed a cosmopolitan department with so many eminent academics. Only later did I learn how influential the Leicester department was in the development of British sociology (Goodwin and Hughes, 2011). I expected sociology to be 'relevant', and involved in contemporary issues, but I was largely disappointed. Instead, the Leicester syllabus included Evans-Pritchard, Malinowski, Bloch, Witfogel, Barrington Moore and, of course, Norbert Elias' work on the sociogenesis of courtly behaviour in Europe in the middle ages. This was most definitely not what I had imagined. Instead of the tumultuous events and social movements of the day, we studied cargo cults, feudalism, Chinese Confucianism, millennial religious movements and social and political power in Ancient Egypt. Courses in 'race relations' were as likely to focus on the history of Brazil as on the city of Leicester. Of course this emphasis on long-term historical and comparative processes was a distinctive feature of the work of a department that gave a home to Norbert Elias. Like many of my generation, our involvement in sociology was characterised by battles between varieties of Marxism and activist politics. Deep involvement in social movements and a strong ideological commitment was seen as virtuous. I clung to my position as a Marxist until my supervisor, Eric Dunning, encouraged me to read more Elias. My interest was in nationalism and the apparent 'break up of Britain'. Tom Nairn challenged the scientific pretensions of Marxism and its failure to comprehend nationalism, describing it as, 'Marxism's greatest historical failure' (Nairn, 1975). Eric and other colleagues in Leicester suggested that Elias offered much more in the attempt to understand state formation and disintegration. It was also the start of a process of grasping the importance of what Elias termed, 'involvement and detachment'. This was particularly challenging at a time when political engagement was highly valued and detachment parodied as (bogus) 'objectivity'. Elias also questioned the tendency of sociologists to seek to apportion blame arguing that however psychologically satisfying it may be to point the finger of blame, it is rarely sociologically illuminating.

In the 1970s, displaced Kenyan and Ugandan Asians settled in Leicester and the city became a focus of racist agitation. Along with many others, I was active in the protests against racist politics, and one of the rallying cries was, 'One race, the human race'. Elias took me aback by claiming that such a slogan was meaningless to the majority. People make attachments to place and to group, so positing a bond to the whole human race was simply too abstract to make sense to anyone apart from a handful of intellectuals. He argued that we should struggle to make sense of all social movements, even those we might consider reprehensible, through the prism of figurational analysis and with a degree of detachment. He suggested that the conflict was best understood as a particular example of an insider–outsider configuration and not 'racism'. The approach at Leicester was to analyse power as a central concept and to see it as a property of dynamic social relations, with many dimensions. Power is not a static concept in which one or other party possesses 'it' at the expense of another. This relational approach to power taught me that, though there may be profound inequalities in terms of power relationships, it is sociologically absurd to conceive of any group as 'powerless'. Contra Marxism, and the idea of bourgeois control of the State, Elias claims that social forces and processes are unplanned – that there really is no group in charge. Predating the analogy of modernity as an out of control juggernaut, Elias urges us to see people as chained together by invisible ties of interdependence, 'No one is in charge. No one stands outside. Some want to go this, others that way…No one can regulate the movements of the whole unless a greater part of them are able to understand, to see, as it were, from outside, the whole patterns they form together' (Elias, 1956, 232).

Subsequently I was research associate for Professor Joe Banks on a Social Science Research Council (subsequently ESRC) project on the consumer co-operative movement. Joe and his wife, Olive Banks, the first female professor at Leicester, were generous supporters of many early career sociologists. Their intellectual influence reinforced the importance of an historical perspective in sociology, and both were feminists and committed teachers of sociology. What sustained me in the efforts to complete a thesis, find a job and get something published was the support of so many friends at Leicester and elsewhere, but also the realisation that the core ideas of sociology are powerful and resilient. The idea of 'social context' is a simple concept and rather obvious, but it opens up a depth of analysis and it is revealing how often colleagues in cognate disciplines, from economics to psychology – proclaim to have discovered the importance of 'social context'. Later I taught at Northampton where sociology 'serviced' a wide range of professional courses for teachers, social workers, health visitors and careers advisers. I was seconded to work at a nursing college to help integrate nurse education into higher education, and worked on a GP training scheme in the Oxford region. These experiences were useful in broadening my understanding of sociology beyond the narrow specialisation of a PhD. The discipline has flourished in the UK precisely because its insights and research findings have been shown to be of interest to wider constituencies and professional groups. It is chastening to recall the claim of a former President of the British Sociological Association (BSA) that the UK needs only two or three departments to reproduce the discipline. The rest of us must make a case for our existence by demonstrating that sociology is central to a broad-based humane education, as well as for delivering sociological research and insights to wider constituencies in such a 'service' capacity (Albrow, 1986). When sociology produces useful and practical knowledge of relevance to occupational groups – doctors, teachers, nurses, planners, social workers, and so on – there is a tendency for such insights to bleed away from the 'parent' discipline. In the case of medical sociology the contributions of sociological research to understanding, for example, the medical consultation, health beliefs, the patient experience, and so on – tend to become absorbed into medical education. The distinctive findings of applied sociology become part of the common sense of wider social groups and are lost as distinctive sociological knowledge. According to Abrams, this leaves sociology with 'theory', the esoteric and the abstract, and the task of continuous reconstruction (Abrams et al, 1981).

Around 2000 I completed a project with Eric Harrison on assessment and standards of undergraduate sociology as part of the Higher Education Funding Council (HEFCE) *Fund for the development of teaching and learning*. Only then did I realise how little thought I had given to the social process of learning, and how little interest we showed in the scholarly work on higher education teaching. The sociology of education focused almost exclusively on schooling and we tended to leave research into adult learning to psychologists or educationists. Later I worked with the National Subject Centre for Sociology Anthropology and Politics (CSAP) at the University of Birmingham. It funded small-scale research into sociology teaching and learning and provided a forum for dissemination of this work. Over the ten years that the Birmingham Centre operated I learned a great deal from an impressive group of social scientists who took seriously the need for a scholarly approach to pedagogy. Surely now is the time to subject our routine practices – lectures, seminars, exams and essay setting – to critical scrutiny? Sociologists are in an excellent position to research the implications and impact of changing patterns of higher education as well as new modes of communication, and to experiment with new ways of teaching. The 'digital generation' expect (and demand) that universities take proper account of new technologies. How much longer can we expect students to travel to the same place to hear someone give a lecture that could have been posted on YouTube? The routine delivery of content is untenable when students can draw on unlimited content from the web. The rhetoric of learning as an exchange between teacher and student must be turned into reality because even the most experienced lecturer is unable to manage the scale of knowledge 'out there'. As for assessment of sociology, the endless repetitive essay writing, where students regurgitate material that we have 'delivered' must surely be questioned. We ought to give our undergraduates the skills and confidence to work in cross-disciplinary groups to address tasks that makes them draw on subject understandings and methods. Sociologists need to master new technologies of communication and data gathering as objects of research and curriculum design. Early career sociologists are in a strong position to be innovative and offer a lifeline to departments staffed by greying baby boomers.

Any advice to early career sociologists is bound to reflect some analysis of the discipline and its discontents, as well as some stocktaking about the future for universities as a whole. We all know that the landscape of higher education is being transformed in the UK and recent speculation predicts that some institutions could become unviable over the next five years. If true, this could include many sociology departments. There is, though, a persistent strand of gloom-mongering, so much so that we must have eclipsed economics as 'the dismal science'. Martin Albrow identified a pessimistic collective belief he labelled 'the myth of heroic struggle', in which sociology is engaged purportedly in an on-going battle against hostile forces – the State, rival disciplines or the spectre of 'managerialism' – and they always threaten to get the upper hand. Currently, if some commentators are to be believed, we are to be swept away by the tsunami of neoliberalism. While the prospect of retrenchment of academic departments is real, we must be careful not to turn a perceived threat to sociology into Armageddon. Even if there is a blurring of distinctions between public and private providers, there is no reason why sociology should not flourish. It is likely that a super league of research-based institutions will be consolidated after REF2014 and the bulk of state-funded sociological research will be channelled to fewer than 20 institutions. Early career sociologists must make some critical choices. A research-oriented career requires developing a particular set of skills – preparing funding bids, project management, staff management, report writing for funding agencies, and so on. A majority of sociologists in higher education will find employment in the other 80 per cent of universities where there will be a greater emphasis on more modest scholarship, producing teaching material, good quality teaching and various types of community engagement.

One of the ways in which I negotiated career challenges was through the intellectual friendships made through the BSA and other networks. Conferences, study group meetings, teaching events and committee work were critical in developing my understanding of the discipline and my self-identity as a sociologist. It puzzles me why membership of the BSA is so low. For a discipline that understands the importance of collective organisation, ignoring the BSA has always seemed a bit daft. I have been surprised and annoyed when sociologists young and old, famous and not so famous, have aired their prejudices about the BSA, often with a complaint that 'it' has done something to which they object. Beware the tendency to reify, for, apart from the handful of permanent staff in Durham, the BSA is run by an ever-changing group of volunteers.

British sociology has an unfortunate tendency to parochialism. Most of us are acquainted with some US sociology, but detailed knowledge of what is happening in sociology elsewhere in the world is short on the ground. This will not be sufficient in the future as the balances of power shift away from the global north, and the foundational concepts of the discipline are subjected to greater critical scrutiny. Ignorance of theoretical and empirical developments in the wider world will be inexcusable. One more 'health warning' – beware theoretical fads and fashions. So many young academics spend hours trying to master the obscure work of a theorist only for the tide to turn and for their work to be consigned to the dustbin. This is why it is important not to ignore earlier 'classics'. Apart from the inspirational work of Norbert Elias, I would recommend the work of Robert Merton. Although hailing from a different theoretical tradition, Merton's essays in *Social theory and social structure* are impressive for their clarity, the modesty of the claims being made and the range of issues covered – with essays spanning the sociology of science, deviance, bureaucracies, reference groups and so on. It is valuable to turn again to a sociologist who puts forward empirically justified theories about social structures and social behaviour. Merton requires us to take proper account of the cultural networks in which we are embedded and the inevitable constraints these impose on our choices. Finally, I think we should try and write academic social science that is clear, free of jargon and hopefully elegant (Billig, 2013).

References

Abrams, P, Deem, R, Finch, J, Rock, P (eds), 1981, *Practice and progress: British sociology 1950–1980*, London: Allen and Unwin

Albrow, M, 1986, BSA Presidential address 1986. The undergrdauate currriculum in sociology: 'A core for humane education', *Sociology* 20, 3, 335–46

Billig, M, 2013, *Learn to write badly: How to succeed in the social sciences*, Cambridge: Cambridge University Press

Elias, N, 1956, Problems of involvement and detachment, *British Journal of Sociology* 7, 3, September, 226–52

Goodwin, F, Hughes, J, 2011, Ilya Neustadt, Norbert Elias, and the Leicester department: Personal correspondence and the history of sociology in Britain, *British Journal of Sociology* 62, 4, 677–95

Jackson, B, Marsden, D, 1965, *Education and the working class*, Harmondsworth: Penguin

Merton, R, 1957, *Social theory and social structure*, Glencoe, IL: Free Press

Nairn, T, 1975, The modern Janus, *New Left Review* 1, 94, November–December

Savage, M, 2010, *Identities and social change in Britain since 1940: The politics of method*, Oxford: Oxford University Press

THIRTY

A career spent orbiting sociology

Eric Harrison

Eric Harrison is senior research fellow in the Centre for Comparative Social Surveys at City University London, and since 2006 he has been a member of the Core Scientific Team of the European Social Survey. He has held teaching and research posts at the universities of Manchester, Plymouth, Oxford and Essex. In addition to research interests in social stratification and social inequality, he is also the deputy coordinator of the City Q-Step Centre, a new national initiative to improve the teaching of quantitative social science in the undergraduate curriculum.

I've been a sociologist as long as I can remember. So it was surprising to recall that I've spent as much of the last 25 years outside the mainstream of the discipline as I have in it.

I came to the subject relatively late. My sixth form did not offer sociology as an A-level option and in any case I was totally besotted with my main choices of history and economics. In both cases I think what attracted me to these was the search for patterns, for structure, for answers to big questions. I was always more interested in macroeconomics and found the simple logic of Keynesian demand management intuitively appealing. I still do.

I went to Cambridge to read history in 1985. I enjoyed it, but increasingly found myself getting swamped by the vast quantity of detail we were required to absorb. The only lecture course I regularly attended was a year-long series on political thought from Montaigne to Rousseau. This more schematic approach – and the imminent threat of studying medieval farming methods – led me to investigate the still novel Social and Political Sciences Tripos, and in my final year I switched over to this option. It was mostly political sociology really and very international, so I gained a solid appreciation of European, American and Soviet societies. In an early example of sociologists' poor predictive record, I remember in 1988 our lecturer expressing much scepticism as to whether perestroika would get very far in liberalising the Soviet Union. Within two years the regime had collapsed.

After I finished my degree it never entered my head that I might become an academic. My overriding aim in life was to become a personnel manager in charge of industrial relations. After unsuccessful interviews with Pedigree Petfoods, Rank Hovis MacDougall and Nissan, I discovered that I was more likely to be optimising car parking space than sitting through the night averting strikes. But my enthusiasm for industrial relations remained undimmed and I took a short-term post teaching at the Manchester School of Management while doing a Master's thesis in the subject.

This was fine as far as it went but at that time I felt my project was an interesting MSc but not a PhD. Besides I was fed up with being broke so I got a job as a graduate trainee accountant at Lancashire County Council. This was the period during which I realised that there was unfinished business between me and sociology. While the double entry bookkeeping left me cold, I found the politics of the workplace and the daily rituals of resistance to managerial authority compelling. I carried on writing up my MSc thesis in the evenings and scoured the pages of each Tuesday's *Guardian*. Soon I landed a research assistant post in a large team doing an evaluation of the Thatcher government's urban policies. That was a fascinating and complex project but it now seems to belong to a different era. My colleague had to run his multilevel models overnight and if you wanted a government document you wrote a letter to a civil servant and sent an envelope, then waited eagerly. You could now download an entire library of literature in a couple of hours. It was also an early indication of the trend towards evidence-based policy that would later define the New Labour governments, though the *Independent*'s headline '£10m on urban policy wasted' seemed an oversimplification of our 500 pages of output.

As this drew to an end I applied for a lectureship in sociology at the University of Plymouth to get some interview practice. I ended up working there for eight happy years and of necessity expanded my repertoire across the discipline. It's a long way from Cambridge to Plymouth, both geographically and in terms of institutional mission, and my time by the sea shaped my outlook for my subsequent career. After an initial year of youthful and slightly stubborn resistance, I pretty much threw away my received ideas about teaching. I'd previously seen this as a missionary role, aiming high, displaying my academic credentials and not worrying too much if the message didn't stick with the whole cohort. If you asked me to sum up my teaching philosophy now, I'd use that bit of modern vernacular, 'It's not all about you.' The central task is to start from where the student is, and work from there. Moreover, there's often a sales job to be done, because the material doesn't enthuse or embed itself on a single attempt. Getting to know a subject is like getting to know a person – it doesn't always happen quickly and it can take a number of iterations – and your job is to show the student all the good things it can offer them and the way it might change their outlook and their life. In many cases I was aware that students – particular mature returners – were actively remaking their lives through their degree, and that I was in a small way contributing to that process.

Perhaps inspired by the many mature students with whom I had contact, as the new century dawned I became a PhD student at the age of 34. For any self-respecting sociologist, this was a fascinating experience. For a start I exchanged the role of teacher, 'expert', authority figure that I had held for eight years for that of learner, ingénue, eager apprentice. But on top of this I was moving from a former polytechnic to the oldest institution in the country, Oxford University (albeit one of its most modern manifestations, Nuffield College). The research-intensive hothouse of a college with 90 postgraduate students and at least half as many Fellows could not have been more different from the large lecture halls and the semi-anonymity of a complex modular system. This was a throwback to an earlier era of sociology, steeped as it was in the British empirical tradition, with a touch of American seasoning. Words like 'evidence', 'claim', 'explanation' and even 'prediction' punctuated the many seminars and lectures I attended, while concepts around 'postmodernism' were met with a despairing shrug and a glance to the heavens. It became a joke among my cohort (ferociously bright, admirably international) that there were two ways to carry out any task – the Nuffield way and the wrong way. It is worth reflecting – as a sociologist – that this was a classic example of the 'incommensurable paradigms' phenomenon. I'm extremely proud to be associated with Nuffield, but I wasn't prepared for the way the association divides opinion and skews people's perceptions of what I believe or what I can offer. The Nuffield tag has helped me get two jobs since and probably stopped me getting another, so I'm still in credit.

Nuffield sociology (I won't say Oxford sociology, which is a much more diverse beast altogether) left me two legacies. The first of these was that research ought to be problem or question driven, regardless of the type of data collection and analysis in which one was engaged. The Master's class I attended in my second term, as part of my doctoral training, was called 'Sociological puzzles'. Pairs of students would take turns to select a puzzling phenomenon and look for possible explanations and evidence that could support them. For a few weeks I felt this was a breakthrough – why did we not all do sociology in this practical and empirical way? But after a while I remembered Keynes's old dictum from my A-level economics, the one that says 'even the most practical man of affairs is usually in the thrall of the ideas of some long-dead economist'. And I started to notice that what one chose to define as a puzzle tended to be driven by one's underlying theoretical model of the world. And this being Oxford, any behaviour that appeared to run counter to rational action theory was deemed puzzling. This doesn't detract from the value of the puzzle paradigm as a pedagogic strategy; it merely reminds us of the importance of theory in the process of problem-definition. So the research question, 'Why does social inequality persist?' is only a puzzle if your underlying theoretical position makes it seem so. If you believe that talents are unequally distributed at birth and that this will be reflected in the distribution of rewards, there is not much of a puzzle.

This leads me to the second legacy from my Nuffield period, namely that technical virtuosity is no replacement for a sociological imagination. There is a widely-held misconception among our students that quantitative methods are about precision, and about 'proving' things to be true (this probably stems from all those textbooks using the 't' test to compare exam scores of different groups of students). In sociology, we are more interested in establishing relationships between predictor and response variables (my first lesson was 'don't call them dependent and independent variables – there's no such thing as an "independent" variable'). The power of quantitative analysis is its ability to reveal these associations and to estimate their strength in a way that adds to our knowledge about the world. Another quotable *bon mot* from my time as a postgraduate is that 'any decent sociologist should be able to think of at least three different explanations for empirical findings'. What I like about this maxim is that it acknowledges a) the possibility of 'flipping the causal arrow' (another favourite from the Puzzles class), and b) the need to understand the mechanism through which the relationship operates. So I know that when I'm driving my car and I press the accelerator, there is an effect. The car speeds up and there is a change in the engine noise. But given my indifference to all things mechanical, I have no idea how this is being achieved under the bonnet. I tend to view the division of labour between methods in the same terms. Large datasets are very useful for agenda-setting, for establishing patterns and relationships, and indicating where deeper probing is required. To borrow an old statistics joke, 'Correlation does not imply causation, but it does waggle its eyebrows suggestively and gesture furtively while mouthing "look over there".' When it comes to zoning in on the way a process unfolds, qualitative approaches (such as through in-depth interviews or observations) offer sharper-edged tools.

Since leaving Oxford my 'second career' has involved no great masterplan. It's mostly happened by accident. I was shortlisted for a Nuffield Foundation New Career Postdoctoral Fellowship, to study the self-employed using the British Cohort Studies, but I didn't get the funding. If I had I wouldn't have left Oxford and gone to work with David Rose on a large European research project based at Essex's Institute for Social and Economic Research. And David wouldn't have sent me to the Essex summer school to do a week-long course on the European Social Survey, which we were planning to use to help validate a cross-national socio-economic classification. At a series of international conferences and workshops I met first Rory Fitzgerald and then Roger Jowell, and grew more interested in their ambitious new cross-national attitude survey in over 30 countries. And if ISER had offered me a new contract sooner I might not have applied for a post as part of the European Social Survey team at City University. I have worked here since October 2006. The lesson I take from all this is that, to borrow from John Lennon, 'life is what happens when you're busy making plans'. The advice I would give someone in early career is that, of course it pays to take the long view, but if you concentrate on being the best you can be in your chosen field, the opportunities will find you.

What advice would I give to someone starting out now? The best advice I ever had on this was from my Master's supervisor in Manchester. 'Just because you're in academia doesn't mean you shouldn't plan your career.' What he meant was that we're often so committed to higher education for itself, to our discipline, to students and so on, that we think it's almost a bit unseemly to want to be a success. It is much more 'professional' than when I started, and if you want to prosper you should take the whole self-promotion thing seriously.

If you're starting a PhD – and you can't get by without one – think about it in terms of three papers for publication, with some topping and tailing. Think about where these papers might get sent. Present your work at conferences to get practice and to impose artificial deadlines on your writing. Know who the main figures are and where they work. Put yourself about. Join the BSA, and join a study group, or form one. Get involved with the postgraduate forum, then the early careers forum. Be known. Bring in money.

Have a five-year research and publications plan, so you don't drift. Make links with other disciplines, with other institutions, with other countries. Be international.

Have good web pages; let people download your working papers; join email lists; have a blog, engage with others about topics that relate to your research.

Update your CV every year, even if you already have a job, even if you like your job.

Be lively. Be different. Be better.

THIRTY-ONE

Researching children's lives: on becoming and being a sociologist in education

Daniela Sime

Daniela Sime is a senior lecturer in the School of Social Work and
Social Policy at the University of Strathclyde. Her research focuses
on the life experiences of migrant children, the impact of poverty on
children's educational achievement and well-being and approaches to
service delivery for families. She has received funding for her research
from the Economic and Social Research Council, British Academy,
Save the Children and the Scottish Government. Daniela is a fellow of
the Higher Education Academy and, since 2014, an elected member
of the Young Academy of the Royal Society of Edinburgh.

When I received the invitation to contribute to a collection of 'stories' by established sociologists, I expressed doubt that my experience would be relevant to this valuable project, as I did not decide be a sociologist, sociology happened to me. The notion of professional identity and the multiplicity of one's identity as a professional have received considerable attention in recent years. In this essay, I share some of the dilemmas I encountered in my career and explain how these have contributed to the development of my professional identity and the strategies I used to adapt to an ever-changing academic environment. My experiences, to a greater or lesser extent, involve personal narratives and I make no claims as to the 'rightness' of my decisions and strategies, only that they made sense and helped my learning and becoming as a sociologist. While many careers are mapped out rigorously, mine did not follow 'a plan' – strange things happened on the way and I moved from a degree in languages and a career in primary school teaching to a career in research with children and marginalised groups. Hopefully, my 'story' will provide some insight for other sociologists starting out, to help them find answers to their own professional dilemmas.

In 2003, I had submitted my doctoral thesis and, as most graduate students, was confronted with the big question of 'What now?' My thesis looked at the value of teachers' gestures and other non-verbal behaviours to students' understanding in language classes, a very interesting and relatively new field, but I felt I needed a change. While I was waiting for my viva to take place, I came across a research post for a project led by two high-profile colleagues, one from the field of education (Lydia Plowman) and one from the field of sociology of childhood (Alan Prout). Given the 'boom' in the use of technologies at the time, the project aimed to look at the impact of technology on young children (aged 3–10), through fieldwork conducted in their homes. I can picture vividly the job interview and how hard I tried to remember all the reading I had done the night before on Prout's work on the sociology of childhood. Securing this six-month post was career-changing; it opened up my mind to an entirely new field and approach to research. I always had a fascination with children's lives through my previous work as a teacher, but my degrees in foreign language teaching had given me limited sociological knowledge. What started as a short-term job to keep me going financially until the viva, became a crucial experience in re-orienting my academic interests and repositioning myself as a researcher. I knew little at the time of the theoretical developments in the sociology of childhood or new conceptualisations of children as social actors, competent and active participants in their lives. Conducting ethnographic fieldwork in children's homes, while listening to their stories and examining their resistances to the impositions of adults, made me rethink my approach to research and interest in sociological work. It taught me about the importance of locating myself amidst the ongoing construction of experience, able to witness day-to-day moments where participants could relax and share thoughts, experiences, emotions and how much more revealing these insights were to other approaches to research. These home visits, while allowing participants to share aspects of their identity as (non)technological beings, provided me with an opportunity to engage aspects of my own identity as a researcher. I knew that from then on I wanted to position myself as a 'listener' to children's (and adults') voices, in order to be able to access meanings and identities which otherwise might have remained unheard.

Working with two eminent academics at the start of my 'new life' post-doctorate also meant self-imposed pressure to become knowledgeable in the sociology of childhood – and I fully embraced the challenge! I discovered the work of James, Jenks and Prout (on theorising childhood); Qvortrup (on childhood as a social phenomenon); Mayall and Morrow (on children's experiences in a range of settings); Skelton and Valentine (on children's geographies and cultures). This immersion in the readings on the sociology of childhood, guided by wonderfully stimulating discussions with my newly found mentors, made me think of children in a completely changed way: not as lesser than adults and in need of protection, but as mainly powerful, resilient, confident and creative, immensely resourceful individuals and actively engaged in promoting their own knowledge and position in society. It also made me realise, as a social scientist, that I had to find ways of giving them a 'voice' and made me aware of my duty of empowering children through the research that I was doing. Sociology has also helped me come to understand that outdated ideologies, mainly based on theories of developmental psychology which conceptualised children as 'incomplete adults' and vulnerable or in need of monitoring, dominate policies and provision of services in education, health and welfare and ultimately serve to oppress children in our society.

I continued to work as a contract researcher and soon added another dimension to my identity as a researcher. I was drawn quite early on to the marked social inequalities and the negative impact that poverty had on children's experiences in the UK. Being originally from an ex-Communist country, I expected that children's lives in the UK would not be blighted by lack of food, decent clothing or adequate living conditions. While conducting fieldwork in some of most deprived areas in Scotland and seeing first-hand the social worlds of poverty through children's eyes, I began to wonder about the scope for using research to tackle social disadvantage and advocate social change. By engaging with the sociological literature on social structures and individual agency, social mobility and social capital, I began to develop my ideas on how tackling social disadvantage through education can be a source of change. Working as a researcher on a grant jointly funded by the Big Lottery Fund and Save the Children exposed me to a different way of doing research, as it involved collaboration with a major voluntary sector organisation, whose interests in campaigning for children's rights meant that research needed to have direct value to policy and practice. Undoubtedly, all research seeks to make an impact – on the discipline, for the individuals involved or for others who might use the findings (public sector organisations, policy makers, companies and so on). In my work, it became crucial that children's participation in research was not wasted and the knowledge they shared became a tool for action. Working with Save the Children made me think of myself not only as a sociologist, but as a campaigner. Giving children a voice through research that looked at the multiple layers of social class and social inequalities and how these affected their chances from a young age and working to identify the best ways of using research to have impact on practice (in education, health, welfare) has remained a key theme of my research since.

After two years of contract-based research work (and several nerve-racking visa applications to the Home Office, as required for researchers from non-EU countries), I secured my first permanent lectureship. My initial experiences as a researcher on short-term projects had collectively contributed to what I learnt about children and the sociology of childhood in a relatively short period of time, and that practical knowledge became immensely useful when I started to apply for my own research grants. Working with experienced academics has also taught me about the culture of academia and the skills required in securing research funds. In an environment which has become more and more competitive for (sometimes string-attached) public funding, pressures through research assessment exercises and calls for research to demonstrate an 'impact' in society, researchers need to adapt and find ways of marrying academic interests with policy, practice and funders' priorities and requirements. Securing research funding in an increasingly cash-strapped and competitive environment means that researchers need to be versatile grant writers, aware of the funders' expectations of a good proposal and assessment criteria, perseverant and prepared for rejection. I was shown once a wall in the office of a well-known professor, covered in rejection letters from prospective funders. Her advice was that 'once rejected, you just need to try again... and again' and eventually the hard work and original ideas would pay off. Securing funding has however become more and more difficult for early career academics. A combination of 'learning the rules' of the funder targeted, persevering, getting support from an experienced mentor and applying through schemes aimed at early career researchers was in my case a recipe for successful applications.

In the last decade, my research has focused on social inequalities, examining issues such as the lives of migrant children, ethnic minority parents' engagement with schools, ways of working with families in disadvantage and intergenerational learning. Involving children through innovative methodologies and getting service providers and policy makers interested from the early stages of a project have remained key features of my work. Conducting research with traditionally marginalised groups has given me a new perspective on the social issues that research can help address. I see my research as a medium through which marginalised people's voices are heard. Being a sociologist, in my case, is a way of informing and facilitating social change. In the years since I have started my research with children, children's rights and interest in their well-being have moved higher up the political agenda and in the public consciousness and it looks likely that research will have a key place in the years to come in improving children's lives around the world.

For those entering the field of sociology now with an interest in children's lives, the opportunities are endless; from the need to identify better child-centred methods and involve children as co-researchers, to better ways of theorising childhood and documenting the complexities of children's lives in an increasingly global world. Looking back on my career, I did not have 'a career plan' and have often reacted, rather than proactively seeking projects that interested me. Over years, I found this is quite common in contract-based research work. Limited funding for long-term projects means that researchers need to become versatile in terms of issues on which they are able and willing to do work in order to build a competitive curriculum, which allows them to eventually move into more stable, lecturing or research posts. Practical circumstances, especially in times of economic recession, such as the growing number of graduates on an international level, the limited funding available, and the pressures to ensure research has an 'impact' are factors which will bring considerable changes to the field and the type of research which we will be able to conduct in the years to come. For early career researchers, this may mean more uncertainty in terms of a permanent position and a need to diversify in terms of 'specialisms' and skills in working with a wide range of organisations (for example, public services, museums, community-based organisations, private companies), as well as finding creative ways of funding, conducting and disseminating research. Publishing research in academic journals, although still a key feature of accountability in academia, will rarely secure a wide audience for one's research. The impact of social media on how research is conducted and disseminated, as well as ways of engaging with those who might use research findings to effect social change, is already changing the way in which research is being disseminated. This means that the sociology of the future will need to combine intellectual argument on theory with a new way of ensuring that those whose voices it researches are also benefiting from its outcomes. Conducting research which is innovative, ground-breaking, field-changing, but also relevant and accessible to the wider audiences and which ultimately benefits those who helped us produce it, remains to me the main challenge (and reward) for new and established sociologists.

References

Corsaro, W, 2011, *The sociology of childhood*, 3rd edition, CA, London: Sage

James, A, Jenks, C, and Prout, A, 1999, *Theorizing childhood*, Polity

Mayall, B, 2002, *Towards a sociology for childhood: Thinking from children's lives*, Buckingham: Open University Press

Morrow, V, 2008, Ethical Dilemmas in Research with Children and Young People about their Social Environments, *Children's Geographies*, 6, 1, 49–61

Qvortrup, J, 2000, Macroanalysis of childhood, in P Christensen and A James (eds) *Research with children: Perspectives and practices*, London: Routledge Falmer

Skelton, T and Valentine, G, 1998, *Cool places: Geographies of youth cultures*, London: Routledge

THIRTY-TWO

Following my star

Jeffrey Weeks in conversation with Andrea Scott

Jeffrey Weeks is emeritus professor of sociology at London South
Bank University, where he was previously executive dean of Arts
and Human Sciences. He has held posts at the London School of
Economics and Political Science, and the universities of Essex, Kent,
Southampton and the West of England. He is the author of over 20
books, and more than 100 articles and papers, chiefly on the history
and social organisation of sexuality, family and intimate life. His books
include *The world we have won: The remaking of erotic and intimate life*
(Routledge, 2007), *Sexuality* (Routledge, 2009; third edition) and
The languages of sexuality (Routledge, 2011) and *Sex, politics and society*
(Routledge, 2012; third edition). He is currently working on a book
entitled *What is sexual history?*

Andrea: Tell me how it was that you came to be a sociologist?

Jeffrey: [Laughs] Well, I actually started as a historian and my first degree was a history degree. When I was doing that, a very traditional history degree at UCL, I became interested in the more theoretical side of issues and gravitated towards the history of political theory, and that led me to an interest in social theory and sociological debates, because I was looking at political theory at the end of the nineteenth century, early twentieth century and it overlapped with sociological debates.

Especially as my MPhil thesis was called *The search for community* and that was in political theory but obviously overlapped with debates over community in sociology. So, I had a very strong interest in the subject from being an undergraduate but instead of doing a sociology master's, which was an option, I decided to do what became my MPhil, and then I became interested in a completely different subject, which was the history and sociology of sexuality.

My earliest adventures in this field, as it happens, overlapped, to some extent, with the debates at which I had been looking at the end of the nineteenth century. I became interested in the history of sexology, in Havelock Ellis, the emergence of theories of homosexuality at the end of the nineteenth century, in Edward Carpenter, and the debates about sexual identity, gay identity and all of that. This was the early 1970s. There was no help at all within traditional history for what I was trying to do. I found the most useful insights from within sociology and a particularly key moment was encountering Mary McIntosh's essay on 'The homosexual role', which inspired my research in its early stages (McIntosh, 1968) . This was passed around in early gay liberation meetings, which I used to go to at the LSE, and here I got to know Mary, and other young sociologists, like Ken Plummer, and eventually other people in the Essex sociology department. I went to Essex for a while to work with Mary, by then it was the late 1970s. I found that sociology was much better as a home for the work I was doing, which was, by its nature, interdisciplinary, than any history department was.

History departments weren't interested in my teaching there, and were not interested in my research, whereas sociology departments were. Intellectually, sociology was much more exciting to me than the empirical history in which I had been brought up and subsequently I got jobs in sociology departments in various universities.

Sexuality studies were pretty marginal, not only to history but even to sociology at that period. Ken Plummer wrote about the fact that then writing about sexuality made you morally suspect, and certainly I felt that, but nevertheless I was able to get short research contracts and so on within sociology or related departments. So that is how I came into sociology, and my PhD ultimately was in a sociology department at the University of Kent, where I was teaching.

By the early 1980s, I was a recognised sociologist, and identified myself as a sociologist. I have always preferred to call myself a historically-minded sociologist or a sociologically-minded historian. I have always tried to bridge the gap in my writings and so be historical as well as sociological. I have almost alternated, in fact, between the historical approach and the sociological approach through various things I have done.

So that is where I was in the early 1980s, teaching sociology at the University of Kent on a three-year contract, when someone was on leave of absence. That came to an end, so I then went to a social work department at the University of Southampton as a researcher. That of course came to an end, in 1985, and I thought, "Well, this is the end of my academic career" because there weren't any university jobs for me to move into, or at least none that wanted me, and anyway I was pretty fed up with endless short-term contracts, so I took a job outside the universities and became an administrator in CNAA, the Council for National Academic Awards which was responsible at the time for validating and awarding degrees in the old polytechnics.

Lo and behold, I found myself responsible for sociology, social work, the social sciences and research policy within the organisation, so I kept an intense interest going in developments in these fields. So that is where I was by the time I was in my mid-30s, I suppose. I certainly, by then, saw myself as a sociologist, writing books within sociology series and so on; a fully-fledged sociologist. However, I was still unable to get a permanent teaching job. Just to finish the narrative, three things then changed my fate, in an unexpected way.

First, by the 1980s, I found myself a heavily published researcher, partly at least because having to get a job at the end of a contract meant you wrote and wrote, so I had a lot of publications. I was suddenly marketable, in the new climate of publish or be damned. Second, I also had a lot of experience by this time as an administrator and educational policy person, responsible for the development of approaches to social sciences and research policy in a national body, CNAA. With the renewed growth of social sciences in the former polytechnics/new universities from the late 1980s, I had skills that made me employable at more senior levels.

Finally, the tragedy of the Aids crisis during the 1980s unexpectedly made research into sexuality more or less respectable. My research and publications were no longer so marginal. In fact, they might help us understand sexual practices better. So, rather to my surprise, by the end of the 1980s, I found myself well qualified enough to apply for chairs, a sudden and unanticipated leap from nowhere. I got my first chair in the University of West of England as professor of social relations, and head of research in the social sciences, and then a few years later I was head hunted from there to come to South Bank as a professor of sociology, and that is roughly the trajectory of my career. Not really steady progress, more leaps and falls till the mid-1990s, but somehow I got there.

Andrea: What would you say that sociology means to you?

Jeffrey: Well, what sociology offered to me and continues to offer to me are theoretical insights. I always loved the great sweep of history. I was always less interested in the nitty gritty, empirical detail, grubbed from dusty archives, so I wasn't at home with traditional history at all (of course, the best history is not like that at all, but perception is all). Sociology offered me broader theoretical perspectives, about which I was always fascinated. More precisely, it offered me keys to the sort of research that I wanted to do.

With no strong tradition in this country, or anywhere indeed at that period, of research into the social and historical shaping of sexuality, I couldn't glean many insights from traditional historiography, whereas sociology, in certain aspects, and especially at Essex, was very alive to the issues. I was very influenced by new deviancy studies, by symbolic interactionism and labelling theory, and so on in the early 1970s.

Then of course, like many of my generation, I encountered French theory. Michel Foucault, who of course is not a sociologist or a historian, and perhaps not even a philosopher, was nevertheless enormously influential in reshaping thinking on sexuality and I was very influenced by my reading of Foucault, critical reading, I hope. I never became a 'Foucauldian' in the classical sense, but I certainly gleaned a tremendous amount from my reading of him. But it is important to stress that I was already well on my way in working towards what became known as social constructionist theories of homosexuality and sexuality more broadly long before I encountered Foucault. Friends and colleagues such as Mary McIntosh and Ken Plummer, from quite different traditions, had got me going along that road.

Sociology provided me with the insights, the theoretical backing as well as many of the empirical findings, which I couldn't find elsewhere. Sexuality by its nature is inter-disciplinary and cross-disciplinary and I needed the strength of the sociological tradition to understand that.

I felt at home with that tradition. So in a sense, I was an accidental sociologist in my origins, but sociology came to be the key to many of the insights that I tried to develop. Both in the historical work and in the more conventionally sociological work which I went on to do.

Andrea: Have your ideas about what sociology is changed at all over your career?

Jeffrey: Well, when I began, I identified very much with those areas of sociology which were perhaps then the most dynamic to my mind, like interactionism, like deviance theory and so on, which were enormously creative, but which were still fairly marginal to the profession as a whole. I never identified particularly with the great Parsonian tradition. I never felt the need to engage in Durkheim versus Weber, though I read, and taught, both.

I certainly, like many of my generation, had a critical engagement with Marxism, but because I came from the outside, I never felt really fully involved with that great patriarchal tradition, the master thinkers of sociology. I was much more interested in the sociology which looked at the marginal, the sub-cultural, the deviant (as it was then called) and all of those areas that fitted in with my own interests in gay history, gay subcultures, and sexuality generally, and in gender issues and so on.

Andrea: Would you say that you would now advise your, say, younger self to study sociology?

Jeffrey: Well, I do indeed advise people to study sociology, and sociology of course has become much more pluralistic as a discipline. It is very difficult these days to point to an agreed canon in sociology and, in fact, I am deeply grateful for that because the various would-be canons could become tyrannies and even the alternative theoretical traditions with which I did engage have in a sense become intellectual tyrants for some.

The debates I have engaged with or listened to, which have accused people of not being a proper Marxist or a proper Parsonian, not understanding Althusser or Gramsci, or not being a proper Foucauldian – I feel I have lived through all of that, and it's been the enemy of genuine creativity. There are many intellectual traditions which have been important in opening up debate, but they are not carriers of the truth and I think what I have learned from sociology is to avoid the search for truth. What one is engaged in is exploring different problems in the real world by drawing on various theoretical traditions. I have never felt aligned to a single theoretical tradition. I am methodologically pluralistic and theoretically pluralistic in my approaches. The key thing is the problem which you are trying to solve, which is an empirical problem but it also raises all sorts of theoretical issues and I have never wanted to be hidebound by theoretical rigidity or correctness or whatever.

One of the phrases of Foucault I have always liked is that we should treat theory as a bag of tools that you use in different contexts and certainly that is how I approach theoretical issues. I have written theoretical articles, I have really been interested in theoretical issues and continue to be, but not in the search for theoretical absolutism, which I think is the bane of our profession.

Andrea: Would you advise somebody to use sociology in order to work in academia or are there other ventures or other ways of using sociology that aren't academic?

Jeffrey: Well, there are many ways of using sociology and there are good sociologists in all sorts of professions in the public sector and the private sector, so sociology still provides good intellectual training. I think the important thing is not your disciplinary commitment, as important as that is actually, but that is not the only thing. What is important is that you have a star that you want to follow, an idea, a concept, a research area that you think is important, and shapes your thinking.

That is what you should pursue and use whatever theoretical aids, disciplines and methodologies are at hand to understand that problem. To my mind, it is more important to have an intellectual interest that you are following than to be a pure sociologist. I often say to the people I have mentored or managed or appraised that you should follow your star and see where that leads you, in research terms, rather than being hidebound to a particular tradition.

Having said that, I think it is important that you get a good intellectual grounding and these days, well even in the 1970s when I started, that can come from many sources. My generation of sociology teachers rarely had a sociology degree to start with. Their first degrees were in history, geography and so on. Today, they could be from cultural studies, they could be interdisciplinary like gender, queer or post-colonial studies and they could even be from English. Finish it off, yes, with a master's in a particular discipline and a PhD that might use a whole series of disciplines. Just take my own particular area of sexuality; today is very difficult to say what the sociology of sexuality is or even the history of sexuality because so many other disciplines are drawn in: geography, critical race studies, gender studies, queer studies and so on. People should use the tools that are appropriate to them.

Andrea: How would you advise someone who wanted to carve out their own career in sociology? Are there certain things they need to do?

Jeffrey: I think, as I have suggested, the important thing is to make your reputation in an area that is of supreme interest to you. There are essentially two sorts of researchers: there is the researcher who has the star that they want to follow, their own particular area of intellectual interest and they might obsessively research it, but it provides a framework for imbibing disciplines and approaches; then there is the jobbing researcher or the jobbing academic, who does what turns up. In a sense, I have been both.

In order to survive career-wise, job-wise, I have been a jobbing sociologist and a jobbing researcher. I have done all sorts of odd research in my career just because that is where the money was or where I could get jobs. What gives coherence to my interest, looking back, is the fact that I had a range of central questions with which I was preoccupied. For example, the nature of sexual identity, how important is it to develop specific sexual identities, like the lesbian and gay identities. What are the implications of the sexual categories that we take for granted as natural but actually have a history? What is the relationship between regulation and agency? All sorts of issues that are specific to the research I developed, but of course they also resonate with much wider questions, so I have been able, through exploring them specifically with sexuality, to look at broader issues of agency regulation, the role of theory, the importance of categories and so on, which go much wider than the specific area. I think that is the important thing, it is through having a particular range of interests, which may be narrow to start with but you get interested in all of the concepts, ideas, theories and methodologies, which are combined within sociology and related disciplines.

Andrea: Do you think there is anything you would do differently if you were to have your career again?

Jeffrey: Well I have often pondered on this because, during the course of my career, particularly crises in my career like when a job came to an end, I would seek advice from more senior people. I remember in particular two very senior academics who took an interest in what I was doing and were very supportive. One of them said to me, "I think writing on sexuality is not going to get you anywhere, you will not get a senior job there. The best thing you can do is retrain as a social worker and after you have got some experience in the field, you could come back to academia and eventually become a professor of social work." Well I totally ignored that advice. I didn't want to become a social worker, I wanted to stay as a researcher and anyway, I stuck to my lathe and, you know, it has not been unsuccessful.

The other, a professor of sociology, whom I greatly admired and still do, who played an important role in my development, once said to me, "Your career would be much easier if you wrote on something else other than sexuality" and because I respected him and so on, I did seriously think, "Well, perhaps I should write a book on something else." I certainly have written articles and books and other things in my career, but I realised that I didn't want to abandon my specific research interest because despite all of the ups and downs in my career for a long time, the coherence was given by my research interest.

Not just my research interest because it was also my personal interest, my cultural interest and my political interest. They all came together, which is why I think it is so important that yes, take advice, yes, be mentored. All of that is very important but in the end you have got to decide what you want to spend 30 to 40 years of your life doing and it is much more important to have a project that is yours and develop it as best you can, even if it means doing paid work for a while in an area that is completely different but gives you the space to do your own project. That is much more important than having a smooth-running career. I look at some of my friends, colleagues, contemporaries, who went straight from university into a lecturing job, often without doing a further degree of any sort and had careers for life but have been stultified by the lack of challenge, the routineisation of their careers.

My career was so up and down in its early stages that I feel it stirred me out of my natural laziness to do things, to always be on the go, to always find a new research project, new research income, a new idea. It is a terrible thing to say and it is not something that I would wish on anyone, but insecurity can be a spur to imagination and creativity.

Andrea: Lastly, if there was one book, reading or essay that you would say has inspired you or has provided you with your own unique perceptions of sociology that you would recommend to someone, what would it be?

Jeffrey: The book that I think inspired me way back when I was an undergraduate and it has continued to be an influence is neither conventional history nor sociology and it is Raymond Williams *Culture and society* (Williams, 1963). That is because it had a historical perspective, exploring the changing meanings of culture, but through that, offered a particular analysis of British thinking about capitalism, industrialisation, community, agency, progressive thinking particularly, but not only progressive thinking. Its themes still resonate.

It brought in all sorts of other theoretical cross-currents. I read it as an undergraduate and I was thrilled by it. I identified with the project, not least because Williams was from South Wales, as I was, so there was a personal, political as well as an intellectual affinity. That book was enormously influential in my early career and I avidly read every book by Raymond Williams as it came out for the next 20 years, even as I developed a quite different perspective myself. There were many others obviously that I can name that shaped my early thinking Edward Thompson's *The making of the English working class* (1968), Michel Foucault's *The history of sexuality* (1979), Ken Plummer's *Sexual stigma* (1975), Gagnon and Simon's *Sexual conduct* (1974), and many more.

I have already mentioned Mary McIntosh's article 'The homosexual role'. Those were enormously influential in shaping my particular range of interests. In a strange sort of way, I have never gone away from them. They are always there despite all the work that has followed and critiques and revisions of them, they are the background noise to my whole intellectual trajectory and looking back, it is fascinating to see how much has come out of those books in different traditions, different disciplines. Raymond Williams's book, for instance, is one of the founding texts for what became cultural studies, so there was enormous creativity in those works, which still resonate.

References

Foucault, M, 1979, *The history of sexuality: Volume 1, An introduction*, Harmondsworth: Allen Lane

Gagnon, JH, Simon, W, 1974, *Sexual conduct: The social sources of human sexuality*, London: Hutchinson

McIntosh, M, 1968, The homosexual role, *Social Problems* 16, 2, 182–92

Plummer, K, 1975, *Sexual stigma: An interactionist account*, London: Routledge and Kegan Paul

Thompson, EP, 1968, *The making of the English working class*, Harmondsworth: Penguin.

Williams, R, 1963, *Culture and society, 1780–1950*, Harmondsworth: Penguin

THIRTY-THREE

'The epoch of belief…the epoch of incredulity'

Howard Wollman

Howard Wollman graduated with a BA in modern history from
University of Oxford in 1971 followed by a BPhil in sociology in
1973. He took early retirement from Edinburgh Napier University in
2010 where he was head of the School of Health and Social Sciences
following many years of teaching sociology to a wide variety of
students. He is currently an honorary fellow in the School of Social
and Political Science at the University of Edinburgh, chair of the BSA
and in his non-academic life a volunteer adviser with Citizens Advice
Bureau. He has written on nationalism and ethnic identity.

In October of 1968, that annus mirabilis of radical opportunity and reverse, I went to Oxford to study modern history. This was a subject that had been my favourite at school and I had few doubts that I wished to study it at university. Doubts, which began to surface, focused mainly on my wish to study the modern and contemporary. (Oxford history in those days only just made it to the Second World War.) I thought about switching to politics, philosophy and economics because of my interest in politics, not realising at the time that hidden within PPE was the possibility of studying a course or two in sociology.

I had begun to be radicalised by the events of 1968, particularly the French student revolt of May, the Prague Spring and the Russian invasion of Czechoslovakia in August, and reading books like *The dialectics of liberation* and the seemingly radical work of RD Laing and the other anti-psychiatrists and I began to engage with Marx and Marxist writing. History at Oxford at the time was very traditional, with little in the way of conceptual or theoretical focus or discussion. Yet all around things were changing with the new social history, and the start of the 'History Workshop' movement at Ruskin inspired by Raphael Samuel. I attended the early conferences and found a more engaged history more open to theory and also to radical concerns.

I wanted to go on to postgraduate study but in what subject area? While thinking about this I had met through friends of friends John and Jean Comaroff, then postgraduate social anthropology students themselves in London, now eminent professors in Chicago. Both were enormously dynamic and enthusiastic and they spoke of the exciting insights and potential of the social sciences. I read *The sociological imagination* and was influenced even more by Peter Berger's *Invitation to sociology: A humanistic introduction*. I began to think that I needed (and wanted) to study a subject that offered more analytic and conceptual tools for understanding the world than the history that I had studied up till then. Maybe after studying sociology I would return to history invigorated and with more theoretical sophistication. I applied for the two year BPhil course at Oxford (it seemed easy to stay where I was), which promised a conversion course into sociology plus the likelihood of employment in university level teaching. In retrospect, I was very fortunate to be assigned to Jean Floud (who sadly died in 2013) as my supervisor. It was my loss when she departed after my first year to be Warden of Newnham College, Cambridge. But before that, she had applied a cold logic to my arguments, including, no doubt, at that point, my somewhat simplistic Marxism. Most usefully of all she had instructed me, when I first went to see her with some weeks to go before the course started, to read the sociological classics. I had already read quite a lot of Marx so I read my way through lots of Durkheim – *Rules of sociological method, Elementary forms of the religious life* and (my favourite) *Suicide* and then onto Weber, most notable *The Protestant ethic and the spirit of capitalism*. While still considering myself to be a Marxist I developed a soft spot for Durkheim which has never left me!

We were a close knit group – we BPhil students and in the years from 1971 to 1973 at Oxford there seemed from my student vantage point to be a struggle for the soul of sociology between a positivistic concentration on quantitative empirical work and a more theoretical, historically informed and qualitative sociology. From a later standpoint I realise that this is and was simplistic and although there were and are real differences in the discipline, sharpening and emphasising these at the expense of common ground can be unhelpful. But at the time it seemed bound up with political differences as well – and what was sociology for if not, à la Marx, to change the world?

My year after the BPhil was in terms of career building a wasted year. I had not been very instrumental in choosing my dissertation topic. Writing on 'social stratification and political change in postwar Czechoslovakia' had been interesting and addressed the central issues of class, state socialism and political change in which I was interested. But I had studied this from English language sources only, and, as I was no great linguist, did not feel it was realistic to learn Czech and carry on my researches. Colleagues who had chosen more strategically found a more straightforward path to doctoral study – a lesson perhaps in the need to be strategic as a postgraduate . So I spent a year passed between potential supervisors and not really settling down to a fixed topic within political sociology, but spending my time on useful projects like taking part in a reading group on Marx's *Capital*.

So it was out to the real world – or rather the world of higher education. I went to a lot of interviews and saw a lot of Britain, but only had one firm offer and thus accepted a research officer post at Sunderland Polytechnic (as it then was). I spent a year there, had some great colleagues, but felt that the role, shared as it was between several researchers in different disciplines, was too much of a dogsbody role to lead to any significant achievement. Also, I wanted to teach and so headed north to Edinburgh and have remained there ever since. I took a job at the then Napier College of Commerce and Technology, which became a polytechnic, which became a university in that strange elimination of the binary divide by Kenneth Clarke.

What role was there for a sociologist in an institution like Napier in 1975? At the time I arrived there was an increasing amount of degree level work but there was no sociology degree and no general social science degree. The philosophy of the college was firmly, but also narrowly, vocational but it was aspirational and adding yearly to its degree courses. I started on a Friday in October and had a full timetable the following week. Lectures had to be developed quickly and in some areas I was only just ahead of the students – without a first degree in sociology there were significant areas of the discipline that I had to teach which I had never encountered before. But new undergraduate courses had been developed in which sociology played an important, if secondary role as part of science and business degrees. Needless to say the challenge over the years was often to persuade reluctant students of the value of sociology alongside their other, more central, disciplines. And just occasionally, I do run into former students who say, 'Well I didn't think much of it at the time, but on reflection the sociology was really useful.'

As the institution developed towards university status, things did change. Research began to grow. But we were primarily, for many years, a teaching institution. My political interests, and a sociologist's commitment to the collective, led me to early involvement with the local trade union (in Scotland this was the EIS – the same as for the teachers). Much of my time was devoted to being a trade union rep, branch secretary, then chair and on national committees. I did not carry out much in the way of research. But my hankering for something a bit different took the form of tutoring for the Open University from the early 1980s to the mid-1990s. I learned a great deal from tutoring for the OU. Through it I met many people, students and staff, with whom I am still in contact. Some former students have done brilliantly well. I was always lost in admiration for the commitment, drive and dedication of those who were studying on top of day jobs or major family commitments. And the fact that they had chosen sociology made them more motivated than many of the 18 year olds I taught in my day job. And then there was the quality of the teaching materials, the updating of my own sociological knowledge as I taught 'Beliefs and ideologies' as well as more conventional sociology introductions, the joy of watching Stuart Hall, now sadly deceased, inspire an audience of students at Stirling in a day school. My time with the OU – thanks, Jean, Greg and Bram – gave me an enormous boost in my sociological thinking and improved me, I hope, as a teacher.

I took a decision in the mid-1990s to stop doing the OU work so as to have some time for research and writing. The wars and ethnic cleansing that accompanied the breakup of Yugoslavia stimulated an interest in nationalism. Conversations and long discussions with my oldest friend – a politics lecturer at Kingston University led to a series of joint articles about nationalism – first of all in the post-communist context and then more generally and theoretically culminating in our 2002 book *Nationalism: A critical introduction.* We had similar backgrounds – brought up as moderately orthodox Jews in the shadow of the holocaust in north west London, same schools, same university, same political views. Our starting point was a horror of racism and a critique of the exclusions that were the other side of the inclusive promises of the nation. We wanted to understand what had produced a seeming resurgence of ethnic nationalism and were dissatisfied with some of the dominant explanations in both academic writing and much of the political discourse of the time. As nationalism was an interdisciplinary field of study, there was great pleasure in reading history, politics, anthropology and other literatures. In a way I had come full circle back to the idea that my sociology could inform historical understanding and vice versa.

Meantime I had drifted into management. I first became the subject leader in sociology when a colleague retired in 1997 and was keen to shape the curriculum and take the subject forward in the university. And then through a chance and somewhat accidental sequence of events I became first jointly, temporarily and provisionally and then more substantively a head of school with other disciplines to manage and support. I was no longer doing much teaching although I kept up two areas of interest – nationalism and the sociology of welfare. It would be somewhat self-serving to claim that management seemed in some way an extension of the collectivism that had brought me into trade union activity. But fighting for the interests of the school and the subjects that lay therein did not seem that different.

During all this time I had also been a member of BSA. I went to my first conference in 1974 or 1975 and have been intermittently attending ever since. (I tried to count up the other day and I have certainly attended 15 and probably more.) In the 1990s I became a mainstay of the BSA's then Scottish Committee from which Paul Littlewood, ahead of his time, produced the first UK sociology promotional video 'So what's sociology, anyway?' We organised events and brought sociologists working in Scotland together, carrying on work that had been going on since the 1970s when others before us had tried to get sociology onto the Scottish school curriculum. (It eventually did manage to squeeze into schools and colleges competing with the 'Modern Studies' that had kept it out in the earlier period.) Getting reinvolved with BSA as a trustee a few years later enabled me to focus on sociology when my day job was now more wide ranging. It was also a decision taken out of a sense of collective responsibility for the discipline in which I had worked that seemed normal to me, although I think that academics have tended to become more individualistic and less collectivist – even sociologists.

So at the time of writing this, I am chair of BSA but no longer an employed academic. Edinburgh University have kindly given me a home as an honorary fellow and I have enjoyed contact with new colleagues and also the thought that there is more similarity between the problems of Russell Group and post-1992 universities than I had previously thought! In both kinds of institutions the challenges of inspiring students, meeting their expectations of feedback and support against the pressures of marketisation are great. In a world of spreading workload models for staff, it does remain the case that there will still be more opportunity and time for research in larger departments in research intensive departments such as Edinburgh. But sociological careers can take many different forms and directions and those taking up careers in the subject can benefit from entry from a range of disciplinary backgrounds (such as mine in history) and practical experience in the real world outside of academia. In this post-employed phase of mine I have taken my sociological imagination into the work of the Citizens Advice Bureau as a volunteer. The world of human difficulty I witness there puts all the concerns of higher education into a very different perspective. But it convinces me of the continuing need for a challenging, critical, public sociology in order to help change the world.

References

Berger, P, 1963, *Invitation to sociology: A humanistic perspective*, Harmondsworth: Penguin.

Cooper, D (ed), 1968, *The dialectics of liberation*, Harmondsworth: Penguin

Durkheim, E, 1938, *The rules of sociological method*, New York: The Free Press

Durkheim, E, 1951, *Suicide: A sociological study*, New York: The Free Press

Durkheim, E, 1995, *The elementary forms of the religious life*, New York: The Free Press

Marx, K, 1972, *Capital*, London: J.M. Dent

Mills, C Wright, 1959, *The sociological imagination*, Oxford: Oxford University Press

Spencer, P, Wollman, H, 2002, *Nationalism: A critical introduction*, London: SAGE

Thompson, EP, 1963, *The making of the English working class*, London: Gollancz

Weber, M. *The Protestant ethic and the spirit of capitalism*, New York: Scribners

Recommended readings

We asked our authors to recommend a text that has been inspirational to them and/or shows the kind of sociology which they aspire to.

Les Back selected: Du Bois, WEB, 1903, *The soul of black folks*, Chicago, IL: AC McClurg & Co

> It is a book about black history that was itself history-making. It shaped an African American political imagination through combining moving personal testimony with sociological explanation – a book that is a compound of anger and love, science and poetry. Also, *Soul of black folks* is an academic book that will cost as little as the price of a coffee! I would recommend the 1994 Dover Thrift Edition, which at the time of writing can be acquired for just £2.49.

Mel Bartley selected: Wilkinson, R, Pickett, K, 2010, *The spirit level*, Penguin

> A great example of the application of ideas from sociology to understanding population health. The modern successor to Durkheim's *Suicide* (1897), also a book with enormous impact.

Zygmunt Bauman selected: Barber, B, 2013, *If mayors ruled the world: Dysfunctional nations, rising cities*, New Haven, CT: Yale University Press

> An attempt to answer the most intriguing and urgent while the least answerable question of our time: 'Who is going to do it?'

John Brewer selected: Mills, C Wright, 1959, *The sociological imagination*, Oxford: Oxford University Press

> The short reason why – 'I believe in social justice and in a kind of sociology that tries to make a difference to ordinary people's lives.' This book captures that sentiment.

Judith Burnett selected: Rhys, J, 1966, *Wide Sargasso Sea*, Harmondsworth: Penguin

Rhys was 76 when this came out after a publication gap of almost 30 years. It was met with both huge and astonished acclaim since most people had assumed that she was long since dead. What can be learned from this slim novel is for each to discover for themselves, but by way of encouragement I would suggest the value of perspectival imagination.

Jocelyn Cornwell selected: Benyon, H, 1975, *Working for Ford,* UK: EP publishing Limited

> This book examined the experiences of those working in car factories, written mostly by people who are placed inside organisations for years.

Mark Featherstone selected: Bauman, Z, 1990, *Thinking sociologically,* Oxford: Blackwell

> This book captures the meaning of the discipline and the need to apply conceptual and critical thought to everyday problems which have an impact upon people in every society.

Anthony Giddens selected: Goffman, E, 1959, *The presentation of self in everyday life,* New York: Anchor books

> Accessible to a beginner but which repays endless further readings later on in a sociologist's career.

Richard Giulianotti (also) selected: Goffman, E, 1959, *The presentation of self in everyday life,* New York: Anchor Books

> This classic text is a recommendation for a number of reasons: in terms of its substantive content, as Goffman advances exceptional insights into the structure of social interaction; in terms of its organisation and structure, as Goffman provides a systematic development of a basic theory of social life; in terms of the lucidity of the writing, for how precisely the concepts and keywords are explained and integrated; in terms of its explanatory power, for how skilfully Goffman sets out his general arguments with reference to particular illustrations; and, in terms of its originality, for establishing a new analytical framework for social scientists, which went on to be hugely influential.

Eileen Green selected: Barker, D, Allen, S (eds), 1976, *Dependence and exploitation in work and marriage,* London: Longman/BSA

> This edited collection was ground breaking in its emphasis upon the interrelationship between work and marriage. It forged a

route to new ways of conceptualising sexual divisions in both spheres and provided the building blocks for gender theory. Having struggled with the home and paid work paradigm, reading this proved a 'light bulb' moment for me, laying out exciting possibilities for theorising the impact of gender.

Eric Harrison selected: Kumar, K, 1978, *Prophecy and progress: The sociology of industrial and post-industrial society*, London: Penguin Books
What first attracted me to sociology was its attention to large-scale macro questions about the overall shape and trajectory of modern societies. These were the preoccupations of the discipline's founders. This book is a brilliant overview of 200 years of social development in the West and the thinkers who have tried to make sense of it. A historian-turned-sociologist, Kumar combines 'big picture' theory with a judicious use of empirical evidence. The text is clear, authoritative and uncluttered by ugly and unnecessary jargon, or forests of bracketed referencing. This is Public Sociology done properly.

Anthony Heath selected: Young, M, Willmott, P, 1957, *Family and kinship in East London*, London: Routledge and Keegan Paul
This was a classic in the tradition of British community studies, which has now rather disappeared. I was actually down in Bethnal Green at the Young Foundation (which Michael set up) a couple of weeks ago talking at a workshop organised by Operation Black Vote on how to increase electoral registration among ethnic minorities in time for the 2015 general election. It was good to feel part of that tradition of British sociological research engaging with real-world issues to which Michael Young was a major contributor.

Paul Hodkinson selected: Foucault, M, 1978, *The history of sexuality: Volume 1*, London: Allen Lane
Not very original, perhaps, but the first volume of Foucault's *History of sexuality* was of great importance to the initial lighting up of my own academic imagination. The deconstruction of sexual categories therein led to broader questioning of the relationships between doing and being and interest in the ways identities are constructed. It connected up with one or two things of importance to my own life at the time as well as inspiring me academically, most directly by forming the basis for my undergraduate dissertation. My work subsequently was not so

directly connected to Foucault, which in some ways is a shame, but I'll always remember how inspired I was – and am – by this text.

John Holmwood selected: Allen, D, 2006, *Talking to strangers: Anxieties of citizenship since Brown v Board of Education*, Chicago, IL: University of Chicago Press

> This is an exemplary exercise of the sociological imagination by a classicist and political theorist. It offers a sensitive account of the injuries of segregation, sacrifice and misrecognition, a critical engagement with political theory from Hobbes to Habermas, and a 'manual' for community action to redress injustices.

Lara Killick selected: Elias, N, 1978, *What is sociology?*, New York: Columbia University Press

> Elias's work pushes me to think 'so much it hurts'. This particular book has helped me grapple with some of the age-old debates within sociology (agency–structure; power relations; society–individual) and has never been far from my hand.

Gayle Letherby selected: Stanley, L, Wise, S, 1993, *Breaking out: Feminist consciousness and feminist research*, London: Routledge

> While browsing the library shelves as a second year undergraduate I came across this. This book helped me to understand the importance of reflecting on the relationship between the process and the product of social research and the importance of the knowing/doing relationship.

Carol McNaughton Nicholls selected: Cohen, S, Taylor, L, 1976, *Escape attempts: The theory and practice of resistance to everyday life*, London: Routledge

> A great sociological read which also enables you to consider your own life in context – and a text that has been influential to how I interpret human behaviour in my own research.

Claire Maxwell selected: Reay, D, Crozier, G, James, D, 2011, *White middle-class identities and urban schooling*, Basingstoke: Palgrave Macmillan

> This is a fascinating book exploring how social class, ethnicity and place shape education – choices, trajectories, possibilities for privilege and exclusion. It offers a strong sociological engagement with the issues and draws on psychosocial understandings to help explain the perspectives of those who participated in this

large empirical study. It is one example of rich empirical data having been collected and analysed through a strong conceptual framework – sociological writing, with significant policy implications at its best!

Berry Mayall selected: Qvortrup, J, 1985, Placing children in the division of labour, in P Close and R Collins (eds) *Family and economy in modern society*, London: Macmillan
> This chapter really started me off thinking sociologically about childhood.

Linsey McGoey selected: Rorty, R, 1989, *Contingency, irony and solidarity*, New York: Cambridge University Press
> This book made a deep impression on me. I read it the second year of my PhD. I loved the book, but also sensed limits in his argument that I hadn't heard others voice – a powerful feeling at the time. My version featured a somewhat baffling photo of Rorty dressed like a Boston Brahmin (white linen sports jacket; regally bemused facial expression), reclining good-naturedly in a sort of floral woodland setting. I thought I was alone in noting the unintentional irony of this, until I found myself at a conference in Ghent and other students commented on the same book jacket. None of us could say what the joke was, but we all got the joke. Moments like that stand out: the remembrance of a camaraderie built among those who look to books as if they were friends or fodder or both.

Rob Mears selected: Merton, RK, 1968, *Social theory and social structure*, New York: The Free Press
> Merton's essays are impressive for their clarity, the modesty of the claims being made and the range of issues covered – with essays spanning the sociology of science, deviance, bureaucracies, reference groups etc. It is valuable to turn again to a sociologist who puts forward empirically justified theories about social structures and social behaviour.

Ann Oakley selected: Mills, C Wright, 1959, *The sociological imagination*, Oxford: Oxford University Press
> Its very title suggested to me an amalgamation of the (for me) newly discovered sociology with a writer's imagination. C Wright Mills calls 'the sociological imagination' a tool for grasping the social relations between history and biography, one capable of

ranging from the most impersonal transformations to the most intimate features of people's lives. He is clear that this imagination is *not* confined to academic sociology, and is particularly wonderful on the deficits of what he calls 'grand theory'.

Ann Phoenix selected: Brah, A, 1996, *Cartographies of disapora: Contesting identities*, London: Routledge
This is a collection of previously published and original chapters that brings together a range of Avtar Brah's research and ideas. It addresses issues of culture, identity and politics from feminist perspectives and different historical periods. Re-reading the discussions of 'difference' and 'diversity', even from a distance of two decades, produces new ideas and shows how original and far-sighted a thinker Brah is. The chapters are richly theoretical, addressing the intersections of racialisation, gender, class, sexuality, ethnicity, generation and nationalism and post-structuralism and paying attention to gender and generation as they are played out in Asian women's lives.

Yvonne Robinson selected: Tonnies, F, 1887, *Gemeinschaft und Gesellschaft*, Leipzig: Fues's Verlag, translated in 1957 as '*Community and society*'
This text helped to crystallise my thinking on what the 'community' of community theatre might mean.

Sasha Roseneil selected: Craib, I, 1994, *The importance of disappointment*, London: Routledge
I think he was saying some very important things to sociology and it certainly opened up for me the possibility of exploring the relationship between sociology and psychoanalysis that's been really important to me in the last ten or twelve years, and I think will continue to be. It's a book that expands what sociology can do, and that is, I think, far more interesting than policing the boundaries of the discipline.

Liza Schuster selected: Mills, C Wright, 1959, *The sociological imagination*, Oxford: Oxford University Press
It is difficult to choose one book to recommend to a new sociologist – instead I would urge any sociologist to read widely and far beyond their area of special interest. Read the works of philosophers and historians, geographers and economists, political scientists and psychologists.

John Scott selected: Talcott Parsons, 1937, *The structure of social action*, New York: The Free Press, reprinted 1968

> This was one of the first theoretical works that I read. While it has often been criticised for being an 'unreadable' text, it stands up well against the far greater obscurities of more recent theories. For all its many limitations, it is a model of intellectual rigour that embodies the comprehensive approach to sociology that is essential to its success as a discipline. It is a detailed engagement with the classical work of Durkheim and Weber and draws out a model of 'analytical realist' theorising that is both analytically precise and empirically relevant. We can all learn a great deal from this style of sociology, even if Parsons himself did not always exemplify it in his later work.

Daniela Sime selected: Corsaro, W, 2011, *The sociology of childhood* (3rd edn), London: SAGE

> Since first published in 1997, Corsaro's book has been heralded as a key text in the sociological study of children's lives. The author gives a reflective overview of the major developments in the theoretical and methodological approaches to the study of children and focuses on children as active agents in their own lives. The 'stories' and pictures on children's friendships and other relationships, their views of the world and societies in which they live, and the useful insights into how to approach these as an adult researcher will fascinate any reader.

Bev Skeggs selected: McClintock, A, 1995, *Imperial leather: Race, gender and sexuality in the colonial context*, London: Routledge

> Anne McClintock's text is a brilliant study of class, race, gender and sexuality through the history of colonialism. It is one of the most impressive analyses that I have read that can hold together all the difference indices of power.

Yvette Taylor selected: Toila-Kelly, DP, 2010, *Landscape, race, memory: Material ecologies of citizenship*, Farnham: Ashgate Publishing

> This is a really vivid account of belonging among British Asian women. Engaging with questions of Britishness in calling for attention to landscapes of memory and race, Tolia-Kelly recollects drinking tea and learning the manners and cultures of 'quintessential Englishness', via nursery rhymes and CS Lewis stories. In reading this, alongside interview accounts of working-class and middle-class women inhabiting the post-

industrial landscape of the north east of England, and not really feeling present 'then' (in industrial times) or 'now' (in a 'feminised' economy), I was inspired to think through inclusions and exclusions, familiarity and strangeness, and also the elisions between Britishness and Englishness, apparent in regional dis-identification (and felt personally through my own 'Scottishness'), I think what this book shows is the ways that histories – and futures – are carried; this was important theoretically but also methodologically as I occupied different entry points in researching the north east of England as, for example, 'resident', 'researcher', 'citizen', and in moving to New York in 2010 (as 'foreigner', 'tourist', 'mobile academic').

Jeffrey Weeks selected: Williams, R, 1963, *Culture and society 1780–1950*, Harmondsworth: Penguin

A book that I think inspired me way back when I was an undergraduate and it has continued to be an influence which is neither conventional history nor sociology. That is because it had a historical perspective, exploring the changing meanings of culture, but through that, it offered a particular analysis of British thinking about capitalism, industrialisation, community, agency, progressive thinking – particularly but not only progressive thinking. Its themes still resonate.

Howard Wollman selected: Thompson, EP, 1963, *The making of the English working class*, London: Victor Gollanz

It is chosen because I think history and historical understanding is so important for really good sociology. Thompson's wonderfully written account of a class in the making, of class as a process and the way he gives voice to the downtrodden and the marginal, rescuing them 'from the enormous condescension of posterity' (Thompson, 1963, 12) is a model from which sociologists can learn so much.

Kate Woodthorpe selected: Ritzer, G, 1993, *The McDonaldisation of society*, Thousand Oaks, CA: SAGE

As a sociology undergraduate student this book made so much sense at the time! I enjoyed how it felt academically 'robust' but was also written in a highly accessible way. It opened my eyes to the potential application of theory to 'the real world', and this has remained a key text for me ever since.

Resources for readers

Find a course in sociology

www.thecompleteuniversityguide.co.uk/careers/sociology/

Job searching

www.jobs.ac.uk/categories/sociology
http://careers.theguardian.com/sociology-degree-career-choices
www.britsoc.co.uk/about/Jobs.aspx

Funding opportunities

Economic and Social Research Council (ESRC) for UK funding: www.esrc.ac.uk For early career researchers, the ESRC has PhD studentships and the 'Future Leaders' programme for those within the first four years of submitting their PhD thesis.

The **Leverhulme Trust** has a number of grants and fellowships, including a study abroad award and an early career fellowship: www.leverhulme.ac.uk/

The **British Academy** also has postdoctoral fellowships as well as other research grants: www.britac.ac.uk/funding/

The **British Federation of Women Graduates** offers scholarships for female postgraduate students: http://bfwg.org.uk/bfwg/

The **Wellcome Trust** and the **National Institute of Health Research** also offer grants and fellowships, if your topic falls within sociology of health and illness: www.wellcome.ac.uk/funding/ and www.nihr.ac.uk

The following website gives some more general advice and links for funding: www.gov.uk/funding-for-postgraduate-study

Writing resources

Becker, H, 2007, *Writing for social scientists*, Chicago, IL: University of Chicago Press
Johnson, WB, Mullen, CA, 2007, *Write to the top! How to Become a prolific academic*, Basingstoke: Palgrave Macmillan

The **Writing Across Boundaries** project is dedicated to supporting social science researchers who are seeking to engage more effectively with the practical and intellectual issues that arise in the quest to produce texts that are engaging, accurate and analytically insightful. More information, including about courses they run and other resources found here: www.dur.ac.uk/writingacrossboundaries/

The **Thesis Whisperer** is a blog for and about PhD students and early career academics, including many tips on writing a PhD thesis: http://thesiswhisperer.com/

For help in writing funding applications, check out: www.researchfundingtoolkit.org or see the book: Aldridge, J, 2012, *The research funding toolkit: How to plan and write successful grant applications*, London: Sage

Advice for early career academics

http://beyondthephd.transitiontradition.com

www.nadinemuller.org.uk/category/the-new-academic/

Resources for teaching

Rubistar is a free online resource that will help you design rubrics for a range of formative and summative assignments: http://rubistar.4teachers.org/index.php

The **Centre for Excellence in Teaching and Learning** have an online resource that will help you develop effective student learning objectives: http://rubistar.4teachers.org/index.php

Giddens, A, Sutton, PW (eds), 2010, *Sociology: Introductory readings*, Cambridge: Polity
Scott, J (ed), 2006, *Sociology, The Key Concepts*, Abingdon: Routledge

Think, Educate, Share (TES) have a section where teachers share and download free lesson plans, classroom resources, revision guides and curriculum worksheets. Sociology resources can be found here:

www.tes.co.uk/sociology-secondary-teaching-resources/

AQA is an independent education charity and the largest provider of academic qualifications taught in schools and colleges. They have resources here: www.aqa.org.uk/subjects/sociology/as-and-a-level/sociology-2190/teaching-and-learning-resources

Increasingly lecturers are expected to become fellows of the Higher Education Academy to demonstrate their dedication and expertise in teaching. For further information see: www.heacademy.ac.uk/workstreams-research/disciplines/social-sciences

Associations and organisations for sociologists and social scientists

The **British Sociological Association (BSA)** is the national subject association for sociologists in the UK and its primary objective is to promote sociology. The BSA has special interest study groups, regular events including an annual conference, a newsletter and a jobs board: www.britsoc.co.uk/ (includes links to the BSA Early Career Forum and Postgraduate Forum).

The **Guardian Higher Education Network** posts blogs and articles of relevance to those who work and study in Higher Education: www.theguardian.com/higher-education-network

Sociologists Without Borders is a US-based non-profit, scientific and educational organisation of sociologists: www.sociologistswithout borders.org

The **Campaign for Social Science** was launched to raise the profile of social science in the public, media and Parliament. For news and upcoming events, see https://campaignforsocialscience.org.uk

The Academy of Social Sciences is the National Academy of Academics, Learned Societies and Practitioners in the Social Sciences. Its mission is to promote social sciences in the UK for the public benefit. For more information see http://acss.org.uk

Blogs, news, and radio on sociology and social science

BBC Radio 4, **Thinking Allowed**, in which Laurie Taylor explores the latest research into how society works and discusses current ideas on how we live today: www.bbc.co.uk/podcasts/series/ta

Discover Society is an online magazine published by Social Research Publications, a not-for-profit collaboration between sociology and social policy academics and publishers at Policy Press to promote the publication of social research, commentary and policy analysis: www. discoversociety.org

The Conversation is a collaboration between editors and academics to provide informed news analysis and commentary that's free to read and republish: https://theconversation.com/uk

The Sociological Imagination Blog: http://sociologicalimagination. org/

British Library Blog on the Social Sciences: http://britishlibrary. typepad.co.uk/socialscience/

Global Dialogue is the electronic newsletter and magazine of the International Sociological Association. It appears five times a year and in 15 languages. It offers a sociological lens on current world events, underlining our continuing relevance to public debates: http://isa-global-dialogue.net

Index

Page numbers in **bold** refer to that person's own tale.

grant applications 66, 132, 138, 156, 159,
177, 193, 239, 260–1, 288
Green, Eileen **153–60**, 280
Greenwich, University of 77
Greenwood, Walter 79
Gross, Matthias 117
Grossberg, Larry 43
group (psycho)analysis 62, 63
Gunaratnam, Yasmin 90
Gutiérrez, Lucio 118–19

H

Habermas, Jürgen 53
Hall, Stuart 85
Halsey, AH (Chelly) 111, 231, 232
Haralambos, Michael 78–9, 136
Harding, Sandra 175
Harlow, Harry 183
Harré, R 173
Harrison, Eric 247, **251–6**, 281
health service, sociology in 187–95
Health Studies 189
Heath, Anthony **225–33**, 281
HEFCE (Higher Education Funding
Council for England) 81, 156, 203, 247
Heidegger, Martin 25, 26
Hepworth, Mike 237
HESA (Higher Education Statistics
Agency) 81
heteronormativity 105, 133
Hey, V 130, 131, 133, 134
Higher Education Academy 257, 289
hindsight (what contributors would have
done differently)
John D Brewer 75–6
Judith Burnett 82
Jocelyn Cornwell 195
Richard Giulianotti 240–1
Eileen Green 160
Anthony Heath 229, 230–1, 231–2
Paul Hodkinson 139–40
John Holmwood 53–4
Lara Killick 210–11
Berry Mayall 185
Carol McNaughton Nicholls 217
Ann Oakley 114–15
Ann Phoenix 177
Sasha Roseneil 69
Liza Schuster 21
John Scott 150
Daniela Sime 261
Beverley Skeggs 46
Jeffrey Weeks 269–70
history
academic discipline 56–7, 252, 264–5,
266, 274
historical perspectives in sociology 244,
246

historical sociology 3, 265
history of sociology 2–4, 28
History of sexuality, The (Foucault, 1978)
136, 271, 281
Hodkinson, Paul **135–40**, 281
Hoggart, Richard 85
holistic nature of sociology 149–50, 175
Holland, Janet 131
Hollway, Wendy 61–2, 175
Holmes, R 113
Holmwood, John **49–54**, 282
homelessness 214
'Homosexual role, The' (McIntosh, 1968)
264, 271
Honneth, A 131
honours 143, 150, 225
hope 27–8
hospice, as research location 90
housework 112
Hughes, J 244
Hughes, Martin 184
Hull, University of 32, 38
'hybridic sociologies' 3

I

ideology 43–4
*If mayors ruled the world: Dysfunctional
nations, rising cities* (Barber, 2013) 279
ignorance 121
imagination, sociological *see* sociological
imagination
'impact,' demonstrating 13, 260, 261
Imperial leather (McClintock, 1995) 285
Importance of disappointment, The (Craib,
1994) 284
improving society, as goal of sociology *see*
changing the world
In place of fear (Bevan, 1952) 79
'incommensurable paradigms' 254
individualisation 24, 30–3, 228
individualism 166
inequality
and children 259–60, 261
health inequality 199, 202
and 'powerlessness' 245
social class inequality 52–3, 199, 226–7
structural inequality (in academia) 100,
125
insecurity, in university sector 13, 33,
101, 112, 130, 132, 197–203, 270
insider research 58, 140, 191
insider-outsider configurations 245
Institute of Education, London (UCL)
109, 181, 183, 185, 201
Institute of Health and Community
(Plymouth) 163
Integration of a child into a social world, The
(Richards, 1974) 174